BUY THIS, NOT THAT

BUY THIS, NOT THAT

HOW TO SPEND YOUR WAY TO WEALTH AND FREEDOM

SAM DOGEN

Portfolio / Penguin

PORTFOLIO / PENGUIN
An imprint of Penguin Random House LLC
penguinrandomhouse.com

Most Portfolio books are available at a discount when purchased in quantity for sales promotions or corporate use. Special editions, which include personalized covers, excerpts, and corporate imprints, can be created when purchased in large quantities. For more information, please call (212) 572-2232 or e-mail specialmarkets@penguinrandomhouse.com. Your local bookstore can also assist with discounted bulk purchases using the Penguin Random House corporate Business-to-Business program. For assistance in locating a participating retailer, e-mail B2B@penguinrandomhouse.com.

All tables from FinancialSamurai.com unless otherwise attributed.

ISBN 9780593328774 (hardcover)
ISBN 9780593328781 (ebook)

Printed in the United States of America
1st Printing

BOOK DESIGN BY TANYA MAIBORODA

This publication is designed to provide accurate and authoritative information in regard to the subject matter covered. It is sold with the understanding that the publisher is not engaged in rendering legal, accounting, or other professional services. If you require legal advice or other expert assistance, you should seek the services of a competent professional.

Some names and identifying characteristics have been changed to protect the privacy of the individuals involved.

For my father, Allen, for encouraging me to start.
And for my mother, Kathy, for always
letting me pursue my dreams.

Contents

Financial Freedom, Sooner Than Later

Starting in 1999, my alarm clock began going off at 4:30 a.m. so I could get to work by 5:30 a.m. For someone who had dropped calculus because he had difficulty thinking straight at 8:00 a.m., sitting at my desk under bright fluorescent lights at 5:30 a.m. felt like a special type of torture.

Not only did I have to get to work while it was still dark, but I often had to stay until after sunset to connect with my colleagues in Asia. Over the next two years, I gained twenty pounds, I developed plantar fasciitis, sciatica, allergies, and chronic back pain, and my scalp started creating daily snowstorms because I was incessantly scratching my head due to stress.

Working in international equities at Goldman Sachs in New York City was supposed to be my dream job, but I quickly realized that if I made a career out of banking, I would probably die prematurely.

So I came up with an escape plan. Like Andy Dufresne from *The Shawshank Redemption*, I knew I would have to crawl through a tunnel of excrement to achieve freedom. But unlike Andy, who was trapped in prison for nineteen years until he escaped at fifty-eight, my plan was to escape by age forty.

I figured hustling for eighteen years after college was about as much work stress as I could handle. If I saved and invested aggressively, eighteen years would also be a long enough runway to build a passive-income portfolio that could pay for all my living expenses. With potentially forty years left to live after age forty, I would have time enough to heal and enjoy life to its fullest.

In the end, I was able to leave banking in 2012 at the age of thirty-four, partially thanks to negotiating a severance package that paid for about six years of living expenses. In other words, the severance package bought me the most precious commodity of all: *time*.

Life is both long and short, fast and slow. We must try to make the most of each day so we can minimize looking back with regret. "Financial freedom, sooner than later" is a personal mantra and the guiding theme of *Financial Samurai*, the website and community I have been running since July 2009.

It is also at the heart of this book.

Financial Freedom Means Something Different for Everyone

Ultimately, **financial freedom means you get to do what you want when you want.**

Financial freedom is also a defensive and offensive position at the exact same time.

Defensive because when the shiitake mushroom hits the fan in ways that are completely out of your control (hello, 2008–9 financial crisis; hello, 2020–21 pandemic; hello, never-ending geopolitical risks), you and your family will still be okay. Your finances are strong enough that you get to live your life mostly unimpeded.

Life is hard, and we all experience significant stress at times. None of us are immune. So hopefully this book, among other things, will be able to make a strong contribution toward reducing that kind of emotional upheaval and contributing to your peace of mind.

Just as important as living life on your own terms, financial freedom is also an offensive position. This is the mental difference between playing to win and playing not to lose. Once you nail survival mode, you can level up to win mode.

When you're free to play offense, you can make new investments, spin up cool projects, and work on crazy entrepreneurial ideas that you'd never have tried otherwise. Some of the wealthiest people in the world owe their wealth to being able to afford to take tremendous risks.

Success is often a numbers game, and money itself is just a means to an end. But money, *applied*, can open doors to things you want to do with your finite time. Understand how you ultimately want to spend your time each day and use money to achieve your goals.

For now, as a father with two young children, having financial freedom for me looks like this: spending as much time as possible with my family, writing, playing tennis and softball, and constantly looking for new ways to learn from and connect with people.

The Motivation to Keep Going

Figuring out how to best apply (grow, spend, save, invest, give) your money, at whatever age and stage of life you're in, is what I have been writing about at *Financial Samurai* since 2009.

As of this writing, more than ninety million people have stopped by *Financial Samurai*, most of them looking for a change. I've been privileged to hear from readers around the world who have eradicated their debt, fixed their spending habits, bought their first homes, left toxic environments, created thriving side hustles, built substantial retirement portfolios, and so much more.

Success stories like these are what drive me to keep writing about money issues that impact real life, and I make it a point to write directly from personal experience. Money matters are just too important to be left to guesswork. In the pages that follow, I'll take the mystery out of achieving financial independence so you can take the necessary steps to get there yourself.

Taking the Fear Out of Financial Decision-Making

I wrote *Buy This, Not That* because I know, from my own experience and hearing from thousands of my readers, how hard it can be to take action with your money. The breadth of choices is intimidating. The fear of making a wrong move is paralyzing. On a very basic level, this book will help make your financial decisions simple, or at least simpler, in this chaotic world.

A big challenge holding folks back is the fact that most of us grew up on financial advice centered around saving. We're urged to budget, avoid consumer debt, stash an emergency fund—and it's all solid advice. But the truth is, it's difficult to become financially independent by simply putting money in the bank. To achieve financial freedom, we need to know how to *spend our money* in ways that will build wealth now, and in the long run. The spending piece is where most financial advice falls flat, and where the most opportunity lies. It's also where most people panic because they're scared of making the wrong move with their money.

Here's another truth: there are no "perfect choices" when it comes to making financial decisions. Let's get that common misconception out of the way. The best we can do is make *optimal* financial decisions using logic, clear reasoning, and an understanding of how things worked in the past. Every money decision I discuss in this book is rooted in those three factors.

My first hope with *Buy This, Not That* is to help you let go of the fear of making a wrong financial choice. Let that sink in: there are no wrong money choices, just as there are no perfect choices, only optimal or suboptimal. That fear of making a wrong move stops too many people from *spending* in ways that will build wealth. Fear keeps us clinging to safety (and cash). It's easier to do nothing when the fear of failure and embarrassment has such a strong hold on us. It's the same fear that prevents us from asking someone out, asking for a promotion, or starting that new project. Fear stops us from taking chances that can change our lives.

But even when we set fear aside, figuring out the optimal choices can be overwhelming. For many Americans, financial decision-making feels like a never-ending trade-off between now and later. How can we make sense of the yin and yang of finances? Spend or save? Save or invest? Invest here or there? Rent or buy? Stay at the job or quit? Kids or travel? Big city or little city? Private or public school? Go corporate or go start-up? Invest in 401(k) or pay off debt? Organic or conventional? The list goes on and on.

That's why the title of this book is *Buy This, Not That*. There is an avalanche of decisions rushing down at you every day. More choices often create more stress, anxiety, and confusion. Amid skyrocketing costs, debt out of control, jobs in constant flux, and decreased spending power, I will help you tune out the noise. Step by step, chapter by chapter, I will show you how to make optimal money choices that focus on wealth building—not saving for saving's sake—in order to live your best life now while also ensuring a financially independent future.

Buy This: You Have the Power to Become Financially Independent

The title of this book is a bit of a sleight of hand, for two reasons. First, because financial decisions are never quite that binary. There are always many nuances, sacrifices, and cross-category effects. "This or that" is rarely the full expression of your options.

For example, sure, you could decide to buy the Honda Fit over the Porsche 911, but that's not going to help you accumulate any wealth if you are also afraid to put money in the stock market, or you're sitting complacently in a low-paying job, or you go and blow it all at the craps table. That's why the "this or that" method challenges you to look at your complete financial picture as you gauge money choices in any area of your life.

Yes, you will eventually need to choose *this* or *that*. If you don't, you're sitting idle and accomplishing nothing. Taking action is the way. But backing those choices with a full understanding of your money situation will get you closer to the optimal move.

The second trick of the *Buy This, Not That* title is more cultural. Society at large paints a certain picture about wealth. It's flashy. It's rude. It's a winner-takes-all, get-ahead-at-all-costs story.

At the same time, there's also a long history of sucking it up in a single career—a kind of "live with the cards you're dealt" industrial mentality. Sure, there's a noble work ethic in this attitude, but not a lot of creative thinking about how to achieve financial independence.

The punch line is don't buy it. Buy *this*, not that. Buy your new mindset. Buy this idea that you are in control of your path to financial freedom. Don't buy the old story that you are stuck.

My goal for this book is to provide you with at least a hundred times more value in the short term than what you paid for it. In other words, if you bought this book for $30, I want you to come away with at least $3,000 in value through the knowledge you will accumulate and the actions you will subsequently take. In the long term, I want this book to create at least one thousand times more value for you, thanks to making optimal financial moves that will compound over time.

Each chapter will provide you the tools you need to make optimal choices in some of life's most common and biggest decisions.

My Method for Slicing Through Money's Mysteries

Back in 2009, the world was falling apart and my net worth declined by roughly 35% in six short months. I had been putting off starting *Financial Samurai* since 2006. But once the financial crisis hit, I decided to finally launch the site. If I got laid off, I needed a backup plan.

I also thought it would be a good idea to start writing to help myself and others make sense of chaos. After all, by that point I had spent ten years working in the finance industry, studied economics at William & Mary, gotten my MBA from UC Berkeley, saved aggressively, diversified my investments, and . . .

I *still* got financially rocked.

I wanted to help others learn from my experience and from my mistakes. And, to be frank, I also needed some therapy to cope with all the fear and uncertainty. Chaos is a great motivator to change. The pain and suffering you feel today might be the best thing that could ever happen to you. Still, wouldn't it be much better if you could make some changes *before* the pain happens?

For example, instead of waiting for a heart attack to force us to eat better and exercise more, why not start now? Instead of getting a divorce because we neglected to work on our communication skills, why not actively work on listening better today?

As I started writing, I created a methodology for developing the advice and conclusions I'd share with my readers. It's the same methodology I bring to this book, and it comes in four parts:

1. **I draw from my education, experience, and writing.** I worked in finance for thirteen years, and have published two thousand–plus personal finance–related articles.
2. **I spend the bulk of my time on research and rigorous analysis.** I put days into researching minutiae and always "show my work" in the analysis. I've never met an Excel sheet I didn't love. Real numbers tell real stories.
3. **All analysis is paired with firsthand experience because money is too important to be left up to pontification.** This is my favorite part of what I do, and I sometimes get weird looks for it. For example, a few years back I decided to become an Uber driver. I set a goal of five hundred rides, not the three or four I saw some others do before writing their story. My friends called me crazy, but firsthand learning is what makes *Financial Samurai* special, and it's a big part of my approach.

4. **I incorporate as many viewpoints as possible to provide well-rounded perspectives.** Given that there are no perfect choices, only optimal and suboptimal ones, it's important to listen to other people's experiences, especially divergent ones. So many times I've dogmatically believed one point of view, only to see the other side of the story once I've taken time to listen.

The chapters ahead are driven by this methodology.

Part 1 starts with a personal reality check so you can figure out what financial freedom looks like to you. It lays out the math required to achieve your goals, the hard questions you need to answer on your journey to building wealth, and smart changes you can make right now to improve your outcomes.

Part 2 shows you where to put your money to maximize your wealth potential. I'll help you design an investment strategy that will generate passive income to cover your best life's expenses sooner than later. We'll cover stock market investing, along with my favorite way for everyday people to build wealth: real estate.

Part 3 helps you optimize your career. You'll see why everyone has the ability to earn more money, and I'll show those on the lookout how to target high-paying industries and get paid and promoted quickly once you're hired. We'll also explore side hustles so you can have multiple income streams contributing to your wealth.

And finally, part 4 helps ensure that your money choices are contributing to a lifestyle that keeps you fulfilled and at peace *today*. Not when you retire "someday." Yes, you'll need to work hard and sacrifice in your early days, but even those sacrifices should put your wellness first. If your grind has you running on three hours of sleep and a diet of Spam and Cheerios, you won't be here long enough to enjoy the fruits of your sacrifices. I'll help you see where to set boundaries as you make lifestyle choices that influence your bottom line.

In the end, *Buy This, Not That* will give you an approach to your finances that will bring you peace of mind and financial freedom sooner than you ever thought possible.

Making Decisions Using the 70/30 Philosophy

In *Buy This, Not That,* I hope to give you a new framework for decision-making across all of life's big buckets. Because while life is rarely black-and-white, we need to make definitive choices all the time. Rent this house or buy that apartment? Invest in a growth stock or an index fund? Live in San Francisco, California, or Raleigh, North Carolina? Order sushi delivery or suck it up and cook?

These choices all involve an expense of time and capital and bring risk and reward. I will help you navigate each with a focus on smarter spending for building wealth. We will go through the reasons why the optimal choices vary for each person based on their specific circumstances as we develop the habits that will kill the self-doubt that stops many people from making even the first steps to financial freedom.

You see, the problem, most of the time, is that we don't have enough information to confidently choose this or that. My approach helps you overcome that information gap. And you'll do this by thinking in probabilities instead of in binary terms, where it's an all-or-nothing proposition. If you start thinking in probabilities instead of absolutes, you will develop a stronger analytical mindset to make more winning decisions over time. You will also likely be able to make more winning decisions on risks that others never dare take.

One of the biggest decision-making fallacies people fall victim to is thinking they must take action only when there is 100% certainty. Here are three examples.

1. Only if you are certain someone likes you—because they told their friend, who told you—do you feel confident asking them out. But you might find out years in the future that they liked you as well and were just waiting on you to make the first move. What a shame to miss out on love due to the desire for absolute certainty.

2. Most people put in an offer on a house only once it's listed for sale. But at any given moment, there may be several homeowners in your neighborhood looking to sell, unsure whether they want to go through the hassle of listing their property. By sending out friendly letters of interest, you could very well start a dialogue and end up buying one of the most coveted houses on the block for a good price.

3. Or consider that the typical job seeker applies to jobs only once they are posted online—a 100% probability that a company is hiring. However, there are always plenty of job openings that are not publicized. If you take the initiative to inquire with your manager or a hiring manager at another firm, you just might get a coveted job because you decided to take initiative on imperfect information.

Your goal is to constantly make positive-expected-value decisions in everything you do. A positive-expected-value decision is when you have a greater than 50% probability of your desired outcome coming true.

Some decisions have higher expected values than others, such as accepting a job offer with a guaranteed raise and promotion with a growing company rather than staying at a place that just got acquired by a company known to cut costs. Some decisions, on the other hand, have murkier expected values due to an overwhelming amount of incomplete information.

It is up to you to do your due diligence to bring your probability of success as close to 100% as possible (while also accepting that very few decisions ever have 100% positive outcomes).

There are few sure things in life. So think in probabilities.

When you go to a casino, the house always has an edge. The edge ranges from as low as 0.5% in blackjack and 0.8% in craps to 17% for slot machines and 25%+ for keno. In the long run, the house always wins. Therefore, if you must gamble, you should gamble at games where the house's edge is the lowest. But an even better scenario is gambling on only those decisions where the odds are in *your* favor.

The more important the decision you need to make, the higher the edge or positive expected value you should have.

The 70/30 Philosophy

Now that you understand the importance of making positive-expected-value decisions, let me introduce you to my 70/30 philosophy in decision-making.

The 70/30 philosophy states that you should seek to make a decision only if you have *at least* a 70% probability of making an optimal decision. At the same time, you have the humility to understand that 30% of the time, you will make a suboptimal decision and have to live with the consequences and adapt.

With more than a two-to-one reward-to-risk ratio, over the long run you will become very profitable with your overall decision-making philosophy. You will most certainly have regrets where you will wish for do-overs. However, you will also constantly be learning from your mistakes so that you can make even higher positive-expected-value decisions in the future.

Just be careful not to get too cocky. That's when you run the risk of financial and personal ruin. There's a classic saying on Wall Street: "Bulls make money, bears make money, pigs get slaughtered." Being overconfident and not properly recognizing risks will be your downfall. The worst mistake you can make is not realizing when a good decision was mostly due to luck, not skill. Proper risk management is paramount.

Expert marketing has also made so many things seem like attractive products, experiences, or investments. But of course, not everything you spend money on or invest in turns out to be as great as expected. Therefore, it's up to you to continually hone the accuracy of your predictions so that they aren't too far off from reality. If your predictions are way off, it's imperative that you study why—and make adjustments.

How to Improve Your Forecasting Abilities

The best way to improve your forecasting abilities is to constantly make predictions about uncertain outcomes. For example, if you watch any type of sporting event, before the game starts, make a forecast of who will win, by how much, and why. Jot your forecasts down to keep yourself honest. Then compare the outcome with your expectations and see what you got wrong and why.

You can practice improving your predictions on practically any type of activity that has an uncertain result. You can make forecasts on:

- which dog will win the dog show
- how long a friend's relationship will last
- how much a house will ultimately sell for and by when
- how long your injury will take to heal
- whether your leaky roof will still leak if there's no wind during the next rainstorm
- how many whales you'll end up spotting off Makapu'u Point in January
- whether your son will stay in his bed and not bother you in the middle of the night if you bribe him with blueberry cheesecake

Soon you will start to naturally see everything as a probability matrix. Where others make decisions based solely on gut instinct, you go into every decision-making process based on extensive practice, logic, and self-awareness. This is your competitive advantage.

When you are dead wrong, you must review the reasons why and learn from them. Eventually you will narrow the gap between various outcomes and your expectations to the point where you can confidently say something has at least a 70% probability of succeeding. If you feel your desired outcome has more than double the chance of coming true over the undesired outcome, you are on the right track.

Buy This, Not That is a book about making optimal choices for some of life's most important decisions. For each decision, I will present to you the rationale for why I think you should go a certain way based on various circumstances. Then it will ultimately be up to you to decide what's best for your particular circumstances.

Not everything will turn out according to plan. We must embrace this truth. However, so long as you continually keep learning from your mistakes, your decision-making skills will only improve over time.

You Don't Have to Be Born Special

Sadly, many folks never try to achieve financial freedom because they believe wealthy people have or know something that the rest of us don't. This is a damaging misconception.

Not everyone with a healthy income is a doctor or a lawyer or a CEO. Many don't have MBAs or formal business training. Nor do they have stock market intel that gives them an edge over everyone else. Sure, some lucky ones inherit wealth. But others have qualities that are far more valuable: the *determination* to create wealth and the ability to consistently make good choices that help them build their fortune. So, yes, they do have something that most people don't—it's just a lot more attainable than you may realize.

If you don't know by now, many regular people make or have *a lot* more money than you think. They just don't publicize it. Every week I hear a new story about a person who makes way more than you'd ever expect. I've written about many of them, including:

- a Bay Area Rapid Transit elevator technician who makes $235,814 plus $48,429 in benefits
- a University of New Hampshire librarian who left $4 million to his school
- a stay-at-home food blogger who makes $500,000+ a year
- a YouTuber who makes millions a year reviewing new toys

These people's grit and courage to act have nothing to do with pedigree and lucky breaks. Sometimes it comes from exactly the opposite. There are very real inequalities in our world based on various forms of discrimination. If you ever experience such an injustice, use it as *motivation* to reach your own financial freedom, sooner than later.

The only thing I know about you right now, this minute, is that you are an ambitious person who wants to improve your financial health. Otherwise you wouldn't have picked up this book. You are also logical enough to believe that it's better to learn from someone who has already achieved what you want to achieve, rather than someone still pontificating on what *might* be.

So I have some good news for you: you don't have to be born special in order to achieve financial freedom or live the lifestyle you want.

More good news, which many of you won't believe at first, especially if you're financially underwater at the moment, is that it's also never too late to get started. The more difficult a financial situation you find yourself in, the more opportunity there is to improve!

But determination alone won't make you rich. If that were the case, every person with a fire in their belly would be sitting on a fortune. You need grit, consistency, *and* the confidence to make the right choices that will build your wealth. Most people miss that third part. So this book is not only about optimizing your choices; it's also about optimizing your attitude.

Get on the Damn Bus

I came to America with my family from Kuala Lumpur. I was born in Manila while my parents, who worked for the U.S. Foreign Service, were stationed there. We lived in Zambia, the Philippines, Virginia, Japan, Taiwan, and Malaysia, in that order, before coming to northern Virginia when I was fourteen years old. At the time, only about 6% of the population in our town looked like me. It was quite a shock going from being a part of the majority to being a minority.

I had to start all over and find new friends while also navigating encounters with bullying and racism. I was also a misfit who lacked the ability to think quickly on my feet because my thoughts constantly bounced between English and Mandarin. My grades and SAT score were nothing to write home about either.

I knew my parents weren't rich. They drove beaters and frowned on ordering any drinks other than water when we went out to eat. We lived in a modest townhouse in a grungier part of town. I never had a Nintendo growing up, and all I knew of Air Jordans was a pair of hand-me-downs from a friend that was two sizes too large. We were by no means poor. We just never had more than we truly needed.

After high school I decided to go to William & Mary, a public university in Williamsburg, Virginia, because I could afford the tuition. We weren't able to comfortably afford a higher-priced school, and I wasn't smart enough or athletic enough to get any scholarships. I did well enough at William & Mary, but that's not why I ended up at Goldman

Sachs. In fact, William & Mary wasn't even a target school where Goldman Sachs recruited. The only reason I got a job at Goldman Sachs after college was because I got on a 6:00 a.m. bus one chilly Saturday morning.

The bus was heading from college to a career fair two hours away in Washington, DC. Twenty other students had signed up to attend, but I was the only person who showed up. After waiting over an hour for the no-shows, the bus driver drove me to his company's headquarters, swapped out the bus for a black Lincoln Town Car, and personally chauffeured me to the fair. This was the first time I realized that just showing up is more than half the battle.

Seven months, six rounds, and *fifty-five interviews* later, I finally got the job at One New York Plaza, Goldman's equities headquarters in New York City. All because I woke up early and stuck with it.

Never in my wildest dreams did I imagine I could leave the corporate grind at age thirty-four to focus on my life's passions. But thanks to *Financial Samurai* and my investing efforts, I'm now forty-five and financially free to spend time with my wife and two kids and work on things I love.

One saying helps me keep going whenever things are hard and I feel like making excuses: "Never fail due to a lack of effort, because effort requires no skill." I can fail because the competition was too good or there was an unforeseen event that knocked me off my feet. But if I fail because I just didn't try hard, I know I will be filled with regret as an old man.

Grit, consistency, and confidence are by far the most important attributes for achieving your goals. Don't think you need to have special skills, innate talent, or rich parents to get ahead. Who you are is good enough already.

Now let's get started.

PART ONE

Adopt the Right Money Mindset to Get Rich

Achieving financial independence is largely a numbers game. It's a blend of math, rational decision-making, and consistent action taken over the years.

But before we jump into the numbers, let's start with goal setting. What would you do if you weren't forced to exchange time for money? Paint that picture. Then I'll help you figure out how much money you need to live that dream.

Your financially free life will mostly be funded through passive- and semipassive-income streams. We'll look at the options so you can find the income sources that are right for you.

I'll also help you set up a strategy to drop debt quickly and use it as a wealth-building tool.

Get ready—this may be the most exciting math lesson of your life.

Chapter 1

Find Your Happiness Equation

What's the point of money, anyway? We all want to be rich, but why? To be free—free to live our lives on our own terms and in the way that energizes us.

It's easy to forget that money is just a means to an end. We hustle to pay off debt, set up our automatic investment contributions, obsess about savings and try not to touch it, all because we want to grow our nest egg as large as possible.

But if we don't know why we're putting in all this effort, there's really no point. We must have specific purposes for our money.

Freedom means something different to everyone, and it's worth taking the time to think about what it means to you. You're reading this book because you want to achieve financial independence. Well, why? You're not chasing the money itself. You're after the freedom that the money will bring. What does that freedom look like to you? What will it allow you to finally do?

In order to best make use of this book, you need to answer those questions and get a crystal-clear sense of what your goals are. We'll talk through how to do just that in the next few pages, but for now, let's take a look at the universal benefits that financial freedom can bring:

1. **Your health improves.** Stress kills. During my working days, I developed chronic back pain, tendinitis in my elbow, and TMJ (jaw clenching, teeth grinding). All of this disappeared after I reached financial independence. Our health is priceless. Removing stress from your life related to money and your job will be a huge benefit to your overall wellness. And at the times when you or a family member does need medical care, knowing that you can afford to pay for it—whatever it is—is a tremendous gift.

2. **You work fearlessly.** There's a fear cycle in most jobs. You get the job and try to fulfill big promises, but there will always be hits and misses at work because there are so many things out of your control: A boss who might not like you. A backstabbing colleague. A fundraising round that never materializes. A recession. A merger. Job security is a thing of the past, and having your income exclusively connected to your job will leave you defenseless and on edge.

   Financial freedom lets you enter jobs, projects, or gigs without this fear. It gives you the courage to be more creative and take on bigger risks. It also lets you explore new areas without always worrying about pay. Think about all the other jobs you would enjoy and derive purpose and happiness from if money wasn't a big reason for working. It feels fantastic working on something because you *want to*, not because you *need to*.

3. **You stand up for what's right.** This one is extremely important to me.

   There's a lot of BS in the world that goes unchallenged because people are afraid of the repercussions. How many times have you bitten your tongue at work because you were worried about the consequences?

   The discrimination I have experienced, from the playground to the boardroom, was one of my main motivations for working toward financial freedom. It was a big reason why I decided to save so much and aggressively work on my passive-income streams. My desire to have absolute choice and be beholden to no one was and still is a huge motivating factor.

   Once you are financially independent or are on the path to financial independence, you are more confident to speak your mind when you see an injustice. It's a wonderful feeling to never have to back down from anyone.

4. **You realize you belong just as much as anyone else does.** When you have control over your time, you realize you're equal to the most successful people in society, be they CEOs, celebrities, star athletes, or the most powerful politicians. You have the right to voice your opinions and breathe the same air and be in the same place as them. More importantly, you develop the confidence to pursue your passions without apology.

   Who is the Michael Jordan or Serena Williams in your line of work? In my old industry, that person is a guy named Carl Kawaja, the chair of Capital Research and Management, one of the largest mutual fund companies in the world, with around $2.5 trillion in assets under management. Before getting to know Carl, I was intimidated to speak with him. I was a G-league player hoping to get a ten-day contract while he was a hall of famer with six championship rings. Many people working on Wall Street want his attention, but he's nearly impossible to get a meeting with. But once I got to know him, I realized he was a nice guy with hopes, concerns, and dreams just like everybody else. On the tennis courts, we smack-talk each other all the time because we're just friends having fun.

   When you feel confident that you belong, good things start happening, and your belief in yourself propels you forward. So much about becoming wealthy is believing you deserve to be wealthy, too.

5. **You get to choose your people.** Hell is other people if you are forced to spend time with folks you don't like. You know the people who are always late because they are selfish with their time? They used to bug me to no end. What about colleagues who steal your ideas and don't give you credit? Or how about people who get in touch only when they need something? Or the guy who was rude to a waiter at your business lunch? Now imagine not having to pretend you like someone just because they hold the keys to your future. When you're financially independent, you're more likely to hang out only with people whose company you truly enjoy.

6. **You make your parents proud.** Our parents tend to give us everything and ask for very little in return. They hope we can simply lead happy, self-sustaining lives. When we are financially independent, that is one less thing they have to worry about.

   When we are financially free, we can also start spending more time with our parents because we have more time to spend. It has been pure joy for me to give back to my parents for all their years of sacrifice, and I want to do everything I can to allow them to live great lives.

7. **You get to spend more time with your children.** The sooner you become financially independent, the sooner you can spend more time with your kids. It's hard to juggle work and parenting. Both are full-time jobs!

My wife and I had children relatively late in life (thirty-nine for me, thirty-seven for her), which is one of the downsides of trying to achieve financial independence at a younger age. We focused so much on our careers that we didn't seriously entertain the idea of starting a family until our midthirties.

Now that we are parents, the value of financial independence has grown even more. There's nothing more precious than spending time with your kids. You only get one shot at raising them before they go out on their own. So make the most of it. (And if you don't have children, then make the most of your time with your family and friends.)

Now that we've covered some of the universal reasons that financial independence is worth pursuing, let's unpack the specific ways that it can help you live your best life.

What Does Financial Independence Look Like to You?

It's time to get brutally honest with yourself. What do you want your financially independent life to look like? In 2009, I helped ignite the modern-day FIRE movement when I started *Financial Samurai*. (If you haven't heard of it, FIRE stands for Financial Independence Retire Early.) More than a decade later, there are hundreds of FIRE blogs and dozens of major media outlets writing about FIRE.

There are a lot of different points of view about what FIRE means, but one common definition of FIRE is when your net worth equals 25X your annual expenses. In other words, if your annual expenses are $100,000, you are considered financially independent if you have a net worth of $2.5 million, preferably excluding the value of your primary residence.

However, with low interest rates, declining expected returns of risk assets, exorbitant health-care costs, and longer life expectancies, I don't believe a net worth equal to 25X your annual expenses is enough. My preferred definition of FIRE is when you've achieved one of two things:

1. **Your net worth equals 20X your average annual *gross income*.** When you base your net worth goal on your income rather than your expenses, you can't cheat by slashing

your spending. Instead, you are always encouraged to save and invest more as your income grows. For those of you who still prefer to use a multiple of expenses, consider using a range of between 25X annual expenses and 20X annual gross income before declaring yourself financially independent. For example, let's say you spend $50,000 and earn $100,000 a year. Your FI range is, therefore, $1,250,000 to $2,000,000.

2. **Your investments generate enough passive income to cover your best life's expenses.** So if your annual expenses are $100,000, you are considered financially independent once your existing investments generate over $125,000 a year for you (because you've got to pay taxes on that income). Living off of your investment *income*, without touching your principal, ensures you'll never run out of money as long as you live within your means. That, right there, is freedom.

Since 2009, the FIRE movement has evolved into three distinct FIRE lifestyles: **Fat FIRE, Lean FIRE, and Barista FIRE.** These are all subjective terms based on how one wants to live in retirement—from really living it up (Fat) to living relatively frugally (Lean) to working a part-time job and/or having a working spouse (Barista).

The evolution occurred because FIRE means drastically different things to different people. It's human nature to try to make ourselves feel better about our progress by redefining terms. However, it's important to be honest about what your ideal FIRE lifestyle is—and not to lie to yourself about it.

To me, FIRE looks like living in San Francisco or Honolulu in a home large enough that we each get our own bedroom, providing a great education for our children, traveling a couple times a year, and having enough cash flow each month to continue investing. Unfortunately, this type of lifestyle doesn't come cheap, which is why I'm still so focused on building passive income.

Someone else's best FIRE life may be living in a converted school bus while adventuring across the country with no kids. For them, maybe $30,000 a year is enough to be happy. The beauty of personal finance is that there is no right or wrong way to live your lifestyle. There is only the way *you* want to live your lifestyle and the steps you will take to get there.

When I negotiated a severance in 2012 at age thirty-four, I was technically Barista FIRE for three years because my wife was still working. She is three years younger than me, and we had set a goal for her to also "retire" at thirty-four if everything went well with our finances in that time.

During my Barista FIRE years, I was added to her company's health-care plan while I paid for all housing costs. We kept expenses relatively low, and I spent those years writing a book teaching people how to negotiate a severance like I did and writing at *Financial Samurai*. (I'll share more on negotiating a severance in chapter 11.)

In 2015, my wife left her day job at thirty-four after I helped her negotiate a severance. Within a couple of years we were living a modest financially independent lifestyle because our investments had appreciated while our online income continued to grow. It took us nine years after I first left work to get to our ideal passive-investment income figure because our family, and hence our expenses, kept growing. And we're still working on building investment income because there are no guarantees.

Here it's worth pointing out that the notion of "early retirement," in the sense of never working again, is often a *gimmick*. Many people you see online preaching about early retirement are working as hard as ever, mainly on their own online project. My articles don't write themselves. This book took two years to write. I'm not retired in the slightest. Instead, I'm simply free to do what I want.

After more than ten years of not having a day job, I don't think retiring early is what FIRE is all about. I tried twiddling my thumbs for one year in 2012 while aggressively traveling abroad, and after about six months, I was itching to do something productive with my time. In essence, I never plan on retiring so long as my fingers, voice, and mind are still working!

As you plot your journey to financial independence, I want to encourage you to focus on the FI (financial independence) part of FIRE. Nobody retires early and does *nothing*. Or, if they try, they rarely last long. Life is richer when we fill it with meaningful work. And one of the best parts of financial independence is that you get to do work that you feel passionate about.

Your Happiness Equation

Happiness equals reality minus expectations. When the reality of life is better than anticipated, you're generally much more appreciative of what you have.

As a middle schooler in Malaysia, I was once swarmed by beggars while visiting the island of Penang. Even when I had nothing left to give, they kept pulling on my clothes, pleading. It was a jolting moment that made me realize not everybody had a warm bed to sleep in, and so that Christmas, instead of hoping for a new skateboard deck from Powell-Peralta, I decided I would expect nothing. In the end, when my parents gifted me a T-shirt, I was happy.

People say money doesn't buy happiness because it's true. After you make enough to comfortably survive, whether it's $75,000 in Kansas City or $250,000 in San Francisco, having more money seldom moves the happiness needle significantly.

A recent World Happiness Report ranked Finland as the happiest country in the world. The report highlighted six significant factors that contribute to happiness: GDP per capita, social support, life expectancy, freedom to make life choices, generosity, and perceptions of corruption levels.

Despite the United States having by far the highest nominal GDP in the world, and the ninth largest GDP per capita, it ranked only eighteenth in the survey. What a conundrum to be so rich, yet so thoroughly average in the happiness ranking.

Happiness is subjective and extremely difficult to quantify. But based on the data, it's clear that money is only one part of the happiness equation.

In my opinion, money determines, at most, 40% of your level of happiness. Once you get to where you have enough money to do what you want, your 40% is maxed out.

The remaining 60% that determines happiness often has to do with family, friends, accomplishments, faith, and purpose. If money were a predominant happiness indicator, billionaires would never cry, never suffer, and definitely never get divorced.

Progress is my one-word definition of happiness.

I believe happiness is deeply connected to continually making progress in anything you care about: your relationship with your partner, your relationship with your children, your fitness, your finances, your career, your sports skills, the number of people you help, etc.

Imagine this 40% part of your financial picture is complete. How would you fill the remaining 60% of your masterpiece? I suggest focusing on three key buckets as you think about what makes you happy:

- *What* **do you want the freedom to do?** Having independence and the freedom to do what you want is an enormous contributor to happiness. The more autonomy you have, the happier you will be. Working at a job you hate just for the purpose of making money is a suboptimal choice. There are countless jobs and freelance opportunities that can provide income and excitement. It's up to all of us to keep looking for that better combination.
- *With whom* **do you want to spend your time?** Having someone who loves you as much as you love them brings tremendous happiness. Children give parents a tremendous

purpose: to provide the best life possible for them. This means making money, providing shelter and a good education, and staying alive for as long as possible. If having kids is not for you, whom would you like to share your freedom with? Friends, parents, siblings? It's up to you!

- **Where do you want to live that life of freedom?** This *where to live* piece is inextricably tied to money, and we explore that truth in part 2. Where you live matters more than some people like to admit.

As you think through your full happiness picture, also take this time to acknowledge what makes you unhappy and get intentional about removing those things from your life.

Put a Price Tag on It

Once you have a clear sense of the life you're after—of the ingredients you need to fill your happiness cup—you can calculate how much money you'll realistically need to get there. Don't gloss over this part. You'll see in chapter 2 that the entire *Buy This, Not That* (*BTNT*) method is rooted in answering questions about what you want and what you're willing to do to get it. So get used to being brutally honest with yourself if you aren't already.

As discussed earlier, everybody has a different level of income that will bring maximum happiness due to different desires, needs, and living arrangements. It's up to you to find out your optimal income level. Crunch the numbers.

Let's say you want to live in San Francisco, Honolulu, Paris, Amsterdam, or New York City, some of my favorite cities in the world. You should look up the median rent and housing prices for each city. Now add up your realistic food, clothing, and transportation expenses. If you have children, factor in private education costs in case you can't get your children into a good public school.

Once the necessities have been accounted for, include wants such as vacations and entertainment as well as charity. After conducting the expense exercise, you may be surprised at how quickly costs add up! On the next page is a sample budget for a family of four living in an expensive American city.

I know some of you will be baffled by some of the expenses. That's okay. Just because you don't have the same expenses (or goals, desires, or ideals) doesn't mean one budget is any less realistic than another budget.

HOW A FAMILY OF FOUR LIVES ON $300,000 IN AN EXPENSIVE METROPOLITAN AREA

Gross Income	Annual $300,000	Monthly $25,000
401(k) contribution (two working parents)	$41,000	$3,417
Taxable income after 401(k) contributions	$259,000	$21,583
Taxable income after $25,900 standard deduction and 401(k) contributions	$233,100	$19,425
Tax bill (24% federal, 8% state, 7.65% FICA, 23% effective total)	$53,613	$4,468
Net income + $4,000 child tax credit + $25.9K noncash standard deduction	$209,387	$17,449
Expenses	**Annual**	**Monthly**
Childcare for two-year-old	$24,000	$2,000
Preschool for four-year-old	$26,400	$2,200
Food for four ($70/day on average, including weekly date night)	$25,550	$2,129
529 plan (K–12 and college savings plan)	$13,200	$1,100
Mortgage ($2,100 principal, $1,900 interest)	$48,000	$4,000
Property tax (1.24% on $1.6 million home)	$19,840	$1,653
Property insurance	$1,560	$130
Property maintenance	$2,400	$200
Utilities (electricity, water, trash)	$3,600	$300
Life insurance (two $1M twenty-year term policies through Policygenius)	$2,160	$180
Umbrella policy ($2M)	$600	$50
Health care (employer-subsidized)	$8,400	$700
Baby items (diapers, toys, crib, stroller, playpen, etc.)	$2,400	$200
Three weeks of vacation per year (two destinations, one staycation)	$7,200	$600
Entertainment (Netflix, shows, sporting events, social functions, w/e getaways)	$4,800	$400
Car payment (Toyota Highlander, not Range Rover)	$3,900	$325
Car insurance and maintenance	$1,800	$200
Gas	$3,600	$300
Mobile phone (family plan)	$1,440	$120
Clothes for four (Old Navy, not Gucci)	$1,800	$150
Personal-care products	$1,200	$100
Charity (foster care, nystagmus vision research, UNICEF)	$3,600	$300
Student loans (husband paid off $50K at thirty)	$0	$0
Total Expenses	**$208,050**	**$17,337**
Cash flow after expenses to pay for miscellaneous	**$1,337**	**$112**

Relevant cities: San Francisco, NYC, Boston, LA, San Diego, Seattle, DC, Miami, Denver, Honolulu, Vancouver, Toronto, Hong Kong, Tokyo, London, Paris, Sydney

Source: FinancialSamurai.com

This exercise of adding up your ideal spending is necessary to come up with your ideal income for maximum happiness. When you're shooting for financial targets, be aggressive, so that even if you fail to achieve your goals, you'll likely end up with more of a safety net than if you had more conservative targets.

In my mind, earning a steady $300,000 a year with two children in San Francisco is a good figure to shoot for. If you have one kid and live in Austin, perhaps $120,000 might provide you a similar ideal lifestyle. And if you are a single person living in Raleigh, $50,000 may be more than enough. Everybody has different preferences and costs of living vary wildly by place.

Think about an after-tax monthly income number you'd like to achieve. Keep that goal in front of you because you're about to do a lot of number crunching, planning, and sacrificing to get there. Remember, your goal is not to try to earn this ideal after-tax income. Your ultimate goal is to make the majority of that money through passive income combined with doing something you love.

Personally, I believe the ideal split between active and passive income is 30/70, the exact opposite of my 70/30 decision-making philosophy. In other words, out of a $120,000 ideal income, it feels better if $30,000 of the income comes from doing something you enjoy. By staying active, we get the reward of staying relevant and productive. Meanwhile, with 70% of our ideal split coming passively, we won't feel the stress of running out of money. After all, when we're discussing ideal incomes or spending, we usually input a buffer of safety.

What Does Financial Independence Feel Like?

Since I left my "day job," a number of people have asked how it feels to be financially independent. The quick answer is that it's the same as when you were a kid and excited about a holiday or a birthday or a summer vacation. You go to bed late because you're so excited, and you wake up early because you're so excited!

I've technically been financially independent since 2009, when I realized my passive income could cover all basic expenses. I could have led a simple life in Hawaii tending to my grandfather's mango and papaya trees in the morning while I surfed in the afternoon. Lean FIRE, in other words. But I wanted more because I eventually wanted to start a family with my wife.

By 2012, I had decided an extra three years' worth of capital accumulation was enough to say sayonara to banking for good. That is when I negotiated a severance to be free. It was now or never to make a move.

But the truth is, even if you've accumulated enough capital or built enough recurring income streams to be free, you will always have some financial concerns. The 2008–9 global financial crisis wiped away about 35% of my net worth in just six months. Another prolonged crisis could certainly happen.

However, even if we can't eradicate financial worry, waiting for 100% certainty before taking action is not the Financial Samurai way. Instead, we must live our lives knowing that we've done our best to increase our probability of success to 70%+. At the same time, we must be humble enough to expect that things will go wrong some of the time.

The key is to recognize what went wrong and take action to make things better. Your goal is to continually make progress on the things that matter most to you and your family. Embrace financial independence as a journey of ongoing improvement with no finish line.

THE FINANCIAL SAMURAI WAY

I end each chapter with a list of action items to get you moving on your journey to financial independence. You'll see that by breaking down the *BTNT* method into small, achievable steps, it's entirely doable. So don't skip them! Take your time to work through them, and I promise you'll be on your way to financial freedom. To get started:

- Envision what you would do, whom you would hang out with, and where you would live if you were financially free. This is your North Star.

- Come up with a realistic best-life budget so you know exactly how much passive investment income to shoot for.

- Work to build a net worth equal to 20X your annual income or generate enough passive investment income to cover your desired living expenses. If you prefer using expenses, consider your financial independence number as a range between 25X annual expenses and 20X annual income.

- Ultimately, your financial independence number should give you the courage to change suboptimal situations. If you are unable to act, then you probably need to keep on growing your wealth.

- The difference between your passive investment income and your expenses is called your gap. As your amount of passive investment income rises toward your total expenses and the gap gets narrower, more enjoyable jobs open up that enable you to bridge the gap.

Chapter 2

Do the Math and the Plan Will Come

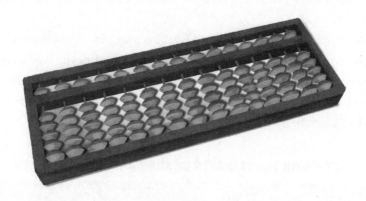

et's do a little number crunching.

If you're the type to set financial goals—and I'll wager that you are—hopefully you enjoy running numbers to figure out how to reach those goals. And if you don't find this fun, well . . . you still have to do it. Remember, financial independence comes when you figure out the math of money *applied*. I have a good feeling that the excitement of reaching your dream life will make all this math pretty interesting. So let's look under the hood.

In the previous chapter, I said that my definition of financial independence is (1) when your net worth equals 20X your average annual gross income or (2) when your investments generate enough passive income to cover your best life's expenses. These two points are highly correlated financial objectives, and ideally you will eventually achieve both.

I'll start with net worth. **Everyone should have a net worth target to shoot for based**

on age, work experience, and income. Net worth targets will help you stick to your financial plan and motivate you to do more if you're falling behind. Too many people wake up after ten years and wonder where all their money went. If only they had a net worth guide they could print out and stick on their refrigerator to keep them on track.

Here is that guide. My table links that 20X net worth target to age sixty-plus, the more traditional age for retirement. However, if you can build a net worth equal to 20X your annual income by a younger age, then you can retire earlier if you wish. By focusing on income as the multiplier, you'll keep yourself challenged as you make more money. Further, focusing on income doesn't allow you to "cheat" by drastically minimizing expenses to achieve financial freedom.

For those of you who may have started working later, due to graduate school or other reasons, you can follow the Years Worked column instead of the Age column as your guide. However, since time waits for no one, ideally you will aim to achieve a net worth equal to 2X income by thirty, 5X income by thirty-five, 10X income by forty, 15X income by fifty, and 20X income by sixty.

NET WORTH (NW) TARGETS BY AGE OR WORK EXPERIENCE

Age	Years Worked	Multiple of Income	NW Based on $50K	NW Based on $100K	NW Based on $150K	NW Based on $200K	NW Based on $300K	NW Based on $500K
22	0	0	0	0	0	0	0	0
25	3	0.5	$25,000	$50,000	$75,000	$100,000	$150,000	$250,000
28	6	1	$50,000	$100,000	$150,000	$200,000	$300,000	$500,000
30	8	2	$100,000	$200,000	$300,000	$400,000	$600,000	$1,000,000
32	10	3	$150,000	$300,000	$450,000	$600,000	$900,000	$1,500,000
35	13	5	$250,000	$500,000	$750,000	$1,000,000	$1,500,000	$2,500,000
40	18	10	$500,000	$1,000,000	$1,500,000	$2,000,000	$3,000,000	$5,000,000
45	23	13	$650,000	$1,300,000	$1,950,000	$2,600,000	$3,900,000	$6,500,000
50	28	15	$750,000	$1,500,000	$2,250,000	$3,000,000	$4,500,000	$7,500,000
55	33	18	$900,000	$1,800,000	$2,700,000	$3,600,000	$5,400,000	$9,000,000
60+	38	20	$1,000,000	$2,000,000	$3,000,000	$4,000,000	$6,000,000	$10,000,000

The ultimate goal is to achieve a net worth of 20X average annual income.

Source: FinancialSamurai.com

Given that everything in life is a gamble, how quickly you achieve financial independence depends on how much work you put in, how much you save, and how much risk you take.

Everything amazing seems impossible until you actually do it. Just as a personal trainer challenges you to get more out of yourself than you would on your own, my charts can be used for the same motivational purpose. Don't let them intimidate you.

Even if you do not achieve the net worth targets, you will still likely achieve a far greater net worth than if you hadn't set goals. The more wealth you accumulate, the more courage you will have to take more risks, try new things, and change things up if you wish. Continue to build financial momentum. You will be amazed by the results over time.

After landing my first job, I made it a mission to save and invest as much as possible each month. This meant living in a studio apartment with a friend, maxing out my 401(k) contributions, investing 100% of my year-end bonus each year, and saving at least 20% of my salary after 401(k) contributions.

My original goal, and the goal that I recommend, was to save 50% of my after-tax income. That's where I started, and I eventually kept pushing until I got to about an 80% saving rate during my peak earning years.

If you can manage to live off what's left each month after saving 50% of your after-tax dollars, it will mean that each year you save is one year of living expenses. If you can get to a 70% saving rate, then each year you save provides for two years of living expenses and so forth. At the very minimum, please save about 20% of your after-tax income. At this rate, it will take four years to save for one year of living expenses.

Save more, invest more, reach financial independence sooner. It's that simple.

A Multiple of Income Is Better Than a Multiple of Expenses

I want to stress again that it's important to **link your net worth goals to your gross income**.

Focusing on an earnings multiple instead of an expenses multiple is a vital shift away from a scarcity mindset and toward an abundance mindset. You can use your highest annual gross income or your average income for all your working years. It's just too easy to lie to yourself if you base your net worth goal on expenses. Even if you manage to get by while living on macaroni and cheese, it's probably not a sustainable lifestyle.

Push to save in your early years but recognize that you'll eventually need more breathing room to live comfortably. Living extremely frugally only to then live extremely frugally in retirement is not the ideal life for most. Instead, you want to focus on maximizing income to improve your chances of living your best life possible.

If you feel strongly about using a multiple of your expenses as a net worth target, go for it. One of the most often used metrics is 25X your annual expenses, and it's based on the popular 4% rule for safe withdrawal rates. I don't recommend withdrawing from your nest egg at a rate of 4%, and I'll explain why in a minute. For now, I'll emphasize that accumulating a net worth equal to 25X your annual expenses is a good goal to shoot for. But once you get there, reassess. If you're satisfied and still have the desire to work, see if you can get to a net worth equal to 20X your annual income. Make it a fun challenge, knowing that in the worst case, you'll likely be fine with what you already have.

Also remember that the younger you retire, the higher your expenses will be compared with retirement later in life. You will have a longer life without full income to cover it. You'll need to pay for health care (whether subsidized or unsubsidized), housing costs (versus retiring later, perhaps with your mortgage paid off), and kids if you have them (versus being an empty nester). Plus, you won't have access to Social Security payments or traditional retirement savings accounts like an IRA or a 401(k). For now, the earliest you can take Social Security is sixty-two, and the earliest you can withdraw penalty free from your 401(k) or IRA is fifty-nine and a half, although there are exceptions. Please see the Further Reading section on Rule 72(t) for those who might want to withdraw from their tax-advantaged accounts earlier than fifty-nine and a half.

With this in mind, the earlier you retire, the greater the likelihood you'll want to generate supplemental income through something you enjoy doing.

Net Worth versus Passive Income

There is a constant balance between net worth and passive income. The two are intertwined and synergistic. If you achieve the various net worth targets, your *passive-income potential* will automatically increase as well. So long as you have achieved the target net worth, you can change the *composition* of your net worth to generate income if you want or need to. When it comes to money, so much about being rich is *feeling* rich and financially secure.

Let's say you make $100,000 and achieve my target net worth of 10X your annual income at age forty. With a net worth of $1 million, perhaps $500,000 is tied up in your primary residence and the remaining $500,000 is invested in growth stocks that pay zero income. Therefore, your current passive investment income is $0.

However, if you decide you've had enough of work and want to downshift for a few years to travel the world, you could *change* your net worth composition to help hold you over. First, you could sell your home and collect up to $250,000 in tax-free income as an individual, depending on how long you lived in it. You could then live off the $470,000 in proceeds, after paying a 5% commission to your selling agent and 1% in transfer taxes and fees. Or you could reinvest the $470,000 in large-capitalization dividend-paying companies to generate $14,100 a year at 3%. Or you could do a combination of both.

In addition to selling your home, you could sell some growth stocks that pay no dividends and reinvest the proceeds in bonds, dividend-paying stocks, REITs, and other income-producing assets. Just be aware of the tax implications. (Don't worry, I cover all of these in detail in later chapters.)

By following my target net worth multiples, you will always (always!) have the *potential* to generate passive investment income if you want to. Knowing that you have this option if you need it brings greater peace of mind. You just need to decide how to change your net worth composition while being aware of the tax implications.

At the same time, if you can achieve your desired passive income amount to consistently cover your desired living expenses, then you will have achieved your target net worth, *regardless of the multiple*. For example, let's say you make $100,000 a year at age fifty and have found yourself happily living off $30,000 a year for the past three years. My guide says you should have a net worth of about $1.5 million based on 15X annual income. However, you find yourself at age fifty with a net worth of "only" $800,000. Well, $800,000 is fine because it has consistently been generating $36,000 a year, enough to cover your desired living expenses. You now have the option to downshift to part-time work or make less money doing something new. Having the freedom to choose is priceless.

Higher potential reward almost always requires taking greater risks. Therefore, if you are risk averse and can't stand volatility, it's likely you will need to accumulate more capital because you will likely receive a lower return. The reverse is true for someone who is risk loving due to personality and circumstance. (We will measure risk tolerance in more detail later in this chapter.)

Let's say you're forty years old with a lot of energy left. Assuming only a 3% to 5% return or yield on your $1 million portfolio to generate $30,000 to $50,000 a year may be too conservative; instead, you may have a greater risk appetite to invest in highly volatile tech stocks that may grow by more than 15% a year. If your investments sour by –20%, you have the time and energy to spend months of your life working to make up for such losses. But if you're seventy years old and time is much more precious, you may decide that you are unwilling to spend even a day making up for any potential losses.

When it comes to risk, always equate monetary loss with time loss.

How much passive income you need is up to you. Once you decide on a number, you've got to figure out how much capital you need invested to generate that target figure. Simply take what you think you need per year and divide by 2%, 3%, or 4% to get your minimum target net worth figure. For example, if you want $80,000 in passive income, you will need between $2 million and $4 million in capital. The 2%, 3%, or 4% is your estimated annual yield or return. However, if you believe your portfolio will go up by 15% a year (unlikely), divide $80,000 by 15% and you'll only need a $533,333 portfolio to pay for your living expenses. Realistically, the largest divisor you should probably use is 8%, if we're talking about creating a sustainable passive-income source. The most appropriate divisor is likely between 2% and 4%.

Investing your savings in a risk-appropriate manner is vital for achieving financial independence. I show you how to allocate your assets based on your goals and circumstances in chapter 5.

For now, it's important to understand that your actions must always be congruent with your goals. If they're not, then you will suffer from delusion. You can't expect to achieve financial freedom if you don't aggressively earn, save, invest, and plan, just as I can't expect to get six-pack abs by eating lemon meringue pie every day and not working out. And delusion may be the biggest risk to your financial independence and overall happiness. When it comes to your money, it's always better to be a little too conservative and end up with too much rather than being a little too aggressive and ending up with too little. There is no rewinding time.

Two Retirement Philosophies to Consider

Once you have a target net worth, you need to figure out your safe withdrawal rate for when you're ready to quit the nine-to-five game. If your net worth is under the estate tax threshold, above which every dollar faces a likely "death tax" rate of 40%, then the ideal withdrawal rate for retirement may be one that does not touch principal. You may want to live off your retirement principal *income* for the rest of your life. This way, you won't have to stress about running out of money. You can also give away some of your wealth to those in need and help create generational wealth for them. The estate tax threshold is $12.06 million per person in 2022 but changes frequently. Which retirement philosophy you lean toward will help determine your net worth target and safe withdrawal rate in retirement.

1. **The YOLO retirement philosophy:** If you adopt this philosophy, then your goal is to die with little to nothing. This retirement philosophy makes sense because it

maximizes the benefits of the time you spent working and the risks you took investing. Further, why not spend as much money helping others as possible while still alive?

2. **The Legacy retirement philosophy:** If you believe in leaving a legacy, then you will want to set up a trust fund or establish an organization that keeps your good name alive for as long as possible while helping others. Leaving a legacy may mean creating a scholarship at your alma mater or establishing a fund to perpetually donate the returns to an organization that helps the disabled. Whatever the case may be, helping others while honoring your family name is something many aspire to achieve.

Most people are likely somewhere in between. Personal finance, like so many things, is on a spectrum. However, the closer you lean toward the YOLO retirement philosophy, the higher your safe withdrawal rate in retirement can be (4% to 8% recommended range). The closer you lean toward the Legacy retirement philosophy, especially if you are below the estate tax threshold, the lower your safe withdrawal rate in retirement should be (0% to 3% recommended range).

A Simple Formula to Determine Your *Initial* Safe Withdrawal Rate in Retirement

I said earlier that I don't recommend withdrawing from your nest egg at the popular 4% rate. It's important to understand why. The "4% Rule" was first published in the *Journal of Financial Planning* in 1994 by William P. Bengen. It was subsequently made popular by three Trinity University professors in 1998 in a study called the Trinity Study.

The rule was based on research showing that historical annual market returns from the years 1925 to 1998 would allow someone to withdraw from their portfolio at a rate of 4% every year with little risk of running out of money. The Trinity Study notes that, if history is any guide, withdrawal rates of about 4% are extremely unlikely to exhaust any portfolio of stocks and bonds for up to thirty years. As a result, the 4% Rule became retirement enthusiasts' favorite guideline for a safe withdrawal rate.

However, a lot has changed since the 1990s. Most of all, the ten-year bond yield has come down from a high of 7.8% in October 1994 to a low of 0.53% in July 2020. Although the risk-free rate has inched up since its all-time low in 2020, it still remains much lower today.

Therefore, we must also change with the times. Here's a safe-withdrawal-rate formula to consider: **the Financial Samurai Safe Withdrawal Rate (FSSWR) = ten-year Treasury bond yield × 80%.**

In other words, if the ten-year bond yield is at 2%, FSSWR recommends retirees limit their withdrawal rate to 1.6%. As the ten-year bond yield increases, so does the safe withdrawal rate, and vice versa.

At a glance, my safe-withdrawal-rate formula may seem overly conservative. Many of you might even call it downright absurd. However, I have devised it based on when the 4% Rule was created. Back in 1998, when the 4% Rule was popularized by the Trinity Study, 4% equaled roughly 80% of the average ten-year bond yield of 5%. In other words, you didn't need a PhD back then to conclude you'd never run out of money withdrawing at a 4% rate when you could have earned a risk-free 5%! Therefore, if you can accept the logic of the 4% Rule, you can accept the logic of the FSSWR. It's my way of simplifying and adapting to different economic scenarios.

But here's the real reason the FSSWR was created: to protect you during one of the most vulnerable periods of your life. After spending a lifetime working, you may find it tremendously jolting to leave work behind. And a bear market may hit right when you retire. (Just ask those who retired in 2007!)

Therefore, I encourage you to be more conservative with your withdrawal rate during the *initial years* of retirement as you figure out your new life. Chances are high that the younger you escape work, the more self-doubt you will have.

In retrospect, leaving a multiple-six-figure job behind at age thirty-four was unwise. I didn't follow my 20X income rule because I hadn't created it yet. I left with a net worth equal to about 8X my average income over the previous three years. If I were my father, I probably would have told myself to gut it out until age forty and then try to negotiate a severance.

Because the FSSWR is so low, it encourages you to either accumulate a larger net worth before leaving work or, more pertinently, find alternative ways to make money once you do leave work, in order to gain more purpose and cover the gap. Feeling lost is terrible. After a couple of years of finding yourself after retirement, you can then resume a more traditional safe withdrawal rate of 3% to 5%.

To read more about the negatives of early retirement that nobody likes talking about, see "The Negatives of Early Retirement" in the Further Reading section, which links to a post that is updated annually with new feedback from readers. Anybody who tells you that early retirement is always roses and rainbows is BSing you.

THE TEN-YEAR BOND YIELD'S IMPORTANCE

The ten-year bond yield is the most important economic indicator to follow. This one figure gives investors, economists, and financial freedom fighters expectations about inflation, the direction of the federal funds rate, employment, investor risk appetite, the health of the economy, and so much more.

It makes sense to put your money into an investment only if it has the potential to give you a return that is above the risk-free rate of return, which is traditionally the ten-year bond yield. In other words, if the ten-year bond yield is 2%, there's no way you'd invest in a stock that has an expected return of 2% or less. You would require a risk premium to compensate you for a potential loss. As a real estate investor, you would never invest in a piece of real estate that had only a 2% expected return or less. Instead, you would demand a risk premium to be compensated for managing tenants, dealing with maintenance issues, and potentially taking on debt.

I could write an entire book about the importance of the ten-year bond yield. However, to keep things simple, I suggest you always look at it as your opportunity-cost hurdle. In other words, before investing in any asset, compare your expected returns with what you could get risk-free by buying and holding a ten-year Treasury bond. As the ten-year bond yield declines, the opportunity cost declines, which is why so much liquidity has flowed into riskier assets.

As the ten-year bond yield inches up, economic activity will slow at the margin because it becomes more expensive to borrow. The yield is a big determinant for mortgage rates and, to a lesser extent, consumer loan rates. At some point, if the ten-year bond yield rises high enough, investors will decide they no longer want to take on extra risk.

Return Expectations for Risk Assets Are Declining

In 2021, Vanguard came out with its return expectations for the next ten years for stocks, bonds, and inflation. Its Vanguard Capital Markets Model calculated only a 4.02% annual return for U.S. stocks, a 1.31% annual return for U.S. bonds, and 1.58% inflation over the next ten years. These figures were down from 10.37% for U.S. stocks, 5.3% for U.S. bonds, and 2.87% inflation over the previous ten years.

HISTORICAL RETURNS ARE NO GUARANTEE OF FUTURE RETURNS

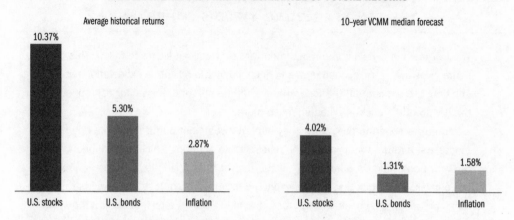

Notes: Past performance is no guarantee of future returns. The performance of an index is not an exact representation of any particular investment, as you cannot invest directly in an index. Data for average historical U.S. stock returns, U.S. bond returns, and inflation figures cover January 26, 1926, through March 31, 2021. U.S. stocks are represented by the Standard & Poor's 90 Index from 1926 through March 3, 1957; the S&P 500 index from March 4, 1957, through 1974; the Wilshire 5000 Index from 1975 through April 22, 2005; and the MSCI US Broad Market Index thereafter. Bonds are represented by the S&P High Grade Corporate Index from 1926 through 1968, the Citigroup High Grade Index from 1969 through 1972, the Bloomberg Barclays U.S. Long Credit AA Index from 1973 through 1975, and the Bloomberg Barclays U.S. Aggregate Bond Index thereafter. Inflation is represented by the U.S. Consumer Price Index. The VCMM forecasts are as of December 2020 and correspond to the distribution of 10,000 simulations for 10-year annualized returns for U.S. stocks and U.S. bonds. The median return is the 50th percentile of an asset class's distribution of annual returns. The 10-year median forecasts for U.S. stocks, bonds, and inflation represent the annualized expectation over a 10-year horizon, though considerable uncertainty in those outcomes remains over the period.

Sources: Vanguard, from VCMM forecasts, and Thomson Reuters Datastream

What this means for you is that if you have a portfolio mix in retirement of 60% stocks and 40% bonds, your portfolio will return just 2.93% a year if Vanguard's forecasts come true.

Vanguard's forecasts seem overly conservative, but what if they turn out to be correct? A bear market could easily hit. Withdrawing at a 4% rate or higher may prove to be too much.

And it's not just Vanguard predicting lower returns for stocks, bonds, and other risk assets in the future. Joining Vanguard are Goldman Sachs, Bank of America, BlackRock, and other large financial institutions. Therefore, if you plan to retire earlier than normal (at sixty-plus), you may have to do the following:

- **Accumulate more capital before retiring:** Shoot to accumulate a multiple of your annual expenses equal to how long you expect to live minus your age of retirement (for example, 30X annual expenses if you expect to live to age eighty and are retiring at fifty), or else 20X your annual income. Aiming for 25X your annual expenses with no supplemental income likely won't be enough. But again, these are financial goals to shoot for, not hard-and-fast rules.

- **Generate supplemental retirement income:** Find something you love to do that also makes money through consulting, part-time work, or entrepreneurship. If you don't plan to accumulate 20X your annual income or a large multiple of your annual expenses, you must find ways to generate supplemental income.
- **Delay your retirement date:** Each year you delay has the double benefit of allowing you to save more and have one less year of life to provide for.
- **Lower your life expectancy by eating more junk food and not exercising:** Not recommended.

Start Conservatively and Then Adjust

Crunching your numbers based on blue-sky, realistic, and pessimistic scenarios is important. However, until you actually leave a steady paycheck behind, you won't know exactly *how you'll feel* in retirement. The longer you've been working, the more jolting retirement will feel.

Therefore, I recommend first living off the FSSWR for at least six months *before* you retire. This way, you can get an idea of what it is like to live on what you have. After you leave your paycheck behind, continue to live off the FSSWR until you figure out your supplemental retirement income needs, if any.

Once you feel like you won't fall through the cracks while in retirement, which may take one to three years, you can gradually adjust your safe withdrawal rate upward if you wish. And if you feel like you need to be more conservative, whether due to a belief in an upcoming bear market or an unexpected expense, you can lower your safe withdrawal rate accordingly.

Stay flexible. No one should retire and expect to withdraw like a robot at a set rate that never changes. We have to be adaptable, and part of being adaptable is paying close attention to our needs, wants, and income streams.

Everybody's needs, risk tolerance, and goals are different. However, the 70/30 decision in retirement is to start conservatively with your safe withdrawal rate and spending for the first couple of years and then adjust depending on circumstances.

Calculate Your Risk Tolerance

I've mentioned that our risk tolerance plays a big role in our financial independence strategy. So you may be wondering how you can measure your risk tolerance. It seems very subjective. The answer lies in how we value our time. As investors, we take risks in order to generate potential returns that will help us reduce the amount of time we need to work. The more we make, the less time we need to spend working to accumulate our net worth objective and vice versa.

Therefore, you can calculate your risk tolerance by measuring how much time you're willing and able to spend working in order to make up for any potential losses from your investments. If you're a healthy twenty-five-year-old, you should have a high risk tolerance since you likely have more energy and willingness to work than an unhealthy seventy-year-old. As a result, you would be willing to invest in more speculative investments for potentially greater return.

Let's dig into what risk looks like in terms of investments: since 1929, the median bear market price decline has been 33.63%, while the average bear market price decline has been 35.62%. (A bear market is any market decline greater than 20%, and the median and average price decline is always adjusting.)

Further, the average length of a bear market has been about 289 days, or just under ten months. The longest bear market—the Great Depression—occurred from March 1937 until April 1942 and lasted for sixty-one months, whereas the bear market in 2020 saw a decline for only about a month and a half, starting on February 14. By August 2020, the S&P 500 had regained a new high.

Therefore, it's reasonable to assume that the next bear market could also bring equity valuations down by ~35% over an approximately ten-month period. Since this is a realistic worst-case scenario, let's calculate how many months you would need to work to make up for a 35% decline in your investments.

Here's a quick **risk tolerance formula** you can use:

(public equity exposure × 35%) ÷ monthly gross income

For example, let's say you have $500,000 in equities and make $10,000 a month. To quantify your risk tolerance, the calculation is $500,000 × 35% = $175,000 ÷ $10,000 = 17.5.

The $175,000 amount is how much you could potentially lose on paper; 17.5 is the number of *additional* months of your life you'd need to work to earn a gross income equal to how much you lost. After taxes, you're really only making around $8,000 a month, so you would actually have to work closer to twenty-two more months and contribute 100% of your after-tax income to be whole.

But it gets worse. Given that you need to pay for basic living expenses, you need to work even longer than twenty-two months. Good thing stocks tend to rebound after an average bear market duration of ten months, if you can hold on.

You've got to ask yourself whether you are truly willing to work an additional 17.5+ more months to make up for your losses. If the answer is no, then your risk exposure is probably too high. If the answer is a resounding yes, then your risk exposure is probably too low.

Because everybody has a different tax rate, I've simplified the formula using a gross monthly income figure instead of a net monthly income figure. Feel free to adjust the risk tolerance multiple based on your personal income tax situation.

Time is money. The more you value your time, the more you dislike your job, and the less you desire to work, the lower your risk tolerance should be. You're simply not willing to sacrifice as much time to make up for potential losses.

Let's look at the scenario of a seventy-year-old retiree with a $1 million portfolio. He lives off $20,000 a year in Social Security and $20,000 in dividend income from his portfolio.

If his portfolio loses 35% of its value because it is 100% in equities, it will be difficult to recover the lost $350,000 on his $20,000-a-year Social Security income alone. His dividend income may also be cut, as companies tend to hold on to their cash for survival during bear markets. The only thing this retiree can do is pray the market eventually goes up while he cuts his spending. Or he might apply for a part-time job to make some supplemental income.

Given the lack of time and ability to make up for such potential losses, this retiree would likely have most of his investments in bonds or other lower-risk investments. That way, he minimizes his chance of seeing such a great investment drop.

Your Risk Tolerance Multiple

Personally, I'm not willing to spend more than twelve months trying to make up for any investment losses because I don't want to go back to work while my kids are still young. Therefore, I consider myself a moderate-to-conservative investor.

My guide below gives you an idea of what your risk tolerance multiple is, along with an idea of what your maximum equity exposure should be based on your risk tolerance. Your risk tolerance multiple equals the number of additional months you are willing to work to make up for potential losses in a bear market. My risk tolerance multiple is 12 (months). What is yours?

RISK TOLERANCE GUIDE FOR EQUITY EXPOSURE

Risk Level	Risk Tolerance Multiple (Months)	Monthly Income	Investment Loss Potential	Maximum Equity Exposure
Extreme	36	$10,000	$360,000	$1,028,571
High	24	$10,000	$240,000	$685,714
Moderate	18	$10,000	$180,000	$514,286
Moderate	12	$10,000	$120,000	$342,857
Conservative	6	$10,000	$60,000	$171,429
Ultraconservative	3	$10,000	$30,000	$85,714

Assumptions:
1. The average bear market decline since 1929 has been 35%.
2. The ability and desire to work declines as we age.
3. Risk tolerance declines with age and as we get more wealthy and less energetic.
4. The value of an asset is based on current and future expected earnings.
5. Maximum equity exposure = (risk tolerance multiple × monthly income) ÷ average bear market decline.
6. This guide can be used for any investment that contains risk, not just equities.

Source: FinancialSamurai.com

The chart assumes that those who are conservative investors aren't willing to spend more than six months of their lives making up for investment losses (risk tolerance multiple of 6 or less). Those with moderate risk tolerance are willing to spend twelve to eighteen months of their lives making up for investment losses, while those with high risk tolerance are willing to spend more than two years making up for investment losses.

For example, someone with a moderate risk tolerance who makes $10,000 a month could have between $342,857 and $514,286 in equity exposure. With an extreme risk tolerance, maximum equity exposure could be $1,028,571 with the same monthly income. Don't forget, during a bear market you could also lose your job or receive a pay cut.

You may not agree with my definitions for the various levels of risk tolerance, and that's fine. Perhaps working for three years to make up for your potential losses is moderate in your book. If so, adjust accordingly.

Your Maximum Equity Exposure

Using simple math, you can rearrange my risk tolerance formula to figure out your recommended **maximum equity exposure**.

maximum equity exposure = (your monthly salary × your risk tolerance multiple) ÷ potential percentage decline

Let's say you make $10,000 a month and are unwilling to spend more than twenty-four months making up for potential investment losses. You also believe the potential decline in your investments is 30%, not the 35% in my initial example.

The calculation would be ($10,000 × 24) ÷ 30% = $800,000.

In other words, $800,000 should be about the maximum in exposure you should have in the investments you think could go down 30%.

If you just got promoted and plan to see 20% year-over-year earnings growth for the next five years, you could use your current monthly salary and a higher risk tolerance multiple to determine your equity exposure.

Now let's say you currently make $10,000 a month and have a risk tolerance of twenty-four months. But you expect to be making $20,000 a month in five years. You also think stocks will go down by 20% at most. Therefore, you could split the difference and change the calculation to ($15,000 × 24) ÷ 20% = $1,800,000, making your maximum equity exposure $1.8 million.

If you decide to live like a hermit in a low-cost town in the middle of nowhere, you could increase your risk tolerance multiple. However, you've got to question your money priorities if you're trying to make a bigger return only to never spend your rewards.

Please speak to a friend or loved one to discuss each variable in the equation. Talking through different scenarios helps to make things less confusing and more realistic. In general, people tend to think they have a higher risk tolerance than they truly do. It's only when you're losing big money that you recognize how much financial pain you can really bear.

Income Tethering: Knock Out Small Goals Immediately

Developing enough passive income to pay all your desired living expenses will likely take at least a decade, if not three. Therefore, achieving true financial independence might feel like an impossible task. Don't let the enormity of the goal make you feel defeated.

Instead, think of one of your small joys and find a way to generate enough investment income or returns to consistently pay for it forever. Maybe it's your Saturday-morning croissant sandwich or Friday-night sushi dinner with your partner. Perhaps you'd love to spend more on camping gear or designer shoes or remodeling your bathroom if you could justify the expense. Do the math and figure out how much you'll need to invest to pay for that little joy.

Let's say your weekend croissant at the corner café costs $8 a week. Multiplied by 52, that's $416. Now pick a realistic rate of return, say 3%. Then calculate how much money you need to invest to generate enough income at a 3% rate to pay for your croissant habit. The equation would be:

cost of joy ÷ interest rate = investment amount

For your croissant, that would look like:

$416 ÷ 0.03 = $13,866

In other words, you'd need to save $13,866 at a 3% rate of return in order for your investments to fully fund your croissant habit. If you could consistently generate an 8% rate of return, then you would need to save and invest only $5,200.

Start with these little joys. Once you knock one out, keep building. Little by little, scale up to other expenses: gas, groceries, insurance, mortgage, kids' education, travel, whatever. Do the math and figure out how much you'd need to invest at a safe rate of return to fund each thing. It makes saving incredibly motivating, rather than saving for saving's sake.

It also helps to take the opposite approach: link an investment you already have, or that you plan to make, to a life goal. When it comes to money, finish your sentences. For example, if you say, "I bought twenty shares of Tesla," it is critical to keep going with the second part of the sentence, ". . . so that I can _____." Or "I will max out my 401(k) for fifteen years so that I can _____." Or "I will take this extra freelance job so that I can _____."

This helps you remember that money alone is never your primary motivation. Money is only a means to an end. We need to connect our financial choices to our goals, and we need those goals to be tangible.

It's not enough for your sentences to end with "so that I can have $100K in the bank" or "so that I can be a millionaire." You have to keep going. Why do you want that money in the bank? Why do you want to be a millionaire? What are you going to do with the money once you have amassed it? Money is simply a tool, and a tool, by definition, needs to be used.

Go through an exercise of saying, "My investment in X paid for Y." Here are some examples:

- My investment in Google paid for my daughter's education.
- My investment in the S&P 500 index paid for my kitchen remodel.
- My investment in Apple paid for the down payment on my house.
- My investment in a private Fundrise fund paid for my parents' two-week cruise.
- My investment in VYM, a Vanguard High Dividend Yield ETF, is paying monthly dividends, which pay for my gym membership.

I call this income tethering. You can also connect your *personal time and effort* investments to real outcomes.

- My investment in blogging for ten years paid for my ability to stay home with my kids.
- My investment in driving for Uber a few days a week paid for my new MacBook Pro.
- My investment in taking that freelance gig paid off my property taxes for a year.
- My investment in teaching tennis pays for family entertainment like movies and shows.

If you find yourself going through the exercise and realizing your time and investments haven't paid for anything, you've got some work to do. You've forgotten your purpose. The goal is to always tether your investments and efforts to real things. As soon as you identify what your hard work has bought, or will buy, you'll be much happier and significantly more motivated.

Get Ready to Buy—This, Not That

We can only do so much goal setting and number crunching. Eventually we need to buy and build up capital so those assets can start throwing income our way. The chapters ahead will help you strategize some of the most important spending choices of your life.

There's a common saying: "If I knew then what I know now, I would have done things differently." The way to never need to say this phrase again is to learn from the many people who've gone through what you're going through. Keep an open mind and be aware of the many variables that might come your way. Be flexible in thought and be open to new possibilities.

THE FINANCIAL SAMURAI WAY

- Tether all income and investments to specific purposes. Start small and work your way up to build momentum. Making money for money's sake is an empty feeling.

- Use my net worth target guide as you would a personal trainer. Even if you don't achieve the exact net worth targets, you will accumulate much more than if you had no guide. The ideal multiple is based on gross income in order to keep you focused as you earn more over your career. Once you hit 20X your annual income or generate enough passive investment income to consistently cover your desired living expenses, you are free to do as you wish.

- Quantify your risk tolerance in terms of time. How many months of your life are you willing to give up to recoup potential investment losses? To find the realistic answer, you must discuss various scenarios with your closest friends or loved ones.

- Be flexible with your safe-withdrawal-rate assumptions in retirement. Life after work may be very different from your expectations. You won't know exactly how you will feel until you leave a steady paycheck behind. Therefore, during the initial retirement years, it's better to be more conservative, using a lower safe withdrawal rate and finding supplemental income opportunities.

Chapter 3

Get the Cash, Put It to Work

So far we've done a lot of goal setting. You have goals for your financially independent life, savings goals, and a framework for buying *this* or *that* with the right mindset.

Now let's get to work. The only way you can make any progress on your big dreams is by taking action with the money you have today. The rest of this book goes into more detail on the money moves I'll recommend in this chapter, but to start, we'll focus on the big-picture steps you need to take to start building wealth.

Your main source of income at the moment is likely your day job, although some of you might get lucky with a financial windfall from a company IPO, a multibagger investment, or an inheritance. Wherever your money is coming from, your objective is to leverage as much of it as possible into passive and semipassive investment income so that you eventually have a massive money army providing for you.

Here is a step-by-step strategy for putting your money to work.

First, you need to set a savings plan that goes *beyond* your traditional retirement investment accounts. Too many people ignore this portion of their net worth. They think that investing in a tax-advantaged retirement account (401[k], IRA, RRSP, SIPP, etc.) is good enough. It's not. In most cases, you can't touch the passive income that those investment vehicles generate before the age of fifty-nine and a half without paying a 10% penalty. That doesn't help us with the "sooner" part of our financial freedom goals. Many of us want to get there way before age fifty-nine and a half. The only way to do that is by building a taxable investment portfolio.

Next, you need to optimize your earning power. Whatever you're saving, you probably need to save more. That means earning more. You can cut expenses only so much.

Then stick to your plan relentlessly. Let your goals guide you, automate your savings, pivot as needed. If you want this badly enough, you'll make it work.

Finally, it's important to figure out what income streams are best for you. Not all passive- and semipassive-income streams are alike, and the best ones for you will depend on a lot of factors, including your age, your risk tolerance, and how much time you want to put into managing an investment. Other factors include personal preference, understanding of the investments, and creativity.

But let's start with making sure you're setting aside enough cash to invest.

Step 1: Set a Savings Plan

Generating passive income starts with savings. Without a healthy amount of savings, nothing works. But remember, when I say *savings*, I'm not talking about squirreling money away in a bank account as inflation eats away its buying power. Keep a six-month emergency fund in the bank. After that, focus on maxing out your tax-advantageous retirement accounts and building your taxable investments.

It is your taxable retirement portfolio that is going to allow you to retire early because those are the investments that will spit out passive income you can access before age fifty-nine and a half without paying a penalty. Although dividends and rental income are taxable, they are usually taxed at a much lower rate than your earned income.

I recommend that everyone strive for this **optimal saving scenario**:

1. **First, max out your pretax retirement contributions if you're able to do so.** In 2022, the employee limit for 401(k) contributions is $20,500 and those over fifty are allowed

to contribute an additional $6,500 in catch-up contributions. The contribution limits for 401(k) accounts tend to go up by $500 every two to three years. The maximum traditional IRA contribution is $6,000. Workers age fifty and older can add an extra $1,000 per year as a catch-up contribution, bringing the maximum contribution to $7,000.

2. **Then save *at least* 20% of your after-tax income in taxable investments.** This may not sound easy to some of you, but nothing good comes easy! The key is to try. This chapter covers the options for where you can put that 20%+ savings. And I go into further detail throughout this book.

On the next page is my Financial Freedom Saving Rate Chart, which shows how many years it will take you to save one year of living expenses at various saving rates. It also shows how many years of living expenses you can save after ten, twenty, and thirty years. For illustrative purposes, the chart uses $100,000 in after-tax income. The saving rates and the results are applicable to any livable income.

The shaded areas indicate when you will likely reach financial freedom, if not sooner, because I haven't assumed any positive investment returns. They represent the start of financial independence after so many years of work and a particular saving rate. For example, let's say you graduate college at age twenty-two and work for twenty years and save 50% a year. At forty-two years old, you will have saved twenty years' worth of living expenses, which will bring you to age sixty-two after full depletion. However, it's unlikely you will fully deplete your capital due to investment returns, expense adjustments, and your ability to earn supplemental retirement income if needed. Further, by the time you reach your sixties, you may be eligible for social security.

In another example, let's say you graduate college at age twenty-three and were able to average a 75% saving rate for ten years. By age thirty-three you will have accumulated thirty years' worth of living expenses. As a result, you could live until age sixty-three if you were to fully deplete your capital. Therefore, I have shaded the box with the number 30.00 to indicate when financial independence may begin. Bottom line, the greater your saving rate, the sooner you will reach financial independence.

The **second-best scenario**, if you can't max out your pretax retirement account, is:

1. **If your employer offers a company match, contribute at least that much to your pretax retirement accounts.** This is nonnegotiable. There is no excuse for leaving free money on the table by contributing less than the company match. If your employer matches up to 6%, get that 6% in—*no matter what*. Not only will you reduce

FINANCIAL FREEDOM SAVING RATE CHART

$100,000 After-Tax Income Example

Saving Rate	Amount Saved	Annual Expenses	Years to Save One Year of Expenses	Years of Living Expenses Saved after 10 Years	Years of Living Expenses Saved after 20 Years	Years of Living Expenses Saved after 30 Years
5%	$5,000	$95,000	19.00	0.53	1.05	1.58
10%	$10,000	$90,000	9.00	1.11	2.22	3.33
15%	$15,000	$85,000	5.67	1.76	3.53	5.29
20%	$20,000	$80,000	4.00	2.50	5.00	7.50
25%	$25,000	$75,000	3.00	3.33	6.67	10.00
30%	$30,000	$70,000	2.33	4.29	8.57	12.86
35%	$35,000	$65,000	1.86	5.38	10.77	16.15
40%	$40,000	$60,000	1.50	6.67	13.33	20.00
45%	$45,000	$55,000	1.22	8.18	16.36	24.55
50%	$50,000	$50,000	1.00	10.00	20.00	30.00
55%	$55,000	$45,000	0.82	12.22	24.44	36.67
60%	$60,000	$40,000	0.67	15.00	30.00	45.00
65%	$65,000	$35,000	0.54	18.57	37.14	55.71
70%	$70,000	$30,000	0.43	23.33	46.67	70.00
75%	$75,000	$25,000	0.33	30.00	60.00	90.00
80%	$80,000	$20,000	0.25	40.00	80.00	120.00
85%	$85,000	$15,000	0.18	56.67	113.33	170.00
90%	$90,000	$10,000	0.11	90.00	180.00	270.00

Note: Gray boxes indicate when you can retire. Remember to focus on the years, not the income.
Assumptions: (1) start work after high school or college, (2) 0% returns, (3) investment income kicks in after retirement, (4) Social Security kicks in by age seventy.

Source: FinancialSamurai.com

your taxable income by contributing, but you're also getting a 100% return on the money you are contributing.

2. **Then push to save at least 20% of your after-tax income in a taxable investment portfolio.** If 20% is not possible, get as close as you can.

If you can't manage this second-best scenario, there is probably a bigger issue at play. In a lot of cases, people think they can't afford to save, and then they spend the money on unproductive things. You can come at me with your "Yeah, but . . ." scenarios, but if you want to achieve financial independence sooner rather than later, it's important to understand that getting there won't come easily.

The chart below shows the power of maxing out your 401(k) every year starting in 2022.

WHAT YOU COULD HAVE IN YOUR 401(K) IF YOU MAXED IT OUT EVERY YEAR

Age	Years Worked	Amount	With 8% Compound Returns
22	0	$0	$0
23	1	$20,500*	$22,000
24	2	$41,000	$46,000
25	3	$61,500	$72,000
26	4	$82,000	$100,000
27	5	$102,500	$130,000
28	6	$123,000	$162,000
29	7	$143,500	$197,000
30	8	$164,000	$235,000
31	9	$184,500	$276,000
32	10	$205,000	$320,000
33	11	$225,500	$368,000
34	12	$246,000	$420,000
35	13	$266,500	$476,000
40	18	$369,000	$829,000
45	23	$471,500	$1,348,000
50	28	$574,000	$2,110,000
55	33	$676,500	$3,231,000
60	38	$779,000	$4,878,000

*$20,500 is the maximum contribution limit for 2022.

Source: FinancialSamurai.com

If you do this properly, not only will you have a 70%+ chance of becoming a 401(k) millionaire by age sixty, but you will also have a 70%+ chance of having over $1 million in your taxable accounts. And even if you don't become a multimillionaire by sixty, you will still be in a much better position than the average person who didn't bother to max out their retirement accounts and focus on building passive investment income. It's win-win.

Step 2: Optimize Your Earning Power

You can't get anywhere with the advice in this book if you don't have money to save and invest. If that's your struggle, your top priority right now is to bump up your income and/or find places where you're spending unnecessarily so you can reroute that cash to your financial independence goals. (And look, even if you *do* earn enough to save, you'll get closer to your goals if you can earn more and save more.) Part 3 offers advice on how to optimize your earning power at your day job and generate income through a side hustle.

Gigs like Uber or Instacart are fine for quick cash now, but an even better move would be to find something you're good at and actually enjoy doing and try to monetize it. Everybody is good at something, be it music, sports, communications, writing, art, dance, or other talents.

A tennis player can teach tennis. A photographer can offer mini photo shoots for local families or wedding photography. A teacher can sell lesson plans for homeschooling parents to incorporate into their curriculum. A graphic designer can sell downloadable prints and calendars on Etsy.

The more interests and skills you have, the greater the chance you can create something that can provide passive income down the road. This is especially important because it's a good idea to try to make supplemental retirement income once you do leave your day job behind.

Step 3: Stick to Your Plan Relentlessly

Olympic champion Mark Spitz reportedly once said, "If you fail to prepare, you're prepared to fail." Once you've determined your optimal savings scenario, you need to create a strategy to get there and to stick to it through the pain. If you don't, you will never make progress. I know these big goals can feel so insurmountable that it's hard to know where to begin. Just remember that everything great started from nothing.

So set aside one day every month to tackle your big-picture financial independence goals. Circle the date on your calendar and cancel all other distractions. Use this time to review your progress and your objectives. If you're not hitting a certain target—like saving a particular amount each month—brainstorm solutions. Also spend a few minutes each week checking in on smaller goals. The more you regularly prepare and work on your strategy, the greater your financial achievements are likely to be.

It's important that you take the time to actually write down your goals. Write down the small income-tethering goals you set in chapter 2 along with your long-term goals for financial freedom. You can keep them in a private journal, but telling several close friends also helps you stay accountable. I use my site to write out goals all the time for my accountability. The last thing I want to do is let my readers and myself down.

If you're working on building new income streams through a hobby or interest, chip away at it every day and be patient. The key is to stay consistent. I thought about starting *Financial Samurai* for three years before I finally hired someone from Craigslist for $500 to help me launch my website. Often the most difficult part of anything is knowing how to start. Therefore, hiring someone who knows what they are doing is some of the best money spent. Once I got my website up and running, it became much easier to keep going. Today you can set up a website in under an hour for less than $100.

As the money comes in—whether it's from your day job or side hustle—set automatic transfers to your investment accounts and be relentless about never withdrawing what you've set aside.

I've set up multiple investment accounts outside of my main operations bank that deal with working capital, e.g., checking, paying bills. By transferring my money to a couple of brokerage accounts and two other banks as soon as it hits my main bank, I'm no longer tempted to spend on frivolous things. As a result, I can wake up in ten years and reap the rewards of compounding.

Determine the Income Streams That Are Best for You

The options for where to invest your income can seem endless. I go into detail about the optimal investment choices for building wealth in parts 2 and 3 of this book. As we take a broad look at your investment strategy, I want to introduce you to some of the most common investment options by ranking them from worst to best.

These rankings are based on my own real-life experiences attempting to generate passive income from multiple types of sources over the past twenty-two years. I rank each one based on risk, return, feasibility, liquidity, activity, and taxes. I give each criterion a score between 1 and 10. The higher the score, the better.

- A **risk** score of 10 means no risk. A risk score of 1 means extreme risk.
- A **return** score of 10 means you have the highest potential of getting the highest return relative to all other investments. A return score of 1 means the returns are horrible compared with the risk-free rate (based on the ten-year bond yield).

- A **feasibility** score of 10 means everybody can do it. A feasibility score of 1 means that there are high requirements to be able to invest in such an asset.
- A **liquidity** score of 10 means you can access your funds instantly without penalty. A liquidity score of 1 means the investment is very difficult to quickly withdraw your money from or sell without a penalty.
- An **activity** score of 10 means you can kick back and do nothing to earn income. An activity score of 1 means you've got to manage your investment all day long, like working a day job.
- A **tax** score of 10 means the investment is generating the lowest tax liability possible or you can do things to lower the tax liability. A tax score of 1 means the investment is taxed at the highest possible rate and there's nothing you can do about it.

We'll base the return criterion on trying to generate $10,000 a year in passive income.

I'll jump to the spoiler by sharing my overall best passive-income investments ranking chart on the next page. The math, and my experience, confirm that physical real estate, dividend investing, online real estate, and creating your own products are the best sources of passive income. The chapters ahead offer insight on each of these.

But first, it's useful to look at each of the most popular investment vehicles, and why some are more effective than others, as you start building your investment strategy. I've tried to be as objective as possible with the variable scores.

Rank #8: Peer-to-Peer (P2P) and Hard-Money Lending

The least good passive-income investment is P2P lending and lending money directly to friends, family, or strangers (hard-money lending). P2P lending started in San Francisco with Lending Club and Prosper in the mid-2000s. The idea of peer-to-peer lending is to disintermediate banks and help denied borrowers get loans at rates potentially lower than those offered by larger financial institutions.

With a diversified portfolio of one hundred or more notes, the leading P2P lenders claim investors can make an annual return between 5% and 7%. The returns used to be higher, but the increased supply of money has brought returns down.

The biggest problem with P2P lending, like hard-money lending, is people not paying investors back, i.e., borrowers defaulting on their loans. Over time, the P2P industry has seen its returns shrink due to higher competition and more regulation. The industry has

RANKING THE BEST PASSIVE-INCOME STREAMS

Passive-Income Source	Risk	Return	Feasibility	Liquidity	Activity	Taxes	Total Score
P2P/Hard-Money Lending	4	2	8	4	7	5	30
Private Equity or Debt	6	8	3	3	10	6	36
CD/Money Market	10	1	10	6	10	5	42
Fixed Income/Bonds	6	2	10	7	10	8	43
Creating Your Own Products	8	8	8	6	7	7	44
Physical Real Estate	8	8	7	6	6	10	45
REC, REITs, RE ETFs	7	7	10	6	10	7	47
Dividend Investing	6	5	10	9	10	8	48

Score methodology: 1–10, with 10 indicating the least risk, highest return, greatest feasibility, most liquidity, most tax efficiency, and least activity required.

Source: FinancialSamurai.com

also changed its business model. As a result, I would not recommend peer-to-peer or hard-money lending.

Risk: 4, Return: 2, Feasibility: 8, Liquidity: 4, Activity: 7, Taxes: 5, **Total Score: 30**

Rank #7: Private Equity or Debt Investing

Private equity investing can be a tremendous source of capital appreciation with the right investments. If you find the next Google, the returns will blow every single other passive-income investment out of the water. But of course, finding the next Google is a tough task, since most private companies fail and the best investment opportunities almost always go to the most connected investors.

Private equity funds include private equity, venture capital, and private real estate. Private debt investing includes venture debt and private real estate. These funds usually have three- to ten-year lockup periods, so the liquidity score is low. Therefore, if you try private investing, make sure you don't need those funds for a long time. Over the fund's operating period, you should see distributions along the way to provide you passive income and returns.

Often the least liquid and the riskiest type of private equity investments is when you invest directly in a private company. You could be locked up forever and receive zero dividends or distributions. The company also has a good chance of being a dud. If you plan to invest in individual private companies, you should probably build a portfolio of at least five to ten. Otherwise, invest in private companies with money you are willing to completely lose.

Access to private investments is usually restricted to accredited investors (those who earn $250,000 income per individual or have a $1 million net worth, excluding their primary residence), which is why the feasibility score is only a 2.

But the activity score is a 10 because you couldn't do anything even if you wanted to. You're investing for the long term. The risk and return scores depend greatly on your investing acumen and access.

Gaining $10,000 a year in private equity investing is difficult to quantify unless you are investing in a real estate or fixed-income fund. Such funds generally target 8% to 15% annual returns, which equates to a need for $83,000 to $125,000 in capital.

Risk: 6, Return: 8, Feasibility: 3, Liquidity: 3, Activity: 10, Taxes: 6, **Total Score: 36**

Rank #6: Certificate of Deposit (CD)/Money Market

There was a time when CDs or money market accounts would produce a respectable 4%+ yield. Nowadays you'll be lucky to find a five- to seven-year CD that provides anything above 2%. Money markets are even worse, because their rates are highly correlated with the federal funds rate. Due to elevated inflation, the real rates for CDs and money markets are often negative.

There are no income or net worth minimums to invest in a CD. Anybody can go to their local bank and open up a CD of their desired duration. Furthermore, CDs and money market accounts are FDIC insured for up to $250,000 per individual and $500,000 per joint account.

Given that interest rates are now so low, and will likely stay low for the rest of our working lives, it takes a tremendous amount of capital to generate any meaningful amount of passive income. To generate $10,000 a year in passive income at 0.5% requires $2 million in capital. At least you know your money is safe, which is great during bear markets.

Additional factors are that your funds are easily accessible (though not without a penalty in the case of CDs), you don't have to do anything to earn the passive income, and it is taxed as normal income.

Risk: 10, Return: 1, Feasibility: 10, Liquidity: 6, Activity: 10, Taxes: 5, **Total Score: 42**

Rank #5: Fixed Income/Bonds

As interest rates have gone down over the past forty years, bond prices have continued to go up. In August 2020, during the height of the COVID-19 pandemic, the ten-year Treasury bond yield hit an all-time low of 0.51%. Since then, the ten-year bond yield and yields for most government and corporate bonds have inched up as risk appetite has returned.

I believe long-term interest rates will stay low for a long time due to technology, globalization, coordinated central banks, and more prescient decision-making. Just look at Japanese interest rates, which are negative (inflation is higher than the nominal interest rate).

Therefore, bonds will likely continue to be a main way that older and wealthier investors diversify their public investment portfolios. If you hold a government bond until maturity, you will get all your coupon payments and principal back. The same goes for most highly rated corporate bonds. But just as with stocks, there are plenty of different types of bond investments to choose from.

Anybody can buy a bond ETF (exchange-traded fund) such as an IEF (seven- to ten-year Treasury bond), a MUB (muni bond fund), or a fixed-income fund like PTTRX (PIMCO Total Return Fund). These funds generate a yield but have no maturity. Therefore, you may be investing more for principal appreciation. You can also buy individual corporate or municipal bonds. Municipal bonds are especially enticing for higher-income earners who face a high marginal tax rate. You can also directly buy Treasury bonds through your online brokerage platform.

The main issue with bonds is their low interest rate and lower historical performance compared with stocks. With rates already so low, how much lower can they get? With low yields and lower potential capital appreciation, bonds are in a tough spot. Instead of bonds, more investors are considering real estate as a "bonds plus" alternative. However, with the combination of lower volatility, coupon payments, and defensiveness during times of uncertainty, there will always be a place for bonds.

Risk: 6, Return: 2, Feasibility: 10, Liquidity: 7, Activity: 10, Taxes: 8, **Total Score: 43**

Rank #4: Creating Your Own Products

If you're a creative person, you might be able to produce a product that can generate a steady flow of passive income for years to come. You often need very little start-up capital to be creative. At the extreme, Michael Jackson makes more dead than alive due to the royalties his estate makes from all the songs he produced during his career. Since Jackson's death, his estate has made over $1 billion, according to *Forbes*.

Of course, it's unlikely any one of us will replicate that level of royalties, but you could produce your own e-book, e-course, award-winning photo, arts-and-crafts product, or song to create your own slice of passive income. The creator economy is now!

If you are always daydreaming, creating your own product is one of the best ways to go. It is incredibly rewarding to make money by yourself. The margins are extremely high once your product is produced. The only thing you need to do is update the product over time. I offer more advice on starting a side hustle in chapter 12.

Risk: 8, Return: 8, Feasibility: 8, Liquidity: 6, Activity: 7, Taxes: 7, **Total Score: 44**

Rank #3: Physical Real Estate

Real estate is my favorite asset class for the average person to build wealth because it's easy to understand, provides shelter, is a tangible asset, doesn't lose value overnight like stocks, and generates income. You don't need much creativity. But you do need to understand how to buy, how to attract and retain good tenants, and how to create value through remodeling and expansion. I will offer an aerial view of my thoughts on real estate here and dig into the details in part 2.

The main downside to owning physical real estate is that it ranks poorly on the activity variable due to tenants and maintenance issues. Further, generating high rental income is tough on the coasts. In expensive cities like San Francisco and New York City, cash-on-cash yields or cap rates (which are similar but don't take into consideration financing costs) can fall as low as 2%. This is a sign that investors are buying more for capital appreciation than for income generation.

In inexpensive cities, such as those in the Midwest and South, cash-on-cash yields or cap rates can easily be in the range of 7% to 10%. On the flip side, capital appreciation may be slower.

The Goldilocks scenario is if you can buy high-yielding real estate that is also rapidly appreciating. In my opinion, these types of properties are found in the heartland of America, which has become a beneficiary of the work-from-home trend.

The tax benefits of owning physical real estate are very attractive. For your primary residence, you can deduct your mortgage interest and property taxes. As a landlord, you can deduct almost all expenses incurred to operate the property, plus a noncash depreciation expense. For homeowners who live in their home for at least two of the last five years that they own it, capital gains up to $250,000 per individual or $500,000 per married couple are tax free. However, please be aware that depending on how long you rented out the property, the tax-free exclusion gets reduced.

Then there's the ability to defer any capital gains tax on a rental property through a 1031 exchange. Conceivably, you could do 1031 exchanges forever and defer any capital gains tax forever.

In an inflationary environment, taking on debt to buy a hard asset like real estate makes sense. Inflation whittles down the real cost of debt, while at the same time acting as a tailwind for price appreciation. If you're young and full of energy, owning rental properties is one of the best ways to build wealth. The double benefit of rising rents and rising home prices is very powerful.

Risk: 8, Return: 8, Feasibility: 7, Liquidity: 6, Activity: 6, Taxes: 10, **Total Score: 45**

Rank #2: Online Real Estate—Real Estate Crowdfunding, REITs, Real Estate ETFs

Owning physical real estate is one of my favorite ways to build passive income. However, as I've gotten older, my patience for dealing with maintenance and tenant issues has diminished. As a result, I've been investing more in online real estate—publicly traded real estate investment trusts (REITs), real estate ETFs, and crowdsourced real estate deals. The idea is to get the benefits of owning physical real estate without having to do any work.

However, publicly traded REITs and real estate ETFs can sometimes be even more volatile than the S&P 500. We saw many publicly traded REITs and real estate ETFs actually sell off as much as or more than the S&P 500 during the March 2020 downturn. Therefore, if you're looking for a hedge against stock market volatility, publicly traded REITs and real estate ETFs may not work. (With owning physical real estate, on the other hand, the hedge does often work since mortgage rates tend to decline as stocks decline because bonds are bid up. As a result, liquidity tends to flow into real estate.)

In 2012, Congress passed the JOBS Act (Jumpstart Our Business Startups Act), which ignited the creation of real estate crowdfunding for the masses. The purpose of the JOBS Act was to make it easier for start-ups and small businesses to access capital, primarily because small business activity had decreased during and after the financial crisis.

Real estate crowdfunding enables retail investors to invest in private real estate investments around the country, either in a fund or in individual projects. A sponsor procures the investment opportunity, which is then highlighted on a real estate investing platform such as CrowdStreet, which focuses on deals in eighteen-hour cities. Eighteen-hour cities tend to have less expensive real estate with higher rental yields. But due to strong demographic and labor trends, eighteen-hour cities may see more rapid future real estate price appreciation as well. Think Charleston, South Carolina, versus New York City, a twenty-four-hour city. Once on the real estate investing platform, retail investors can do their due diligence on the opportunities that make it through the vetting process. Once an investment is made, the platform will earn a referral or management fee.

Alternatively, some real estate crowdfunding platforms have decided to source their own deals, package them into a fund, and offer their investments to retail investors. Platforms like Fundrise have become institutional real estate investors that are effectively competing with behemoths like BlackRock. For those of you who dislike dealing with tenants and maintenance issues, investing in online real estate is something to consider.

To be able to invest in real estate, but 100% passively, is a great combination. Almost anybody can invest in real estate crowdfunding, REITs, and real estate ETFs. The historical returns have been some of the strongest of all the major asset classes as well. However, the tax benefits aren't as great as owning physical real estate.

Risk: 7, Return: 7, Feasibility: 10, Liquidity: 6, Activity: 10, Taxes: 7, **Total Score: 47**

Rank #1: Dividend Investing

The best passive-income investment is investing in dividend-paying stocks. You can buy either individual dividend-paying stocks or a high-dividend ETF such as VYM, the Vanguard High Dividend Yield ETF. Investing in high-quality dividend-paying companies is 100% passive, which is why it gets an activity score of 10.

Dividend stocks tend to be more mature companies with strong cash flow and healthy balance sheets. "Dividend aristocrats" such as McDonald's, Coca-Cola, Clorox, Johnson & Johnson, Procter & Gamble, Realty Income, Sherwin-Williams, and Walmart have historically paid consistently higher dividends over time. However, because these companies are paying a dividend, they are often past their high-growth stage. If they weren't, management would rather reinvest the company's cash flow in potentially higher-return investments. High-dividend-paying stocks and dividend ETFs are usually less volatile as a result. The utilities, telecom, consumer, and financial sectors tend to make up the majority of dividend-paying companies. Tech, internet, and biotech, on the other hand, tend not to pay any dividends. They are growth stocks that reinvest most of their retained earnings back into the company for further growth.

Overall, I give dividend investing a 5 on return because dividend interest rates are relatively low. Further, it's harder to generate as much income from dividend stocks than it is from owning physical real estate, REITs, public real estate ETFs, and real estate crowd-funded projects.

For investors in their twenties and thirties, investing in growth stocks is likely a more optimal decision. For older investors who want less downside risk, more stability, and income, dividend stocks are likely more appropriate.

That said, while dividend-paying stocks are great, you need to pay attention to the dividend yields, which often follow in the direction of the ten-year Treasury bond yield. In other words, when bond yields are declining, corporations won't need to pay as high a dividend to remain attractive. Remember, everything is relative in finance.

Dividend index investing is attractive because it is passive and liquid. In the long run, it is hard to outperform an index through stock picking.

Risk: 6, Return: 5, Feasibility: 10, Liquidity: 9, Activity: 10, Taxes: 8, **Total Score: 48**

The Bottom Line

All eight of the passive-income investments I cover here can be appropriate ways of generating income to fund your lifestyle. Which are the right ones for you depends on factors like your risk tolerance, abilities, energy level, creativity, interests, and personal preferences.

There are certainly other passive-income investments with varying degrees of passivity. However, I've covered most of them here. Further, within each category you could have multiple passive-income sources, e.g., under "creating your own products" you could have online course income, e-book income, music royalties, and affiliate income based on search engine traffic.

Whatever approaches you're most drawn to, the most important thing you can do is start aggressively saving and contributing regularly to the investment as early as possible.

With interest rates likely to remain low, building passive income will take a lot of effort and patience. Don't delay. Saving early and often is no sacrifice at all. Instead, the biggest sacrifice is living a life on someone else's terms due to a lack of funds. At the end of the day, nobody cares more about your money than you do.

THE FINANCIAL SAMURAI WAY

- Set a savings plan. Ideally, you'd max out your tax-advantaged retirement accounts and then save and invest at least 20% of your remaining cash flow in taxable investments for passive income. If you can't max out your 401(k), then at least contribute up to any available company match for a 100% return.

- At least once a month, review your progress and objectives. Also use this time to make adjustments when necessary. The more you stay on top of your finances, the better you can optimize them.

- The best passive-income investments are physical real estate, online real estate, dividend stocks, and creating your own products. Treat your passive-income investments as money soldiers that fight alongside your main source of income.

- It may take between ten and thirty years for you to generate enough passive income to cover your basic living expenses. Therefore, there's no time like the present to start.

Chapter 4

Master Your Debt

People don't want to hear this, but the truth is that most of us get into debt because we want to live a lifestyle we don't yet deserve.

To be clear, when I say you don't deserve something, it's not because you're a morally unworthy or bad person. You don't deserve it because you simply don't have the money to pay for it yet. There was a time when most purchases were made with all cash. However, with the evolution of the credit market, lenders have found ever more ways to profit off consumers. "Buy now, pay later" options now appear everywhere.

Debt is tempting. It allows us to skip the work and jump straight to what we want. It's like letting a D student press a magic button and enjoy the perks of being an A student without having to study, do homework, or turn in papers on time. But here's the thing: if you slack off and don't do your homework, then you probably don't deserve an A lifestyle.

At the end of the day, if you're one of the millions of consumers taking on debt to buy things that you can't afford, you are likely never going to achieve financial independence. Even in the most reasonable circumstances, with the lowest possible interest rates, debt is the opposite of generating passive income. Debtors are helping make someone else's financial goals a reality while digging themselves further down a dark hole.

I get it. Sometimes debt is unavoidable, as in the case of surprise medical costs or a single parent stretched too thin. A benefit to achieving financial freedom is that surprise expenses hurt a lot less. But until you get there, you have to do the work of earning and saving and living below your means. If a catastrophe hits, do what you need to do to handle it, of course. But driving a five-year-old hatchback with ninety-thousand miles on it when you desperately want a brand-new SUV is not a catastrophe. That spiffy new car can wait until you have enough money to buy it outright.

Depending on your interest rate, one of your top priorities should be to pay down any debt you have. Less debt = more freedom. Just think about all the people or institutions that are getting rich off your back. Not even the great Warren Buffett has been able to return greater than the average credit card interest rate over his illustrious career. And Warren is worth over $100 billion thanks to his shrewd investments!

Each debt I've paid off made me feel happier and freer. I'm sure you will feel the same way. So take back your freedom by starting to *think like a lender instead of a borrower.* You want to be earning interest, not paying it to others. You will seldom regret paying down debt, no matter how low the interest rate or how much more in returns you could have earned by putting that money elsewhere. Because once you are debt free, you gain tremendous confidence to live life on your terms. Just imagine having no mortgage debt, student loan debt, car debt, or credit card debt. The world is yours!

But as toxic as consumer debt is, not all debt is bad. When used appropriately, debt can be an extremely useful tool for building wealth. The key is to use debt only in a way that moves you toward your financial goals in a risk-appropriate manner—not backward. Put simply: use debt to purchase historically appreciating assets. I will show you exactly how to do that.

Slash Your Debt from Worst to Best

If you must take on debt, take on debt that is tied to an asset that potentially appreciates faster than the cost of your debt. It's important to understand how other popular forms of debt are holding you back. As you put together your debt-shrinking strategy, aim to get rid of the worst offenders first.

#1 Worst Dept Type: Credit Cards. Your credit card balance needs to be the first thing to go. The average APR on a credit card is around 15%, and this is despite interest rates continually coming down. Some go as high as 29.99% if you have terrible credit.

If you carry a balance, credit card companies are ripping you off. No Financial Samurai should ever have revolving credit card debt. Use a credit card for rewards points, insurance, a free thirty-day loan, and concierge service, but that's it.

Reduce the time spent playing the 0% APR balance transfer game. Instead, focus on making more money. Don't use the credit card as a crutch to support irresponsible spending habits.

#2 Worst Dept Type: Automobiles. Buying too much car is one of the easiest and biggest financial mistakes someone can make. Some people justify their auto debt because it has a very low interest rate. But even a 1% interest rate is too much when that vehicle is depreciating in value every month.

I've developed what I call the One-Tenth Rule for Car Buying to help folks figure out how much they can really afford. The rule states that you should **spend no more than one tenth of your gross annual income on the purchase price of a car**. The car can be new or old. It doesn't matter, so long as the car costs 10% of your annual gross income or less.

If you really want to buy a car that costs $40,000, then shoot to make at least $400,000 a year in household income. You might scoff at the idea of limiting your vehicle's purchase price to only 10% of your income. But if you actually want to save for college, save for retirement, take care of your parents, buy a home, and not stress out about money when you're old, the one-tenth rule will help keep you sane. (We'll dive into my One-Tenth Rule for Car Buying in chapter 15.)

#3 Worst Dept Type: Student Loans. Next to risk-appropriate mortgages, student loans are the least offensive debt you can have. While I'm very pro-education—education is what can get people out of poverty—there is nothing you learn in college that you couldn't instead learn for free on the internet, and colleges aren't guaranteeing you a well-paying job upon graduation. So unless your family is rich, choose a college that provides enough free grant money that you'll be able to pay everything back within four years of graduation.

Yes, education is what will help set you free, but not if the amount of student loan debt overwhelms your income and livelihood. (We'll talk more about education in chapter 13.)

#4 Worst Dept Type: Mortgages. There's a lot to say about the factors that go into buying a home, and I cover it all in chapter 7, including my 30/30/3 Home-Buying Rule. For now, I'll simply say that I consider mortgage debt to be the least egregious because it's tied to an asset that historically appreciates. And at times when real estate prices do drop, the real estate you own still offers value in the form of a roof over your head or rental income as you ride out the downturn.

There are also some appealing tax benefits to owning your home. For example, the Tax Cuts and Jobs Act, passed in 2017, allows you to write off all mortgage interest on debt up to $750,000. If you sell your property, the government allows tax-free profits of up to $250,000 for individuals and $500,000 for married couples if you lived in your property for two of the last five years (although the amount is prorated down depending on how long you rented the house for). Finally, the government allows you to defer taxes on the sale of a property by allowing you to use the sale proceeds to buy another property under the 1031 exchange program.

You can still take steps toward financial freedom while you pay down debt—but the more debt you have, the more limited your options for generating passive income will be. Please make it one of your top priorities to eliminate all consumer debt. You're only making the credit card companies, banks, and loan sharks rich.

Instead, make yourself rich by utilizing debt in your favor. If you purchase real estate with debt properly, I believe you will have a greater than 70% chance of coming out wealthier if you hold on to it for five to ten years. If you take on revolving consumer debt, the exact opposite is true.

Pay Down Debt or Invest?

As CFOs of our own finances, we need to figure out the most efficient use of our capital. Reality for most of us involves some level of debt. So the riddle we face is figuring out how much of our money to invest and how much to put toward paying off our debt. The decision is a personal one that depends on a lot of factors: your risk tolerance, number of income streams, liquidity needs, family expenses, job security, investing acumen, retirement age, and bullishness about your future in general.

Think about investing as trying to get your wealth as far above zero as possible through compound returns. Think about paying down debt as merely getting back to zero.

Choosing between paying down debt and investing is such a prevalent concern that I came up with the Financial Samurai Debt and Investment Ratio, or FS DAIR for short, to help people logically decide how much to allocate to each area. This is the FS DAIR formula:

debt interest rate × 10 = percentage of cash flow after living expenses to allocate toward debt pay-down

In other words, if you have a mortgage with an interest rate of 3%, then allocate 30% of your monthly cash flow after living expenses to paying down that debt. This would be an extra payment toward your mortgage principal that is separate from your minimum monthly payment. Invest the remaining 70% of your cash flow based on your investment preferences.

Prioritize building up a six-month emergency fund before aggressively paying down your debts. Once you have that, you can put any income you have into your FS DAIR strategy.

As you crunch the numbers, you'll notice that FS DAIR suggests you put 100% of your cash flow (after living expenses) toward paying down debt if your interest rate is 10% or higher. I use 10% because 10% is about the average return of the S&P 500 since 1926. Further, interest rates have been coming down since the 1980s, making any debt interest rate over 10% even more comparatively expensive.

The only debts that will have an interest rate higher than 10% in this low-interest-rate environment are debts from loan sharks, payday loans, and credit card companies. One common practice to help lower your consumer debt interest rate is to consolidate your debt under a lower-interest personal loan. However, personal loans also tend to be much higher than the average mortgage rate, student loan rate, and auto loan rate.

Wherever the high-interest debt is coming from, get aggressive about paying it down. Paying down debt is a guaranteed return equal to the interest rate of the debt.

On the next page is an FS DAIR guide to help you figure out what portion of your cash flow should go toward saving and/or investing.

When torn between paying off debt and investing, follow FS DAIR, which seeks to maximize the efficient use of your free cash flow over time.

If you're juggling multiple debts, focus on paying down your highest-interest-rate debt first while you make your minimum payments on the rest. Those minimum payments should be factored into your living expenses like any other bill. When you've paid off the debt with the highest interest rate, move on to the debt with the next-highest interest rate, and keep going until you are debt free.

FINANCIAL SAMURAI DEBT AND
INVESTMENT RATIO (FS DAIR)

Debt Interest Rate	Debt Pay-Down Allocation	Investment Allocation
0.5%	5%	95%
1.0%	10%	90%
1.5%	15%	85%
2.0%	20%	80%
2.5%	25%	75%
3.0%	30%	70%
3.5%	35%	65%
4.0%	40%	60%
4.5%	45%	55%
5.0%	50%	50%
5.5%	55%	45%
6.0%	60%	40%
6.5%	65%	35%
7.0%	70%	30%
7.5%	75%	25%
8.0%	80%	20%
8.5%	85%	15%
9.0%	90%	10%
9.5%	95%	5%
10%	100%	0%
15%	100%	0%
20%	100%	0%
25%	100%	0%
30%	100%	0%

Source: FinancialSamurai.com

Alternatively, you could follow the debt-snowball method to paying down debt. The snowball method dictates that you pay off your smallest debts first, regardless of the interest rate, to create small wins. The small wins give you a psychological boost to help you build momentum to continue paying down debt.

However, from a mathematical point of view, paying down your highest-interest-rate debt will save you the most money over time.

FS DAIR in Action

Let's look at some examples.

Example 1:

Say you have the following combination of debts:

1. 15% interest credit card debt for $5,000
2. 9% interest personal loan for $15,000
3. 4% student loan debt for $15,000 over 20 years

Using FS DAIR, you would allocate 100% of every incoming dollar, after covering your living expenses, to paying down the 15% credit card debt. Once the credit card is paid off, you would allocate 90% of your cash flow after living expenses toward paying down your personal loan debt and 10% to investing. Once the personal loan is paid off, then you'd allocate 40% to paying off your student loans and 60% to investing.

Example 2:

It's important to stay flexible as you keep FS DAIR in mind and consider all financial opportunities. For example, if your employer offers a match on 401(k) contributions, you should absolutely contribute the full match to your retirement savings for the free money.

Here's a common situation where a recent college graduate would like to invest in her 401(k) and pay down student loan debt. Her scenario is:

1. 3% student loan debt of $25,000
2. 100% 401(k) company match up to $3,000

She should allocate 30% of her free cash flow after living expenses to paying down extra student loan debt. This is on top of her normal monthly student loan payments. Given that her employer provides a $3,000 401(k) match, she should also contribute a minimum of $3,000 per year to her 401(k) for an automatic 100% annual return. If she still has leftover cash flow from her 70% investing allocation, she should keep on investing.

Depending on your amount of disposable income, the ideal approach is to contribute the maximum possible to a 401(k) to take advantage of the tax benefits and build up your retirement savings. With any money left over, aggressively build a taxable investment portfolio in order to generate usable passive income before age fifty-nine and a half.

Example 3:

Here's another common scenario where someone might struggle to figure out whether to pay down mortgage principal or invest. Let's say this is your situation:

1. You have a 3% thirty-year fixed mortgage and no other debt.
2. The stock market is at a record high, and valuations are also at all-time highs.

Use 30% of your free cash flow after necessary living expenses to pay down extra mortgage principal. Nowadays, it's easy to pay down mortgage debt online.

Some will argue that paying down a mortgage with such a low interest rate is a suboptimal use of funds. However, that is why the FS DAIR system is so effective. The remaining 70% of your cash flow can be used to invest.

Remember, when it comes to investing, there are no guarantees. With stock market valuations at all-time highs, you could lose money shortly after investing. In comparison, paying down debt is always a guaranteed return.

Therefore, whenever you feel extremely uncertain about investment opportunities, you must at least continue on your journey to paying down debt using the FS DAIR framework. In this scenario, you could use the remaining 70% to pay down more debt or rebuild your emergency fund if it has dipped below six months of living expenses.

When in doubt, always continue to pay down debt. A big reason why people get stuck in so much debt is because they lack the discipline to pay it off consistently. In the same vein, not investing consistently over the long run is the reason why the average person's retirement savings is still under $100,000.

Stick to FS DAIR and methodically pay down debt *and* invest. It's a framework that aims to eliminate emotions, investing FOMO, greed, and fear from your debt situation.

If FS DAIR Isn't for You . . .

I understand that FS DAIR won't work for everyone. Maybe you're not drawn to formulas. Maybe you're not even interested in investing until you can get your debt under control. That's fine. You know yourself, and you have to do what works for you. So if FS DAIR doesn't speak to you, consider testing out these two strategies:

Pay down the most annoying debt first. There's no math involved here, only feelings. Slay the debt that makes you the most angry, the most annoyed, the most worried. For me, the most annoying debt is credit card debt, so I pay it off every month with an automatic payment system. The second-most-annoying debt was my graduate school loan.

Pay off debts from smallest to largest. This is called the debt-snowball method. Paying down a large debt often feels like chipping away at a mountain; you can hardly tell you're making a difference. Paying off smaller debts, on the other hand, provides more visible progress and is mathematically much easier to do. Momentum is a powerful tool that will supercharge your personal finances. The victory of paying off one debt will spur you into action to pay off the next debt, and so forth.

It is sad that the average person has to work more than one hundred days to pay their taxes before earning any money for themselves. This statistic alone makes me never want to work again and aggressively find ways to legally shelter my income. If you have no debt, it's much easier to be free. You don't have to do "forced work" anymore. Instead, you can work on things you absolutely enjoy.

None of these debt payoff strategies are mutually exclusive. The key is to choose the strategy that works best for you and to stay focused.

The Right Asset-to-Liability Ratio to Retire Comfortably

Hopefully, we have all moved beyond using debt for superfluous consumption and agree to use debt only for investing in real estate or other assets that have the potential to increase in value. With this mindset, let's look at the right asset-to-liability ratio to increase your chances to 70%+ of boosting your wealth, while also enabling you to sleep well at night.

If you have a home valued at $2.2 million (asset) with $2 million in debt (liability), you are highly leveraged, since you have only $200,000 in equity. Your loan-to-value is 91% and your asset-to-liability ratio is 1.1:1. Let's say your home declines in value by 10% to $1.98 million. In such a scenario, 100% of your $200,000 is wiped out and you are underwater by $20,000. Of course, if your home appreciates by 10%, your $200,000 in home equity increases by 110% to $420,000.

However, if you have real estate worth $10 million (asset) and "only" $2 million in debt (liability), then you will probably survive a bear market. Your asset-to-liability ratio is 5:1. Your real estate portfolio would have to decline by more than 80% for you to be underwater.

It could happen, but it is unlikely based on previous bear market cycles. If your assets increase by 10% to $11 million, your $8 million in equity increases by only 12.5% to $9 million.

In other words:

- In a bull market, it helps to have a low asset-to-liability ratio to generate the highest cash-on-cash returns.
- In a bear market, it helps to have a high asset-to-liability ratio to protect your wealth from getting crushed.

According to an analysis by First Trust Advisors, there were fourteen bear markets between April 1947 and September 2021, ranging in length from one month to 1.7 years and in severity from a 51.9% drop in the S&P 500 to a decline of 20.6%. However, the vast majority of the time, we are in a bull market—at or close to record highs in the S&P 500 and in the real estate market.

Therefore, taking on some debt to buy risk assets like stocks, real estate, fine art, antique cars, rare coins, and so forth makes sense if the debt interest rate is low enough and your asset-to-liability ratio is manageable.

If the returns on the risk asset you want to buy have historically been under the cost of the debt, then you should *not* take on any debt to invest in that risk asset. You must also make future return assumptions on the risk assets you want to buy with debt. In other

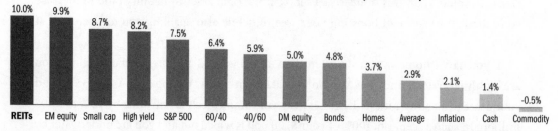

20-YEAR ANNUALIZED RETURNS BY ASSET CLASS (2001–2020)

REITs	EM equity	Small cap	High yield	S&P 500	60/40	40/60	DM equity	Bonds	Homes	Average	Inflation	Cash	Commodity
10.0%	9.9%	8.7%	8.2%	7.5%	6.4%	5.9%	5.0%	4.8%	3.7%	2.9%	2.1%	1.4%	-0.5%

Source: Barclays, Bloomberg, FactSet, Standard & Poor's, J.P. Morgan Asset Management; Dalbar Inc., MSCI, NAREIT, Russell. Indices used are as follows: **REITs:** NAREIT Equity REIT Index, **Small cap:** Russell 2000, **EM equity:** MSCI EM, **DM equity:** MSCI EAFE, **Commodity:** Bloomberg Commodity Index, **High yield:** Bloomberg Barclays Global HY Index, **Bonds:** Bloomberg Barclays U.S. Aggregate Index, **Homes:** median sale price of existing single-family homes, **Cash:** Bloomberg Barclays 1-3m Treasury, **Inflation:** CPI, **60/40:** A balanced portfolio with 60% invested in S&P 500 index and 40% invested in high-quality U.S. fixed income, represented by the Bloomberg Barclays U.S. Aggregate Index. The portfolio is rebalanced annually. Average asset allocation investor return is based on an analysis by Dalbar Inc., which utilizes the net of aggregate mutual fund sales, redemptions and exchanges each month as a measure of investor behavior. *Guide to the Markets—U.S. Data* are as of September 30, 2021.

words, if your debt interest rate is 5% and you expect the asset you want to buy to return less than 5%, you should not use debt to buy the asset.

Obviously, not all asset classes will return similar amounts. On the previous page is a snapshot of the twenty-year annualized returns by asset class between 2001 and 2020. Past returns are not indicative of future returns.

Another assumption to make before deciding on the right asset-to-liability ratio is that younger people have more time and energy to make up for potential losses than older people do. In other words, as we get older, our debt load should decrease while our asset-to-liability ratio should naturally increase. We no longer have as much time to make up for any potential losses. Once you've reached financial independence, or an age when you no longer have the energy or the desire to make more money, leveraging your money for potentially higher returns is a 30/70 suboptimal decision.

Below is my target asset-to-liability ratio for growing your wealth in a responsible manner. By the time you are in your sixties, you should strive to have an asset-to-liability ratio of 10:1 or higher. If you want, by all means pay off all your debt by the time you retire or even before. Having no debt truly feels wonderful. You just have to be okay with not making potentially even greater returns during a bull market.

TARGET ASSET-TO-LIABILITY RATIO FOR GROWING YOUR WEALTH

Age Group	Target Ratio	Target Net Worth
20s	2:1	$250,000 by 30
30s	3:1	$650,000 by 40
40s	5:1	$1,250,000 by 50
50s	8:1	$2,200,000 by 60
60s+	10:1	$3,000,000 by 70

Source: FinancialSamurai.com

Note: The target net worth figures assume a person or a household is making $125,000 to $300,000 per year over their working career. The target asset-to-liability ratio is independent of income.

Personally, I love taking on cheap debt to buy an asset that appreciates in value. Using other people's money to make money feels like you're getting something for free. Meanwhile, paying down debt using the FS DAIR methodology feels equally as rewarding. However, I've also been burned before (during the 2008–9 global financial crisis), which is why I advocate taking on debt in moderation.

For those of you who've been investing only since 2009, it's hard to truly know what it feels like to lose a lot of money for an extended period of time. Yes, March 2020 was a scary time for investors. However, stocks recovered all their gains in a matter of months and real estate prices froze for only about a month before marching aggressively higher. With the global financial crisis, we were wallowing in the mire for two years as firms laid people off left and right.

Given that stocks are the other most popular risk asset, let's now discuss whether taking on debt to buy stocks is a good idea.

Buy This: Risk-Appropriate Mortgages; Not That: Stock on Margin

A great number of people have used debt to enrich themselves beyond their wildest dreams. Just look at the leveraged buyouts (LBOs) of the 1980s, such as when investment firm KKR took over RJR Nabisco with debt and made a fortune once the company relisted. Or when Airbnb took on a $2 billion loan from Silver Lake and Sixth Street in April 2020 so it could have a financial cushion during the COVID-19 pandemic. At the time, Airbnb had an $18 billion valuation. A year later, it was worth over $100 billion.

Using debt to buy stocks is known as margin investing. Spoiler: I don't recommend it. You already know I favor real estate investing, but it's still good to know how margin works, in case you're tempted to try it.

Just like a bank can lend you money if you have equity in your house, your brokerage firm can lend you money against the value of certain stocks, bonds, and mutual funds in your portfolio. That borrowed money is called a margin loan. The margin loan can be used to purchase additional securities or to meet short-term lending needs not related to investing.

In general, after signing a margin agreement, brokerage customers can borrow up to 50% of the purchase price of marginable investments. When people say they are on 50% margin, it means they've purchased double their cash buying power in stocks.

The 50% margin terminology can be confusing, so let me share an easy example.

Let's say you have $100,000 in cash in a margin-approved brokerage account. Your margin agreement says you can borrow up to 50% of the purchase price of marginable investments. You love Apple stock and want to buy more than a $100,000 position.

The margin agreement says you can buy up to $200,000 in Apple stock—you would pay 50% of the purchase price and your brokerage firm would loan you the other 50%. This is where the 50% comes in. Being able to invest 50% on margin actually means you have double the cash buying power in your brokerage account. You have a 2:1 margin.

The amount you can borrow (margin) changes every day because the value of your marginable securities as collateral fluctuates daily. Therefore, don't just assume you have X amount of buying power. Check first, before making an investment. If you run your margin limit to the maximum, a decline in your portfolio's value will decrease your margin buying power and vice versa. You may be forced by the brokerage to liquidate your stock holdings at the most inopportune times.

The Parallel to Using a Mortgage to Buy a Home

The 50% margin figure is like having a 50% loan-to-value ratio when buying a home.

Isn't it funny how it's totally acceptable for people to buy a house with up to an 80% loan-to-value (LTV) ratio (20% down, 80% loan), whereas buying stocks on margin is considered much riskier? Understanding this difference is important for understanding risk and how you want to construct your net worth allocation. (More on this in chapter 5.)

Buying a home with a risk-appropriate mortgage is less risky than buying stock on margin, and ironically, due to lower risk, you could actually end up making much more money from real estate than from stocks. How do we know this? Let me explain.

1. **The government believes so.** Under Regulation T of the Federal Reserve Board, you may borrow up to 50% of the purchase price of securities that can be purchased on margin. This is known as the "initial margin." Some firms require you to deposit more than 50% of the purchase price.

    After you buy stock on margin, the Financial Industry Regulatory Authority (FINRA) requires you to keep at least 25% of the total market value of the securities in your margin account at all times. The 25% is called the "maintenance requirement." Many brokerage firms have higher maintenance requirements, typically between 30% and 50%. The equity in your account is the value of your securities less how much you owe to your brokerage firm.

    On the other hand, the government actively encourages first-time home buyers to put only 0% to 3.5% down and borrow the rest through the following types of loans:
    - VA loans, which are backed by the Department of Veterans Affairs, offer 0% down payment options for borrowers who qualify.
    - USDA loans, backed by the Department of Agriculture, offer 0% down payment options for borrowers who qualify.
    - FHA loans, backed by the Federal Housing Administration, allow down payments as low as 3.5%.

2. **Financial institutions agree.** Just like yours and mine, a financial institution's goal is to make as much money as possible in a risk-appropriate manner.

   If brokerage firms thought stocks were less risky, they would lobby hard to expand the margin cap so their customers could borrow more. After all, a brokerage firm earns a margin interest that pays far more than the interest rate it pays on its client's cash holdings. But brokerage firms know some of their clients could go broke on margin and wouldn't have the capacity to repay their margin debt during swift downturns.

   Most mortgage lenders are gladly lending up to 80% of the value of the real property. If you've got great credit, some lenders will even let you borrow up to 90% of the property's value (10% down payment, 90% LTV).

   If lenders thought real estate was riskier than stocks, they would lower the percentage that a client could borrow. Many of these financial institutions run both a brokerage and a mortgage business. Therefore, they see both sides.

3. **The median purchase price for a home is much greater.** In 2022, the median purchase price for a home in America was around $400,000. This is clearly much greater than the median purchase price of a stock. According to the 2019 Survey of Consumer Finances, the median (not average) retirement account balance in 2019 was $65,000, which would include individual stocks and funds.

   Yet despite the median home price being about six times greater than the median retirement account balance, real estate investors can borrow up to 90% of a home purchase in comparison with 50% for stock margin buyers.

   This fact also signifies that financial institutions believe real estate is less risky than stocks. The greater the purchase price, the more a financial institution has to lose. Therefore, lowering the client borrowing amount would make sense. Yet the opposite is true when it comes to buying real estate.

4. **Average mortgage rates are lower than average margin rates.** Mortgage rates most closely follow the latest ten-year bond yield. The mortgage rate you get is ultimately determined by your creditworthiness. Meanwhile, your margin interest rate will depend on the quantity of assets you hold with your broker. The more money you have with them, the lower the margin interest most of the time.

   However, overall, the average home buyer can borrow at a lower rate than the average stock margin buyer. Depending on your credit and account balance, the average mortgage rate could easily be 3% lower than the average margin rate you could borrow. Given that rates are changing all the time, please do a simple online check before borrowing any money.

MARGIN RATES AT FIDELITY

Debit Balance	Margin Interest Rate
$1 million +	4.250% (3.075% below base rate)
$500,000–$999,999	4.500% (2.825% below base rate)
$250,000–$499,999	6.825% (0.500% below base rate)
$100,000–$249,999	7.075% (0.250% below base rate)
$50,000–$99,999	7.125% (0.200% below base rate)
$25,000–$49,999	8.075% (0.750% above base rate)
$0–$24,999	8.575% (1.250% above base rate)

4.25% rate available for debit balances over $1 million. Fidelity's current base margin rate, effective since March 18, 2022, is 7.325%

Source: Fidelity

A 6%+ margin interest rate is high if the historical return for stocks is 10%, and 6%+ is super high if the lower return assumptions for stocks and bonds by Vanguard, Bank of America, and a number of other investment houses come true.

The last thing you want to do is buy stock on margin, pay a high margin interest rate, and get a margin call because your stock declined in value. If you are forced to sell because you cannot deposit more funds to cover your margin call, you lose twice.

Real estate tends to be much less volatile than stocks. While some stocks can see their prices drop by 30% in one day due to a bad earnings call, real estate valuations tend to move in much smaller magnitudes.

The value of real estate is fundamentally based on the rents the property can receive. Given that rents are stickier in down markets due to yearlong lease agreements and the pain of moving, real estate values don't move down as much. Further, in a bear market, mortgage rates tend to decline, bringing in more real estate buyers.

So long as you are paying your mortgage on time, a bank doesn't really care because it doesn't own your property, nor does it want to. But brokerages set up a maintenance margin that, once crossed, requires more funds. Brokerages know stock investors tend to sell at inappropriate times, whereas with real estate, it's more difficult to panic sell.

If you insist on buying stocks on margin, I wouldn't go beyond borrowing more than your age group's recommended asset-to-liability ratio (more on this in chapter 4). In other words, in your twenties, you may go up to a 50% margin (2:1), where you can buy up to $200,000 of stock with your $100,000 portfolio. This so happens to be the maximum margin most brokerages will give you. By the time you're in your forties, reduce your margin to 20%, and then down to 0% to 10% by your sixties. Reduce your margin debt as you get older. There's no need for margin as your wealth grows.

Embrace the Positives of Debt

Not all debt is bad. Learn how to utilize debt to help you build more wealth and live a better life than you would if you could purchase things only with cash.

Using a credit card as a convenient way to pay for things while also getting rewards points and fraud protection is great. Just make sure to pay off the balance each month. Buying a home with a mortgage to raise your little ones in is wonderful, especially if the home appreciates in value. Just make sure you can always afford to pay your mortgage, insurance, and property taxes on time.

A knife can help you prepare the most amazing dishes for your family and friends, but a knife can also cut you if improperly used. The same thing goes for debt. So long as you are using debt to invest in historically appreciating assets, you will likely come out ahead in the long run.

THE FINANCIAL SAMURAI WAY

- Utilize the FS DAIR strategy to pay down debt and invest at the same time. It's hard to lose if you're always doing both in a logical manner.

- Besides payday loans and loan sharks, revolving credit card debt is the worst type of debt. Not only are credit card interest rates high, the debt is used mostly to purchase a depreciating asset. Always pay off all consumer debt on time.

- Use debt to buy historically appreciating assets, not assets that are guaranteed to depreciate. The best use of debt is to buy real estate, followed by stocks, a distant second.

- By the time you retire, shoot to have an asset-to-liability ratio of 10:1 or higher. Once you've won the game, there's no reason to take on excess risk.

PART TWO

Put Your Money to Work

Successful investing is about putting your hard-earned capital to work in a risk-appropriate manner. You'll build most of your wealth through a mix of stocks, real estate, bonds, alternatives, and doing work you love.

I'll show you exactly where to put your money and when, so that it's working for you as long and as hard as possible. I'll also uncover how certain life decisions—like where you choose to live—can influence your wealth potential much more than people often realize.

Get these pieces in place and you'll be on your way to creating far more wealth than you'd imagine.

Chapter 5

Follow a Proper Allocation Model

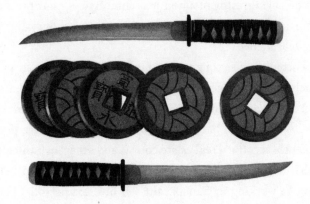

You'll remember that a couple of chapters ago I said everyone should strive for this optimal savings scenario:

1. First, max out your pretax retirement contributions.
2. Then, save at least 20% of your after-tax income in taxable investments.

Once you have a debt strategy in place, your next move is to come up with a plan for *where* you'll put your savings and *when*, to give you the best probability of maximizing your wealth potential.

So let's get your plan going.

The biggest variable in how soon you reach financial independence is how much you save in taxable investments. Since you can't usually access your pretax retirement accounts before age fifty-nine and a half without penalty, it's your taxable investments that will generate passive income for you to live off before then.

I say to save *at least 20%* of your after-tax income, but if you want to be financially free sooner, you really need to save much more.

The chart on the next page provides a base case for how much you need to save in taxable investments in order to live a comfortable, financially free life. Of course, there are lots of variables that influence how much you'll need in passive income. But this chart is a good starting point to see just how aggressively you need to save.

It shows your taxable investment amount as a multiple of your pretax retirement contributions. The greater the ratio of after-tax money to pretax money, the easier it will be to reach financial independence.

Ultimately, I encourage everyone to accumulate 3X more in their taxable investment accounts than their tax-advantaged accounts. There is a limit to how much you can contribute to a 401(k) or IRA, but there is no limit to how much you can invest outside of these accounts. In other words, if you have $200,000 in your 401(k), strive to have $600,000 in your taxable brokerage accounts, real estate equity, and other investments.

Please note that tax-advantaged accounts include the Registered Retirement Savings Plan (RRSP) if you're working in Canada, the self-invested personal pension (SIPP) and company-sponsored defined-benefit pensions if you're working in the United Kingdom, the superannuation system if you're working in Australia, the Mandatory Provident Fund if you're working in Hong Kong, and so forth. Wherever you are reading this book, your goal is to contribute the maximum to your country's tax-advantaged retirement accounts and build your taxable accounts as large as possible.

Once you accumulate your first million, it's much easier to accumulate millions more. At the same time, it's much easier to lose a large absolute dollar amount of money, which is why proper diversification and asset allocation are a must. A goal of a million can seem daunting, but the good news is that once you get to about $250,000 in investable assets, you'll start noticing potentially significant returns. At $250,000 your returns may even start to surpass how much you can contribute to your tax-advantaged accounts.

Most people will start their wealth-building journey by investing in the stock market. The barrier to entry is low—you just need a bank account and a small amount of money— and the potential earnings are high.

But here's an unfortunate truth: only about 53% to 56% of Americans have money invested in the stock market. Sure, some of the people who don't participate are deliberately

TAXABLE INVESTMENT TARGETS BY AGE (BASE CASE)

Age	Years Worked	Multiple	Tax-Advantaged Accounts	Taxable Accounts	Gross Income from Taxable Accounts at 4%	Total Net Worth
22	0	0	$0	$0	$0	$0
23	1	0.5	$10,000	$5,000	$200	$15,000
24	2	0.6	$30,000	$18,000	$720	$48,000
25	3	0.7	$50,000	$35,000	$1,400	$85,000
27	5	0.8	$100,000	$80,000	$3,200	$180,000
30	8	1.0	$150,000	$150,000	$6,000	$300,000
35	13	1.5	$300,000	$450,000	$18,000	$750,000
40	18	2.0	$500,000	$1,000,000	$40,000	$1,500,000
45	23	2.5	$750,000	$1,875,000	$75,000	$2,625,000
50	28	3.0	$1,000,000	$3,000,000	$120,000	$4,000,000
55	33	3.0	$1,500,000	$4,500,000	$180,000	$6,000,000
60	38	3.0	$2,500,000	$7,500,000	$300,000	$10,000,000

Taxable investments include brokerage accounts, rental property, CDs, businesses, private equity, art, etc.
Tax-advantaged accounts include 401(k), 403(b), 457(b), IRA, Roth IRA, SEP IRA, HSA, etc.

Source: FinancialSamurai.com

opting out. Maybe they're sitting on an inheritance that will last a lifetime, or they're swimming in profits from their company equity or real estate holdings. Go, them! But the reality is that many people don't invest in the stock market for one of two reasons: they think they don't have enough money to do it, or they don't know where to start—and often, it's both.

That's disheartening because these folks are missing out on one of the best ways to build wealth over the long term. I failed to invest in a Roth IRA in my twenties because I thought investing a couple thousand dollars a year was a waste of time. I regret this decision now. Even if I'd invested only $2,000 a year between ages twenty-three and thirty-three and never contributed to the account again, I'd have a nest egg of over $71,000 today that would continue to grow tax free. By age sixty, I would have a Roth IRA worth over $243,000. And that's using a conservative calculation of 8% annual returns.

Skipping a Roth IRA was a missed opportunity. But it taught me a major lesson: investing early, in a risk-appropriate manner, can have a bigger impact on our future wealth than we often realize. Do not underestimate the power of compound interest.

In the years since, I've also witnessed how important it is to fit stock market investing into a larger net worth allocation strategy. Stocks, or any other investment, should be just one part of a wealth-building plan. And that plan needs to align with our risk tolerance, life stage, and goals. There's no sense in having a high-risk portfolio if it keeps you up at night and stresses you out all day. Your money should make you feel secure, not constantly worried.

You don't need to be an expert to invest wisely. And you don't need a lot of money. You just need a disciplined strategy that works for you. Then let time work its magic.

The Beauty of Investing in Stocks

Although I love real estate, the average American is either too heavily into real estate or has a net worth that is poorly diversified. The lack of diversification is because most of the average American's net worth is tied up in their primary residence.

Think about what happened during the 2008–9 global financial crisis. By 2010, the median net worth plunged by 35% to about $69,000 from a high of $107,000 in 2005. Meanwhile, the median home equity dropped from about $87,000 to $52,000 during the same period. In other words, the median American's net worth consisted almost entirely of home equity (75% to 81%). No wonder Americans were in such great pain between 2008 and 2010.

This is why I recommend that investors shoot to limit their primary residence value to no more than 30% of their net worth. It will be hard at first, but 30% or lower is the ultimate goal.

With a 30% limit, an investor has enough net worth outside their primary residence to generate investment income. Building more wealth outside your primary residence is a must because those investments can provide you the passive income necessary to live more freely. At the same time, having about 30% of your net worth in your primary residence ensures that you are at least enjoying a good percentage of your overall wealth.

For most people, the optimal approach is to split the majority of their investments across stocks, bonds, and real estate. Then, of course, there is the rise of alternative investments such as cryptocurrency, fine art, farmland, and wine, to which I recommend allocating at most 10% of your net worth. How much you allocate to each asset category will depend on your personal goals, interests, and circumstances. There is no one-size-fits-all approach.

In a minute I will share three asset allocation models for how to approach this. First, it's important to understand why investing in the stock market is such an important part of a strong wealth-building strategy.

The short answer: strong historical performance. If you keep your money in stocks for the long game—and I mean *decades*—your earnings may be in the historical 10% range. Further, stocks are a completely passive investment. But your year-to-year performance is unlikely to look like the historical average. The stock market's short-term performance is extremely volatile.

The S&P 500 index, for example, has had returns as horrific as –43% in 1931 and as glowing as +54% in 1933. Returns were just as manic in more recent years: –37% in 2008, +32% in 2013, –4% in 2018, +31% in 2019, 18% in 2020, and 27% in 2021. But even the most catastrophic bear market losses are eventually evened out by bull market gains if you hang on to an S&P 500 ETF or index fund like VTI, SPY, or VTSAX long enough. That's just how it goes.

Your early years of aggressive saving are critical to helping you achieve this. You're not only saving to build up your net worth and passive income; you're also saving for a down payment on your primary residence. The goal is to get *neutral real estate* by owning your primary residence as soon as possible without draining your entire savings. (Don't worry, I explain what I call short, neutral, and long real estate in chapter 7.)

After real estate, you can branch out to other investments.

Net Worth Allocation by Age

Now let's talk about where to put your money.

Your approach will depend a lot on your life stage and circumstances. A thirty-year-old with dreams of retiring in New York City at age fifty with a family of four will have a pretty different financial plan from a thirty-year-old who doesn't have kids and wants to retire in Billings, Montana, by forty. Whatever your dream, setting age-based goals will help you stay on track.

Your baseline strategy is to own stocks, bonds, and real estate over the long run. If you do, you will likely outperform a large percentage of Americans who own none of the above. Stocks and real estate are terrific beneficiaries of inflation.

- **Stocks** include individual stocks, index funds, mutual funds, ETFs, and equity structured notes.
- **Bonds** include government treasuries, corporate bonds, municipal bonds, high-yield bonds, savings bonds, and TIPs. Bonds are more for defensive purposes.

- **Real estate** includes a primary residence, rental properties, commercial properties, real estate ETFs, private and public eREITs, and private real estate syndication deals.

A small portion of your assets should also go into risk-free savings vehicles such as CDs, money market accounts, and cash. During your financial journey, you will inevitably encounter setbacks. Your risk-free savings or "emergency fund" will help you sleep better at night as you go through the turbulence of life.

You can also diversify your net worth even further by investing in alternative investments. *Alternative investment* is a catchall term for everything other than stocks, bonds, and real estate. Things like art, music royalties, wine, farmland, commodities, cryptocurrencies, collectibles, private equity, angel investing, and venture debt are considered alternative investments.

Lots of people also feel energized to start a side hustle so they can eventually ditch their day job—or quit now and just take the leap. I call this the X factor. And I highly encourage having one. More on this in chapter 12.

For now, let's focus on how you might allocate your net worth among these asset classes. I've put together three models for you to consider based on what has worked for me. My models are also inspired by feedback I've received from some of the tens of millions of readers who've come to *Financial Samurai* since the site began. They are:

- **Conventional:** basic risk-taking
- **New Life:** more aggressive risk-taking; pushes for more wealth through more risk
- **Financial Samurai:** most aggressive risk-taking

I believe following one of these three frameworks can help the vast majority of people looking to achieve financial freedom.

Conventional Net Worth Allocation

The Conventional model consists of investments in stocks, bonds, real estate, and risk-free assets. It is the most basic net worth asset allocation model and also one of the most proven models over the decades.

The Conventional model is for those who like to keep things simple and who are also fine with working until the traditional retirement age of sixty-plus.

RECOMMENDED NET WORTH ALLOCATION BY AGE: CONVENTIONAL

	Risk Level	Medium	Med-Low	None	Medium	Medium	
	Amount of Control	Low	High	Low	Low	High	
Age	Years Worked	Stocks & Bonds	Real Estate	Risk-Free	Alternatives	X Factor	Total
23	1	100%	0%	0%	0%	0%	100%
27	5	50%	50%	0%	0%	0%	100%
30	8	40%	55%	5%	0%	0%	100%
33	11	45%	50%	5%	0%	0%	100%
35	13	50%	45%	5%	0%	0%	100%
40	18	55%	40%	5%	0%	0%	100%
45	23	50%	45%	5%	0%	0%	100%
50	28	60%	35%	5%	0%	0%	100%
55	33	65%	30%	5%	0%	0%	100%
60	38	65%	30%	5%	0%	0%	100%
65	43	70%	25%	5%	0%	0%	100%
70+	48+	75%	20%	5%	0%	0%	100%

Source: FinancialSamurai.com

Highlights of the Conventional net worth allocation model:

- It has you saving 100% of your investment portfolio in stocks and bonds in your twenties, since this is a time to save aggressively and take maximum investment risk. Any losses can be easily made up by work income. The vast majority of your portfolio will be stocks.
- By age thirty, it recommends buying a primary residence and having 5% of your net worth in risk-free assets. One of your main goals should be to get neutral real estate as soon as you know where you want to live and what you want to do.
- By age forty, it suggests having a larger weighting in stocks and bonds than in real estate. As your net worth grows, your primary residence becomes a smaller and smaller portion of your overall net worth. At the same time, you may also be interested in investing in rental properties, REITs, or private eREITs to get long real estate instead of just neutral real estate.
- By age sixty, it recommends having roughly twice the weighting in stocks than in real estate, and about 5% in risk-free assets. As you head into traditional retirement, your

goal is to have more of your investments be truly passive, given that your time is more valuable than ever. Of course, besides a paid-off primary residence equal to no more than 30% of your net worth, you can also own online real estate instead of physical rental properties for more passivity.

- All percentages are based on a positive net worth. If you have student loans right out of school or a negative net worth due to negative equity, use these charts for the asset side of the balance sheet equation. Systematically look to reduce nonmortgage debt as you accumulate your wealth-building assets.

- Alternative investments and your X factor stay at 0%. It's hard enough to get people to save more than 20% of their income, max out their retirement accounts, and buy a house. To then be asked to buy alternative investments may be too much for someone following the Conventional model. When it comes to investing, keeping things simple is often the best way to go.

New Life Net Worth Allocation

The New Life net worth model changes things up around age forty (midlife). After living the Conventional way for around twenty years after high school or college, you may want to experience a "new life" in the second half of your existence. I'm sure many of you have wondered what life would be like if you did something else.

Since starting *Financial Samurai* in 2009, I've discovered many of us start wanting to do something new by age forty. Given that you've had almost twenty years of learning, building wealth, and honing new skills, you may have an itch to try a new career, invest in different assets, or start your own business. For me, doing the same thing for the fourteenth year after college no longer sounded appealing, so I left.

Some call this a midlife crisis. I like to think of this time as a period of discovery and excitement. It's a time when we decide to take more risk because we have more financial security and more experience. When I took the leap of faith in 2012, I once again felt the thrill of the unknown.

The New Life framework essentially includes investments in more alternative assets like venture capital, private equity, and cryptocurrency. It also encourages you to branch into new entrepreneurial opportunities, an X factor, around middle age.

RECOMMENDED NET WORTH ALLOCATION BY AGE: NEW LIFE

	Risk Level	High	Medium	None	Medium	Medium	
	Amount of Control	Low	High	Low	Low	High	
Age	Years Worked	Stocks & Bonds	Real Estate	Risk-Free	Alternatives	X Factor	Total
23	1	100%	0%	0%	0%	0%	100%
27	5	100%	0%	0%	0%	0%	100%
30	8	40%	55%	5%	0%	0%	100%
33	11	45%	50%	5%	0%	0%	100%
35	13	50%	45%	5%	0%	0%	100%
40	18	45%	40%	5%	5%	5%	100%
45	23	45%	35%	5%	5%	10%	100%
50	28	40%	35%	5%	10%	10%	100%
55	33	40%	30%	5%	10%	15%	100%
60	38	40%	25%	5%	10%	20%	100%
65	43	45%	20%	5%	10%	20%	100%
70+	48+	45%	20%	5%	10%	20%	100%

Source: FinancialSamurai.com

Highlights of the New Life net worth allocation model:

- By age thirty, you purchase your first property and allocate 5% of your net worth to risk-free assets now that you have a mortgage. You've also been maxing out your 401(k) or other tax-advantaged retirement accounts while investing an additional 20% in a taxable brokerage account.
- By age forty, your net worth has increased handsomely. Your real estate now accounts for a more manageable 40% of net worth compared with 90%+ for the typical American. You finally diversify some of your risk assets into alternative investments.
- By age forty, you also start a side hustle while you still have a steady job. You've always wanted to consult on the side, start a blog, open an e-commerce store, or teach lessons online. Whatever your X factor is, you're finally pursuing it under the safety of a regular paycheck. You've begun your new life!
- Also around age forty, you begin to wonder what else there is in life. You're getting burned out doing the same old thing for almost twenty years. Maybe you negotiate a severance before working in a different industry. Maybe you just take a long sabbatical and then

transfer departments. Or maybe you decide to join a competitor for a pay raise and a promotion in a different part of the country or world.

- By the time you're sixty, your X factor has grown to about 20% of your net worth. Twenty years is plenty of time to build your side business into something meaningful. Meanwhile, stocks and real estate still account for a majority of your net worth (65%). But your main joy is found in your X factor. The combination of your X factor and your day job has made you far wealthier than the average person who works only a day job.
- In your golden years, a diversified net worth provides stability and security as you plan to live to 110 years old.

Financial Samurai Net Worth Allocation

The Financial Samurai net worth allocation model has you aggressively betting on yourself. You believe the traditional way of building wealth is outdated. You have no desire to work for someone else until long past your forties. Instead, you want to build your own business and have more freedom at a younger age.

Despite your desire for more autonomy, you still diligently build your financial foundation in your twenties and early thirties. Your twenties are when you're learning so that you can start earning in your thirties and beyond. During this period, you are actively building your passive-investment income streams. Once your side hustle starts generating enough to cover your basic living expenses, you take a leap of faith and go all in on your business, as I did in 2012 at age thirty-four.

Ideally, you negotiate a severance with your employer in order to build a nice financial buffer. After all, if you're going to quit anyway, you might as well try to negotiate a severance.

Your ultimate goal is to build an asset that makes up half of your net worth or greater by the time you're sixty. Let's take a look at the chart on the next page.

Highlights of the Financial Samurai net worth allocation model:
- It assumes you have better control of your own financial future than the prior investment models did. When you invest in stocks, bonds, real estate, and alternatives, you are depending on someone else and favorable macro conditions to make you money. When you invest in yourself, you believe you have a greater ability to build wealth.

RECOMMENDED NET WORTH ALLOCATION BY AGE: FINANCIAL SAMURAI

	Risk Level	High	Medium	None	Medium	Medium	
	Amount of Control	Low	High	Low	Low	High	
Age	Years Worked	Stocks & Bonds	Real Estate	Risk-Free	Alternatives	X Factor	Total
23	1	100%	0%	0%	0%	0%	100%
27	5	40%	55%	5%	0%	0%	100%
30	8	40%	50%	5%	0%	5%	100%
33	11	40%	45%	5%	0%	10%	100%
35	13	40%	30%	5%	10%	15%	100%
40	18	35%	30%	5%	10%	20%	100%
45	23	35%	25%	5%	10%	25%	100%
50	28	30%	20%	5%	10%	35%	100%
55	33	25%	20%	5%	10%	40%	100%
60	38	20%	15%	5%	10%	50%	100%
65	43	20%	15%	5%	10%	50%	100%
70+	48+	20%	15%	5%	10%	50%	100%

Source: FinancialSamurai.com

- By your late twenties you get neutral real estate by owning your primary residence. You understand that it's not good to fight inflation over the long term by renting. Your real estate investments provide more stability as you seek to take more investment risks and work on your X factor.

- By your thirties, you are aggressively working on building your side business. After ten years of conventional work, you already know you don't want to do the same job forever. As a result, you're planning for life after conventional work. Your initial goal is to earn enough money from your side business to cover your basic living expenses. Once that is achieved, you can take a leap of faith.

- Before leaving your day job, you will try to negotiate a severance. With a severance package, you gain financial breathing room to build your business the way you want, without the constant pressure of making money. Before you leave your day job, you will also refinance your mortgage and test-drive living off your existing investment income. It may not be much after ten to fifteen years of saving and investing, but it's important to simulate what life might be like without a steady paycheck.

- Despite building your business, you are also focused on building as many passive-income streams as possible. Your goal is to build a large enough passive-investment portfolio to cover your basic living expenses. Once your investment income can cover your housing, food, transportation, and internet expenses, you can really start to take more risks.
- At the same time, you are also trying to generate as much profit as possible from your business. The more profitable your business, the more you can reinvest your profits to grow your business even further. In addition, you can take your business profits and invest them to help you generate more passive income.
- If you are wildly successful in building your own business, the X factor column can easily dwarf all the other columns. Not only can your business generate active income, but it can one day be sold based on a multiple of revenue or profits.

The Bottom Line: The Proper Net Worth Allocation Is Well Diversified

Following any of the three net worth allocation models will likely build you much greater wealth than the average person by the time you are sixty. The question is which net worth allocation model fits your personality best.

There is absolutely nothing wrong with working a day job for your entire career, especially if you enjoy what you do. The work benefits, steady paycheck, and camaraderie can be worthwhile. If there's a nice pension at the end of the rainbow, then even better. In our low-interest-rate environment, having a pension is really like finding a pot of gold. If you choose the Conventional route, you might not end up with the highest amount of wealth, but you may have the least volatility and the most security.

The more risk-loving you are and the more bullish you are on your abilities, the more you should bet on yourself. Many of the wealthiest people in the world are entrepreneurs. They have an X factor within themselves that propels them to take more risks. If you believe you can build a better mousetrap, it behooves you to try. Even if you fail, at least you will never regret having tried. You can almost always go back to getting a day job if you want.

Your investments are there to work for you so you don't have to work for the rest of your life. Your investments also are there to provide more financial security so you can take more risks in your career.

Look, let's be honest: it is not a coincidence that some of the wealthiest people in America also come from very wealthy families. If your dad is a prominent lawyer, your mom is on the board of the directors of a bank, and your grandfather is a bank president, of course you can drop out of school and take more risks. If you fail, you can just kick back at your family's vacation property and try again!

Regardless of your background, just be humble enough to recognize that financial returns are not guaranteed, nor are your entrepreneurial endeavors. Your financial journey will be full of twists and turns. As a result, it's best to keep a diversified net worth mix that can withstand economic downturns. At the same time, your diversified net worth will also benefit from multiyear bull runs.

When it comes to building wealth, I encourage everyone to plan for bad scenarios. Expect the occasional 30%+ decline in your risk assets. This way, you've addressed your biggest fear so you can move on with your financial independence quest.

You are free to follow my recommended net worth allocation guide closely or not at all. The percentages won't be exact over time, and only you know your financial objectives and your ability to withstand shocks. Whatever your beliefs, you must at least come up with your own net worth allocation framework to follow. Just remember to enjoy the journey along the way!

Whatever model you follow (if any), I do not recommend having more than 50% of your net worth in any one asset class after age forty. Once you've built a significant amount of wealth, your goal should tilt more toward capital preservation. The last thing you want to do is go back to the salt mines when you're old and tired to make up for lost wealth.

THE FINANCIAL SAMURAI WAY
FOR STOCK MARKET INVESTING

As you strategize your net worth allocation, let this guide help you keep a level head.

- Investing in the stock market will bring you long-term wealth if you stay in the game long enough. The key is to follow an appropriate asset allocation model to minimize emotion in investing so you can keep on investing during good times and bad times.
- Accept that you will lose money along the way. It's part of the process, and panic selling can be tempting, but it's not an optimal option.
- Stay humble. Even if your portfolio has killer returns for several years, your outperformance is unlikely to continue due to mean reversion. Remember: Bears make money. Bulls make money. Pigs get slaughtered.

- You can build a lot of wealth by investing in the stock market, but you will not build all your wealth this way. The key is to diversify your investment power across a range of asset classes, both in and outside the stock market.
- Given that you will likely underperform the stock market over time as an active investor, invest the majority (80%+) of your equity allocation in low-cost passive index ETFs or index funds.

The Proper Allocation of Stocks and Bonds by Age

You'll notice that stocks and bonds are lumped together in my net worth allocation charts. Let's take a closer look at each, since they require their own allocation strategies.

Age-based benchmarks work well here too, since much of your approach will depend on your life stage. If you allocate too much to stocks the year before you want to retire and the stock market collapses, then you're screwed. If you allocate too much to bonds over your career, you might not be able to build enough capital to retire at all. Everyone's approach will be a little different, depending on their earning power, risk tolerance, and needs.

This stocks and bonds allocation advice applies to both your pretax and posttax investment accounts. For example, if you're thirty years old, aim to max out your 401(k) in the recommended allocation of stocks and bonds, then do the same with your taxable investment accounts.

Aside from your age, your asset allocation between stocks and bonds will depend on three things:

Your risk tolerance. Are you risk averse, moderate, or risk loving? Are you young and full of energy, or are you old and tired as hell? The more risk loving you are, the happier you will be to allocate a greater percentage of your public investment portfolio to stocks and vice versa.

The importance of your various investment portfolios. For example, most people would probably treat their 401(k) or IRA as a vital part of their retirement strategy. For the vast majority of employees, these tax-advantaged retirement accounts will become their largest investment portfolios. However, those who also have taxable investment accounts, rental properties, and alternative assets might view their 401(k), Roth IRA, and IRA portfolios as less important.

Your overall net worth composition. The smaller your public investment portfolio as a percentage of your overall net worth, the more aggressive your portfolio can be in stocks. In other words, if your public investment portfolio only makes up 10% of your overall net worth, then investing 100% of the portfolio in stocks may be fine if you are sixty years old and risk averse. The other 90% of your net worth may be in a cash-generating laundromat empire. Alternatively, if you are fifty years old, work a day job, and have 99% of your net worth in public investments, then having 100% of your portfolio in stocks might not be a good idea.

Let's now look at three asset allocation models for stocks and bonds that should cover the vast majority of readers. For the sake of consistency, they are also called Conventional, New Life, and Financial Samurai.

Conventional Asset Allocation Model for Stocks and Bonds

The classic recommendation for asset allocation is to subtract your age from 100 to find out how much you should allocate to stocks. The basic premise is that we become risk averse as we age, given that we have less ability and time to generate income. Given that bonds are less volatile and lose less than stocks during downturns, having a greater percentage of bonds as one gets older makes sense.

We also don't want to spend our older years working more than we have to. Therefore, we are willing to trade potentially lower returns for more income and higher certainty. The chart on the following page demonstrates the conventional asset allocation by age.

Today you can easily invest in an index target date fund with a reasonable expense ratio of 0.14% or less to replicate the Conventional asset allocation model. A target date fund will automatically rebalance the asset allocation for you over time so you don't have to. All you have to do is keep regularly contributing to the target date fund after you choose the appropriate target date, which is usually the year you'd like to retire. If you choose an actively run target date fund, the expense ratio will be much higher, without a guaranteed higher return. Therefore, I recommend choosing the index option if you don't want to actively manage your stock and bond market allocation.

THE PROPER ASSET ALLOCATION OF
STOCKS & BONDS BY AGE

Conventional Model

Age	Stocks	Bonds
0–25	100%	0%
30	70%	30%
35	65%	35%
40	60%	40%
45	55%	45%
50	50%	50%
55	45%	55%
60	40%	60%
65	35%	65%
70	30%	70%
75+	25%	75%

Source: FinancialSamurai.com

New Life Asset Allocation Model for Stocks and Bonds

The New Life asset allocation recommendation is to subtract your age from 120 to figure out how much of your portfolio should be allocated to stocks. Studies show we are living longer due to advancements in science and better awareness about healthy diet and exercise. That said, the median life expectancy for American men is about seventy-five and for American women is about eighty.

Given that stocks have outperformed bonds over the long run, we need a greater allocation to stocks to take care of us over our longer lives. Our risk tolerance still decreases as we get older, just at a later stage. The classic 60/40 portfolio between stocks and bonds begins at around age sixty.

Financial Samurai Asset Allocation Model of Stocks and Bonds

The Financial Samurai model has the heaviest weighting on stocks. Not only is the Financial Samurai more risk loving in their career, but the Financial Samurai is more risk loving when it comes to investing. However, that love of risk in investing comes from having a strong balance sheet and good cash flow from various sources.

THE PROPER ASSET ALLOCATION OF
STOCKS & BONDS BY AGE

New Life Model

Age	Stocks	Bonds
0–25	100%	0%
30	90%	10%
35	85%	15%
40	80%	20%
45	75%	25%
50	70%	30%
55	65%	35%
60	60%	40%
65	55%	45%
70	50%	50%
75+	45%	55%

Source: FinancialSamurai.com

Candidates for the Financial Samurai asset allocation model have multiple income streams and are personal finance enthusiasts who get a kick out of reading financial literature. Instead of reading the latest fantasy novel, you'd rather read the latest nonfiction book on how to improve various aspects of your life. Watching a segment on CNBC is just as fun as watching the latest hit show on Netflix.

With interest rates so low, investing in bonds is not very appealing. Because the Financial Samurai invests in real estate, real estate acts as a "bonds plus" type of investment. In other words, real estate already helps diversify the stock investor's portfolio because real estate tends to outperform stocks when stocks sell off. When stocks sell off, money tends to flow to bonds, which lowers interest rates. With lower interest rates and the desire for more real assets, real estate helps dampen an overall investment portfolio's volatility.

The *plus* part of *bonds plus* comes in the form of real estate potentially outperforming bonds on the upside. In a bullish environment, investors tend to stay away from lower-risk bonds to buy higher-risk assets with potentially more upside. One such asset is real estate, which tends to increase in value as rents increase. Given that real estate has the greater potential to outperform bonds during good times and bad times, a Financial Samurai often prefers investing in real estate over bonds.

THE PROPER ASSET ALLOCATION OF
STOCKS & BONDS BY AGE

Financial Samurai Model

Age	Stocks	Bonds Plus
0–25	100%	0%
30	100%	0%
35	100%	0%
40	90%	10%
45	90%	10%
50	80%	20%
55	80%	20%
60	80%	20%
65	70%	30%
70	60%	40%
75+	60%	40%

Source: FinancialSamurai.com

The Right Asset Allocation Depends on Your Risk Tolerance

By providing three different asset allocation models, I hope I have allowed you to identify one that fits your needs and risk tolerance. Don't let anybody force you into an uncomfortable situation.

Ideally, your asset allocation should let you sleep well at night and wake up every morning with vigor. But it's not a "set it and forget it" approach. You may want to dial up or down your allocations depending upon changing circumstances. I encourage everyone to take a proactive approach to their investment portfolios. Ask yourself the following questions to determine which asset allocation model is right for you:

- What is my risk tolerance on a scale of 0 to 10?
- If my portfolio dropped 35% in one year, would I be financially okay?
- How many months am I willing to work to make up for my potential losses?
- How stable is my primary income source?
- How many income streams do I have?
- Do I have an X factor to generate additional active income?

- What is my knowledge about stocks and bonds and other investments?
- How long is my investment horizon?
- Where do I get my investment advice and what is the quality of such advice?

Once you've answered these questions, sit down with a loved one to discuss whether there is congruence between your answers and how you are currently investing.

It's important not to overestimate your abilities when it comes to investing. We will all lose money eventually; it's just a matter of when and how much. The key is to choose a framework and stick with it over the long run.

It Comes Back to Mindset

After looking at numbers and percentages for a while, I like to remind myself that our mindset is one of the biggest influences on our potential to build wealth. Investing requires rational thinking. So as you design your asset allocation plan and decide where to invest, please remember these truths.

You are not smarter than the market. I don't care how much you've been able to outperform the stock market over the years. Your performance will normalize over the medium-to-long run. Most professional money managers fail to outperform their respective indices. Don't be so delusional as to think you can. Stay humble!

As you grow your assets to the hundreds of thousands or millions of dollars, you aren't going to be whipping around your capital as easily as before. Your risk tolerance will likely decline, especially if you have dependents and aging parents to take care of. In other words, your risk tolerance usually doesn't increase with the growth of your wealth, unless you grow so spectacularly wealthy that you have money to burn.

The most dangerous investor is one who has experienced only a bull market. They think they are invincible, confusing a bull market with their brains until the next inevitable downturn comes and wipes them out due to improper risk control. If you have only been investing since 2009, please consult those who had significant capital at risk during the global financial crisis between 2008 and 2009 and the dot-com crash in 2000 and previous bear markets.

Get it in your head that you will lose money at some point. There is no riskless investment unless you are putting less than $250,000 in CDs or money markets or buying U.S. treasuries. I've been investing since 1995 and still occasionally lose money on investments

I thought would be home runs. As a result, I've followed a net worth asset allocation model to minimize potential damage.

Your risk tolerance will change over time. When you've got only $20,000 to your name and you're twenty-five years old, your risk tolerance is likely going to be very high. Even if you lose all $20,000, you can gain it back with relative ease. When you are fifty-seven years old with $1 million and are only three years away from retirement, your risk tolerance will likely be much lower. You're so close to the finish line. You can't afford to blow out a knee.

When you're young, you naively think you can work at the same job for years. The feeling of invincibility is incredible. Your energy is the reason why you might be able to rapidly build wealth. However, the longer you live, the more bad (and good) things tend to happen. Your energy tends to fade and your interests will certainly change. The key is to forecast these changes by preparing well in advance.

Do not be delusional and think you're always going to be a certain way. Review your finances every month to assess and adjust your goals. Accept that life doesn't go in a straight line.

Black swan events happen all the time. They are supposed to be rare, but if you've been paying attention for the past couple of decades, you know incredible financial disruption happens all the time. If the economy doesn't get you, maybe workplace politics, a random health issue, a divorce, or a pandemic will! Expect the worst, hope for the best.

Nobody knows when the next panic-induced correction will occur. Nobody knows when your company CEO might drive the bus off a cliff with some ridiculous new product. When Armageddon arrives, practically everything gets crushed that is not guaranteed by the government. It's important to always have a portion of your net worth in risk-free assets.

Further, you should consider investing your time and money in things that you can control. If you want evidence of people not knowing what they are talking about, just turn on the TV. Watch stations trot out bullish pundits when the markets are going up and bearish pundits when the markets are going down.

Always be prepared for a black swan event, especially if you've already reached financial independence. Once you've accumulated enough capital, your main mission is to protect your wealth.

It pays to take advantage of bull markets. Bull markets tend to last between five and ten years. These are periods when you can get incredibly rich. The goal is to know you are in a bull market and allocate your net worth accordingly.

To achieve financial independence, the last thing you want to do is have most of your net worth allocated to risk-free or low-risk investments in a bull market. I've come across many readers who save diligently but just let their savings pile up. As a result of not investing, they fall behind their peers.

You should also be more aggressive in your career during a bull market. Ask for those raises and promotions. If you don't, inflation will eat up your real income. Look for new job opportunities that can immediately boost your compensation and title. In a bull market, demand for labor is high. Take advantage.

These points are essential to maintaining a rational mindset as you build your wealth. Ultimately, the key to wealth creation over the long term is having the right net worth allocation and the right occupation that will take advantage of economic growth and weather any financial storm.

Once you have the right net worth allocation, then you can slowly drill down to the types of funds, ETFs, and individual investments you want to make. But the right net worth allocation will be responsible for most of your wealth gains.

THE FINANCIAL SAMURAI WAY

- Your taxable investments are what will generate your livable passive investment income. Therefore, your goal is to generate 3X more from your taxable investments than from your tax-advantaged investments.

- Follow one of the three net worth allocation models: Conventional, New Life, or Financial Samurai. The models differ based on your risk tolerance, investing interest, and career desires. The more you believe in your ability to generate money, the more you should bet on yourself. Following any of the three models will likely make you much wealthier than the average person by the time you're sixty.

- Instead of investing in bonds in a low-interest-rate environment, consider allocating some of your bond portion into real estate. Real estate is considered a "bond plus" type of investment that provides defensive and offensive characteristics.

- Your 70/30 decision is to stick to an investing model over the long term. It will help you get through difficult times. As an investor, one of your biggest demons is your emotions. By continuing to allocate your capital appropriately throughout your life, you drastically increase your chances of financial success compared with the person who has no system in place.

Chapter 6

Optimize Your Investments

Learning how to optimize your investments can be overwhelming. Even if you know to max out your retirement accounts first, put X amount of your net worth into stocks, X into real estate, and X into alternative investments, there is still an avalanche of follow-up choices:

What kinds of stock should you buy?

Should you buy individual stocks or invest in funds?

Should you invest in that distillery your friend is starting up?

Are you missing the boat completely if you don't invest in crypto?

Deep breaths.

You'll do great—and even if you don't, if your asset allocations are in check, you can't hurt yourself too much. More than likely, by the time you want to retire, you'll end up with a lot more wealth than you first imagined. Compounding has a very sneaky way of surprising us all.

My hope is that everyone reading this will be moved to take action today so they can grow their net worth in an appropriate manner. The goal is to make more money in good times and lose less money in bad times. Think of yourself as the chief investment officer and chief risk officer of your own finances.

Letting your savings sit in a money market account is the suboptimal 30/70 move. You wouldn't believe how many readers I've corresponded with since 2009 who never invested their savings because they were too afraid or simply didn't know where to start. At the same time, even more readers have come back to me and said they now have much more wealth than they ever would have imagined at this stage in their lives. At the end of the day, no risk equals no reward!

Let's start with equity investments. Equity is ownership in a company. You can create equity by starting your own business, or you can invest in the equity of another business. Most of the wealthiest people in the world have tremendous equity in both. Ideally, so should you.

If you're not interested in building your own business, then you should certainly invest in other businesses. There's only so much time you can trade for money. Instead, a more efficient way to generate wealth is to invest in the equity of other businesses whose employees are working hard to generate returns for you. Your equity investments scale up your wealth-building potential, given that your personal labor is limited.

A key decision you need to make is where to place your investments. The choice is between taxable accounts and tax-advantaged accounts. Let's go through the fundamentals under the premise that we must try to always max out our tax-advantaged accounts and aim to build a much greater taxable portfolio.

Taxable versus Tax-Advantaged Accounts

The most common type of taxable account is the brokerage account. You can open one online with giants such as Fidelity and Schwab. In addition, digital wealth advisers, aka robo-advisers, are taxable accounts that manage money for you for a fee. The larger ones are Vanguard Personal Advisor Services, Schwab Intelligent Portfolios, Betterment, Wealthfront, and Personal Capital.

Taxable Account Benefits

Taxable accounts don't have tax benefits. However, there are fewer restrictions and more flexibility compared with tax-advantaged accounts. You can deposit and withdraw money at any time with no penalties. There also is no limit to how much you can deposit or withdraw.

If you hold your investments for over a year in a taxable account and sell, you'll pay a more favorable long-term capital gains tax rate such as 0%, 15%, or 20%, depending on your tax bracket. If you hold your investments for less than a year, you'll pay a higher short-term capital gains tax rate, which is equivalent to your ordinary income tax bracket.

Your taxable accounts are a main source of passive income and liquidity if you plan to retire before the age of fifty-nine and a half or before you are eligible for Social Security benefits. Therefore, even though there are no tax benefits, growing these accounts as large as possible is one of the main goals of a Financial Samurai.

Tax-Advantaged Account Benefits

Tax-advantaged accounts include the 401(k), 403(b), 401(a), 457(b), traditional IRA, Roth IRA, SEP-IRA, SIMPLE IRA, SIMPLE 401(k), and Roth 401(k). Some even use the health savings account (HSA) as a retirement vehicle. Tax-advantaged accounts are either tax-deferred or tax-exempt.

The most popular types of tax-deferred accounts are the 401(k) and traditional IRA. Contributions to these plans are made with pretax income, which means you get an up-front tax break. You then pay taxes when you withdraw your money in retirement, which means the tax is deferred.

In contrast, for tax-exempt accounts such as the Roth IRA or Roth 401(k), contributions are made with after-tax dollars. However, your investments get to grow tax free, and qualified withdrawals in retirement are tax free as well. This is why these accounts are considered tax-exempt.

Tax-Efficient Investing Strategies: Where to Place Your Investments

Your goal is to contribute the maximum to all tax-advantaged accounts possible. Taxes reduce investment returns and are also the largest ongoing liability for most people. Therefore, it behooves us to learn about tax strategies, stay on top of the latest tax laws, and follow this investing framework:

1. **Make contributions to all tax-advantaged accounts automatically.** Given that there are limits to how much you can contribute to each tax-advantaged account, you should be able to eventually hit those limits as your income and desire to save increase. Follow an appropriate asset allocation framework by age and watch your tax-advantaged accounts grow.

2. **Grow your taxable accounts as large as possible for passive investment income.** This is your biggest goal once you're automatically contributing the maximum to all tax-advantaged accounts available to you. This is where saving and investing at least 20% of your after-tax income after contributing to your tax-advantaged retirement accounts comes in. Basically, saving what's left of your free cash flow. The higher you can get the percentage, the better, if you want to achieve financial freedom sooner.

Let's say your salary is $100,000. Saving 25% of your gross income is $25,000. A great goal if you can do so. However, you should try to save $30,500 or more—$20,500 into your 401(k) and another $10,000 after 401(k) contribution and expenses—as in this example below.

$100,000	Salary
$20,500	401(k) pretax contribution
$79,500	Taxable income after 401(k) contribution, ignoring standard deduction
$67,575	Income after paying a 15% tax rate
$27,575	Expenses
$40,000	Income after 401(k), taxes, and expenses
$10,000	Savings amount after saving 25% of $40,000
$35,000	Total savings—$20,500 from 401(k) + $10,000 from free cash flow

As your income grows, the amount you can save from your free cash flow should go up. For example, if your gross salary increases to $200,000 and you keep your expenses and saving rate the same, you could end up contributing $20,500 to your 401(k) and saving an additional $30,000 of your free cash flow. Earning a higher income while keeping expenses stable is a powerful combination.

The main ratio to shoot for between the value of your taxable accounts and the value of your tax-advantaged accounts is 3:1. In other words, have three times more in your taxable accounts than you do in your tax-advantaged accounts. Although this may sound daunting, the amount you can contribute to your taxable accounts is unlimited. Therefore, with consistent contributions and the power of compounding, your taxable account balances should eventually surpass your tax-advantaged account balances. That crossover period is around the eight- to ten-year mark.

Regardless of the imbalance between the amounts of your taxable and tax-advantaged accounts, it's good to understand the ideal types of investments for each account. Ideally, you should hold more tax-efficient investments in taxable accounts and less tax-efficient investments in tax-advantaged accounts.

Here's a chart that shares some examples of what types of investments are most appropriate for which type of account.

TAX-EFFICIENT INVESTING: WHERE TO INVEST YOUR CAPITAL FOR GREATER RETURNS

Taxable Accounts	Tax-Advantaged Accounts
Municipal bonds, treasury bonds, series I bonds	Individual stocks and funds you plan to hold for less than a year
Qualified dividend-paying stocks and funds	Actively managed funds with a high turnover ratio
ETFs and index funds	Taxable bond funds, zero-coupon bonds, high-yield bonds
Individual stocks/funds you plan to hold for more than a year	REITs, eREITs, real estate crowdfunding
Low-turnover funds	Structured notes, investments with uncertain distribution schedule

Source: FinancialSamurai.com

If you're a trader who likes to whip around your capital, do so in a tax-advantaged account. Having to reconcile all your trades in a taxable brokerage account can be a real nightmare. Trust me, I learned this the hard way! One time, when I was in my twenties, I made over a thousand trades in a single year because I was day-trading so much. I had to spend hours making sure I had the appropriate cost basis for each trade before filing my taxes. It was not worth the stress and headache.

Please don't spend time day-trading stocks or ETFs. It's a big waste of time and energy. It may also hurt your career if you're putting in that time during your workday. One year, the head of international equities pulled me into a conference room and asked what the hell I was doing trading so much at work. They could see everything I was doing on my work computer. From then on, I had a target on my back.

Today, all my municipal bond holdings are in my taxable accounts. Most of my growth stocks, which pay no dividends, are in my taxable accounts as well. I'm doing my best to use my rollover IRA to invest in more private investments with uncertain distribution schedules.

I'm also more aggressive in my tax-advantaged accounts because I won't be touching them for about twenty years. For this reason, you may want to have a heavier allocation to equities and other riskier investments in your tax-advantaged accounts than in your taxable accounts. It's easier to stomach downturns when you can't touch your portfolio without penalty.

Forecast Your Income to Reduce Tax Liability

In addition to tax-efficient investing, it is also vital to calculate your expected investment income and active income from your day job and side hustles for the year. Your investment income will be taxed based on the length of holding, the amount of your investment income, and the amount of your overall income. If you have investment income and your modified adjusted gross income is more than $200,000 as a single person or $250,000 as a married couple, you may also owe a 3.8% net investment income tax (NIIT).

The more closely you can forecast your expected investment income, the better you can manage your tax liability. The following charts give you an idea of the difference between short-term capital gains tax rates and long-term capital gains tax rates. It shows that making income from your investments is more tax-efficient. (However, it should be, since you already paid taxes on the money you used to invest in these investments.)

SHORT-TERM AND LONG-TERM CAPITAL GAINS TAX RATES BY INCOME FOR SINGLES

Income	Short-Term Capital Gains Tax Rate (Income Tax Rate)	Long-Term Capital Gains Tax Rate
Up to $10,275	10%	0%
$10,276 to $41,775	12%	0% up to $41,675
$41,776 to $89,075	22%	15% over $41,675
$89,076 to $170,050	24%	15%
$170,051 to $215,950	32%	15%
$215,951 to $539,900	35%	15% up to $459,750
$539,900+	37%	20% over $459,750

Note: Figures are based on 2022 IRS tax rates. Short-term capital gains tax is a tax on profits from the sale of an asset held for <1 year, and its rate is equal to your federal marginal income tax rate. Long-term capital gains tax is a tax on profits from the sale of an asset held for >1 year.

Sources: IRS, FinancialSamurai.com

SHORT-TERM AND LONG-TERM CAPITAL GAINS TAX
RATES BY INCOME FOR MARRIED, FILING JOINTLY

Income	Short-Term Capital Gains Tax Rate (Income Tax Rate)	Long-Term Capital Gains Tax Rate
Up to $20,550	10%	0%
$20,551 to $83,550	12%	0% up to $83,350
$83,551 to $178,150	22%	15%
$178,151 to $340,100	24%	15%
$340,101 to $431,900	32%	15%
$431,901 to $647,850	35%	15% up to $517,200
$647,850+	37%	20% over $517,200

Note: Figures are based on 2022 IRS tax rates. Short-term capital gains tax is a tax on profits from the sale of an asset held for <1 year, and its rate is equal to your federal marginal income tax rate. Long-term capital gains tax is a tax on profits from the sale of an asset held for >1 year.

Sources: IRS, FinancialSamurai.com

Let's say you know that a large distribution in a structured note or private investment is coming due in a given year. You may want to minimize your active income that year, if possible, to minimize your tax liability. As an employee, you may be able to have a portion of your salary or bonus deferred to the following year or across many years. As an entrepreneur, you could increase that year's capital expenditure and delay year-end invoicing into the new year.

The More You Know, the More You Can Optimize

As your net worth grows and gets more complicated, it becomes more important to track all aspects of your finances. Set calendar reminders for when you might receive distribution events. Use a spreadsheet or a free online tool like the one offered by Personal Capital to track your finances. The more you can stay on top of your finances, the more you can optimize your finances.

Further, always think about smoothing out your income to potentially pay a lower tax rate. For example, from a tax perspective, it may be better to earn $130,000 a year for two years than $260,000 in year one and $0 in year two. The $130,000 would face a lower 24% marginal income tax bracket while also enabling you to benefit from more tax credits and less alternative minimum tax (AMT), whereas the $260,000 would face a 35% marginal federal income tax rate and preclude many tax benefits and deductions.

Pay attention to tax laws and benefits when deciding where to put your money. An investment put into a tax-advantaged account over the long term can have a notably different outcome compared with making that same investment in a taxable account and trading it quickly. The results depend on several factors, and your overall tax situation is a huge one.

Roth IRA or Traditional IRA?

You already know I suggest maxing out your 401(k) if you have one. The 401(k) is the most important tax-advantaged retirement account for those without pensions. Not only can you contribute the most each year to a 401(k), but you can also benefit from company matching and profit sharing. The good news is that retirement savers can contribute to both an IRA and a 401(k), provided income limits are met.

Let's start with a quick introduction to IRAs, in case you're not familiar with them. A traditional IRA functions a lot like a 401(k): it's a retirement account that lets you make pretax contributions. You can begin to withdraw from your IRA penalty free starting at age fifty-nine and a half, and you pay income tax on your distributions at that time, just like with a 401(k).

The biggest differences between a traditional IRA and a 401(k) are income limits on tax deductions, contribution limits, the availability of a 401(k) only through an employer, and greater investment options through an IRA (not limited to the options provided by your employer's retirement brokerage). To contribute to a traditional IRA with pretax dollars, there is an income threshold you cannot exceed. However, there is no income threshold to contribute to a 401(k). But there is an income limit that determines how much your employer can contribute/match. Please check the IRS website for the current limits.

Roth IRAs and traditional IRAs differ in the income limits you're able to contribute, and Roth IRAs require you to contribute after-tax income (those dollars then get to compound tax free).

Traditional IRAs and Roth IRAs both have more flexibility than 401(k)s when it comes to making penalty-free withdrawals before age fifty-nine and a half. Both let you take early distributions without paying the usual 10% penalty for expenses like

- qualified higher education expenses;
- a qualified first-time home purchase ($10,000 max); and
- health insurance premiums paid while unemployed.

The choice between a traditional and a Roth IRA is important because the IRS's annual contribution limit includes both types of IRA. In other words, if the annual limit is $6,000, even if you have both a traditional IRA and a Roth, your total contribution across both can't be more than $6,000. The limit should go up over time to keep up with inflation.

So which do you choose?

First, let's assume your modified AGI qualifies you to contribute to a Roth IRA, because many people earn too much to even have that option.

Your first optimal move is to max out your 401(k) if you have one. If you can't do that, *at least* contribute enough to get your company's match if it offers one. On the next page are the historical 401(k) contribution amounts between employee and employer contribution.

If you do max out your 401(k) and can save more, your next optimal move is to contribute to a Roth IRA. Contributing to a Roth IRA when you are paying a lower marginal income tax rate makes sense. Although you pay taxes up front in a Roth IRA, the money compounds tax free over time, and it can then be withdrawn tax free as well. (This can be very valuable if you end up wealthier than you expect in retirement.)

The required minimum distribution (RMD) requires you to withdraw from your IRA and all employer-sponsored retirement plans by age seventy-two. This ultimately means your tax liability will go up. If you're someone who is able to wait until the maximum age before taking the RMD, then you also likely have a higher income and/or net worth. Therefore,

HISTORICAL 401(K) CONTRIBUTION LIMITS

Year	Employee Contribution	Employer Contribution	Total Contribution	Catch Up Contribution (Age 50+)
2022	$20,500	$40,500	$61,000	$6,500
2021	$19,500	$38,500	$58,000	$6,500
2020	$19,500	$37,500	$57,000	$6,500
2019	$19,000	$37,000	$56,000	$6,000
2018	$18,500	$36,500	$55,000	$6,000
2017	$18,000	$36,000	$54,000	$6,000
2016	$18,000	$35,000	$53,000	$6,000
2015	$18,000	$35,000	$53,000	$5,500
2014	$17,500	$34,500	$52,000	$5,500
2013	$17,000	$34,000	$51,000	$5,500
2012	$17,000	$33,000	$50,000	$5,500
2011–2009	$16,500	$32,500	$49,000	$5,500
2008	$15,500	$30,500	$46,000	$5,000
2007	$15,500	$29,500	$45,000	$5,000
2006	$15,000	$29,000	$44,000	$5,000
2005	$14,000	$28,000	$42,000	$4,000
2004	$13,000	$28,000	$41,000	$3,000
2003	$12,000	$28,000	$40,000	$2,000
2002	$11,000	$29,000	$40,000	$1,000
2001	$10,500	$24,500	$35,000	
2000	$10,500	$19,500	$30,000	
1999–1998	$10,000	$20,000	$30,000	
1997–1996	$9,500	$20,500	$30,000	
1995–1994	$9,240	$20,760	$30,000	
1993	$8,994	$21,006	$30,000	
1992	$8,728	$21,272	$30,000	
1991	$8,475	$21,525	$30,000	
1990	$7,979	$22,021	$30,000	
1989	$7,627	$22,373	$30,000	
1988	$7,313	$22,687	$30,000	
1987–1986	$7,000	$23,000	$30,000	
1985–1982	$30,000	$30,000	$60,000	
1981–1978	$45,575	$45,575	$91,150	

Sources: IRS, FinancialSamurai.com

having a Roth IRA to draw from in retirement is very beneficial for tax diversification purposes. You can also pass on your Roth IRA to beneficiaries.

The Ultimate No-Brainer: Open a Roth IRA for Your Kids

Most people only think of IRAs in relation to their own retirement. However, if you have children, opening a custodial Roth IRA for your kids is extremely valuable. Not only will you encourage your kids to build a strong work ethic early, but you also get to teach them about the power of investing in a tax-efficient manner. And since the IRS allows early withdrawals for qualified expenses like education and the first-time purchase of a home, their Roth IRA can help them financially well before their traditional retirement years. Ultimately, your kids will thank you for making them work and open up a Roth IRA while they were young.

If you own a small business, you can hire your children for a reasonable wage. The money you pay them is a business deduction, which reduces the business's taxable income. Meanwhile, the money you contribute to their Roth IRA gets to go in tax free (if their income is less than the standard deduction) or at a low tax rate, then compound tax free. But let me be clear: your kid has to be doing actual work for your business and be treated like any other employee or freelancer. Your child also needs to be earning a "reasonable wage." You cannot pay them $1,000 an hour to organize your home office.

If you don't have a small business, you can encourage your kids to mow your neighbor's lawn, wash cars, work a minimum-wage job at the mall, or whatever to earn money from someone else. They can save the money they earn and invest it in a Roth IRA.

Let's say the standard deduction limit is $12,950 per person and the maximum Roth IRA contribution is $6,000 per person. Someone could essentially earn up to the standard deduction limit of $12,950 tax free, then contribute the maximum of $6,000 to a Roth IRA tax free as well. If a person started contributing $6,000 every year starting at age sixteen, by age twenty-six they would have about $100,000 in their Roth IRA, assuming an 8% compound rate of return. Not bad!

Another benefit is that the money *contributed* to a Roth IRA can be withdrawn at any time and used for anything. So if your kid wants to use the money they earned to buy their first car or take an international trip with college friends, a Roth IRA can help pay for these expenses.

Given that compound interest is one of the most powerful forces in finance, the younger you open up a Roth IRA, the better. Assuming a 6.1% investment return and monthly compounding, if you contributed just $6,000 *once* to a Roth IRA, in sixty years the account would grow to about $210,000.

There are two key things to know about opening a custodial Roth IRA for your kids:

1. **There is no age minimum.** Kids of any age can contribute to a Roth IRA.
2. **The child must have earned income.** Earned income is defined by the IRS as taxable income and wages—money earned from a W-2 job or from self-employment gigs like babysitting or dog walking. A baby can earn income by modeling, even if it's a photo shoot for your own blog or other business. However, always check with a tax professional to be sure of the latest tax rules.

A lot of parents have wondered whether money they pay their kids to do household chores is deductible and eligible for a Roth IRA. Sadly, it isn't. You can obviously pay your kid for doing chores, but that money isn't eligible for a Roth IRA contribution unless they're actually doing work for your business. Instead, you can open up a custodial investment account for them, which doesn't have tax benefits.

If you plan to pay your kid for doing work for your business, make sure your retirement savings are squared away first. After all, you are in a higher tax bracket. If possible, max out your solo 401(k), SEP-IRA, or Roth IRA first. You don't want to risk your family's financial security before your child has the ability to earn an independent living.

There is also a risk that your kids could end up blowing all their Roth IRA money on useless things once they become adults. However, when you spend years working hard for your money, wasting money is harder to do. The more likely scenario is that your kids will want to figure out ways to make even more money because they appreciate the value of hard work. The key is to start educating your children young, so that saving and investing become a natural way of life.

Active Funds or Passive Index Funds and ETFs?

The choices keep coming!

After you decide whether to put your money into your 401(k), Roth IRA, or basic taxable brokerage account, you still need to figure out what to invest in. Let's zero in on funds. There are two main types: (1) active funds and (2) passive index funds and ETFs (exchange-traded funds).

Active funds are funds run by people who are actively trying to pick the best individual investments. The main goal of the long-only active fund manager is to beat its respective index.

Passive index funds are funds that don't pick any individual investments. Instead, the passive index fund invests in positions that make up a particular index it tracks. One of the most common index examples is the S&P 500 index, which is made up of five hundred of some of the largest American companies. A passive fund would simply invest in all the same names that are the S&P 500 with the same weightings.

ETFs are baskets of assets traded like securities. They can be bought and sold on an open exchange, just like regular stocks, as opposed to mutual funds, which are priced only at the end of the day. In addition, there might be cost differences. You can own either. They more or less serve the same purpose of investing in a particular index. Personally, I mainly own ETFs.

The active fund management industry is enormous because everybody has hope that they will outperform the market's average returns—and a small percentage of people do. But most will not, as the data shows time and time again. Not only do most active funds underperform, but their higher fees also cut into returns. It's a double whammy. The more reliable way to build wealth in the long run is by putting the vast majority of your stock portfolio into passive index funds or index ETFs.

The Index Plus Strategy

Given the difficulty of outperforming an index, your 70/30 decision is to **allocate 80%+ of your equity allocation to index funds or index ETFs**. The rest can be allocated to actively run funds and/or individual stocks in companies you use, trust, and like. After all, if you invest only in index funds and ETFs, you'll never outperform the masses of people who do the same. And one of the keys to achieving financial freedom sooner than later is to outperform the masses. I call this equity investment strategy the Index Plus strategy.

Active investing is for you if at least two of the following are true of you:

- Check how the futures market is doing
- Get up at least thirty minutes before the stock markets open to read all the news
- Like to get on quarterly conference calls with management
- Enjoy perusing stock-investing message boards
- Work in the money-management industry
- Write about stocks and the market

Investing is about the long game; compounding returns over decades are a beautiful thing. But investing is also about regret minimization. We can all think of a company that we wish we had invested in ten or twenty years ago. Imagine where we'd be today! It's rare to earn life-changing returns on single stocks, but you can make good money even with just 10% of your portfolio in extraordinary outperformers. That's why I like the 10% approach: it's enough to matter, but it's not enough to blow you up if you make too many bad picks.

There's also an educational component to active investing. Once you take a position by putting your money into an asset, you'll suddenly start to pay more attention to economic news, the stock market, and trends. You'll do your research on that company or asset. You'll start to better understand how investing works overall, what the data means, and how it affects the number in your investment account. Even if you lose money, you'll gain a wealth of knowledge that will, hopefully, make you a more informed investor over the long run.

If you are not enthusiastic about trying to pick winners, then by all means invest 100% of your stock allocation in various index funds or an index target date fund. A simple two- or three-index-fund portfolio will do. You'll never significantly outperform, but you will also never underperform by more than the minuscule fees it costs to own index funds and ETFs.

Today I try to invest in companies with great management and visionary leaders. As an operator of a small lifestyle business, I marvel at the smarts and work ethic of those who have an insatiable desire to win. Once you identify good leaders in a growing sector, the rest tends to take care of itself.

Growth or Dividend Stocks?

If you're drawn to the Index Plus strategy, your next move is to figure out what your *plus* is. A big question, if you want to go with stocks, is whether to go with dividend (also sometimes called value) or growth stocks.

For younger investors (those under 40), **the 70/30 move is to invest mostly in growth stocks over dividend stocks**. With growth stocks, you increase your chances of accumulating more capital quickly. However, you will likely also experience more volatility and bigger sell-offs. Your top priority early in your career is to build as big a financial nut as possible. Owning growth stocks is an optimal way to achieve this. Dividend income is less important when you have job income.

Growth stocks are companies that reinvest the vast majority of their earnings to try to further grow the company. Instead of paying a dividend with a 3% yield, a growth stock's company management believes in investing in new products and business opportunities to potentially boost future profits and shareholder value. Growth stocks are more of a bet on the future, whereas dividend stocks are more a bet on the certainty of the present.

One of the main misconceptions about owning dividend stocks is that the dividend is free money. A dividend is not free money. Paying a dividend lowers the amount of cash on a company's balance sheet, which in turn lowers the overall value of the company. Just think about if you owned a company and it suddenly paid out $1 million to shareholders. If you tried to sell the company the next day, the buyer might offer $1 million less.

The main reason a dividend stock tends to return to its prepayout share price after paying its quarterly or annual dividend is due to expectations that the company will continue to be profitable and maintain its dividend payout ratio. For example, expectations are high that a company like Coca-Cola will continue to generate enough cash flow to pay another dividend, as it has for decades.

If the amount of growth cannot overcome the amount of value lost from a dividend over time, a company will likely decline in value. If you happen to invest in a company that is not growing and is cutting its dividend payout, then you've found yourself a real dud. Further, watch out for growth companies that suddenly decide to start paying dividends. It may signal that management is not finding as many opportunities with its growing cash.

If you invest in dividend stocks while you're young, you may be hoping for filet mignon decades in the future while you eat Hamburger Helper in the meantime. But when you reach your desired age of retirement, you might just be asking yourself, "Where the hell is the feast?"

Of the few multibagger return stocks I've had since 1995, none have been dividend stocks. Over time, dividend stocks may provide healthy returns, especially if you invest in companies with growing earnings and dividend payout ratios. But that doesn't help as much when you're trying to build your fortune sooner rather than later.

How Much to Invest in Growth Stocks by Age

You may recall that in chapter 3 I ranked dividend stocks as my number one favorite source of passive income. However, the best time to turn to them as a source of income is when you're retired, or close to retiring. Here is a guide for how much to invest in growth stocks by age:

Growth versus Dividend Stock Weightings

Age 0–25	100% growth stocks, 0% dividend stocks
Age 26–30	100% growth stocks, 0% dividend stocks
Age 31–35	90% growth stocks, 10% dividend stocks
Age 36–40	80% growth stocks, 20% dividend stocks
Age 41–45	70% growth stocks, 30% dividend stocks
Age 46–50	60% growth stocks, 40% dividend stocks
Age 51–55	50% growth stocks, 50% dividend stocks
Age 56+	40% growth stocks, 60% dividend stocks

Since dividend stocks pay dividends, you will have to pay taxes on that income. If you already earn a high income through your day job, earning more dividend income is sub-optimal, despite dividends getting taxed at a lower rate. Instead, from a tax perspective, it's better to invest mostly in growth stocks when your marginal tax rate is highest and dividend stocks when your marginal tax rate is lowest.

When you have a high active income, you can afford to take more risks. It is when your active income is lowest that dividend stocks are the most valuable. As a result, I recommended an equal split starting in your early fifties.

It's always good to put some percentage of your stock investments in growth stocks. However, as you get older and wealthier, the absolute dollar value of your portfolio will likely get larger as well. If the *plus* portion of your portfolio balloons to $1 million at age sixty, dialing back your exposure to 60% growth stocks still means a $600,000 investment.

REPLACE DIVIDEND STOCKS WITH REAL ESTATE

A powerful investing strategy to consider is buying growth stocks and investing in real estate *instead* of dividend stocks or bonds. In a bull market, this powerful combination provides the best of both worlds: high growth and income. Real estate tends to pay a higher yield than even the sixty-five S&P 500 Dividend Aristocrats, the most established dividend-paying companies. Further, real estate prices tend to perform strongly when the economy is booming.

In a bear market, your growth stocks will likely underperform. However, your real estate holdings may outperform dividend-paying stocks. During difficult times, investors rush to the safety of bonds and real assets that provide utility and produce income.

Finally, here is an interesting way to look at dividend stocks and rental properties from an income perspective. When real estate generates rental income, the value of the real estate does not decline by the amount of rent that is produced each month. Instead, the rent can be considered an addition, or a "dividend plus." When a company pays a dividend, on the other hand, for a moment in time the company's value declines by the amount of the dividend paid. While a company's share price may quickly recover after paying a dividend, real estate investors don't need to worry about a dip in their property value each time their investment generates rent. Only if the expected rental income changes will a real estate investor need to recalculate their property's estimated value.

Angel Investing: Yes or No?

No.

If you are a regular person with no edge and no connections, angel investing is simply not worth the risk.

After twenty years of doing some angel investing, I believe you are much better off investing in an angel fund with connected people rather than making individual angel investments.

To zoom out, angel investing is the early stage of venture capital. However, the definition of angel investing has stretched from preseed investing to include seed investing and even series A round investing.

Even when investments do work out, the numbers are typically not as great as you'd think. I'll show you with an example of a $60,000 investment I made in a gin company back in 2010. After ten years, my investment finally paid dividends—but the returns were bleak. Initially, given that the company was sold for about $49 million after expenses and I had invested in it at a $10 million postmoney valuation, I thought I had made a ~3X return ($180,000). Since shareholders get diluted over time with subsequent funding rounds, I thought that was a reasonable assumption. Well, I didn't come close. Instead, here's what I got:

Gross proceeds: $98,425.88

Federal withholdings: $0

State withholdings: $6,523.82

Net proceeds: $91,902.06

Huh? After almost ten years, with $98,425.88 in gross proceeds, I made only a 64% return on my money. Further, I had zero liquidity and lost hope for years that I'd ever get my $60,000 back. Doing the math, I made only a 5.1% internal rate of return,* barely better than my guaranteed 4.1% seven-year CD that had just expired.

But the company was sold for 5X what I bought it for, so where did all the money go? According to an internal document I received, we had to pay a lot of banker, lawyer, escrow, accounting, and general administration fees. We also had to pay severance packages to all the employees (rightfully so) who were made redundant when the new parent company took over. Then, of course, there is the effect of new investors diluting existing shares. But as an angel investor or later-round private equity investor, you don't get all the financial color.

Don't fall for the glitz of being an angel investor. These are the very real reasons why you should just say no.

1. **You have *zero* edge.** One day I had sashimi and sake with a Sequoia Capital partner. Sequoia Capital is one of the best VC companies in the industry. It has made billions backing Apple, Google, Oracle, PayPal, YouTube, Yahoo!, and WhatsApp. The partner said Sequoia shoots for a hit rate of one win for every seven losses. In other words, to follow Sequoia's ratio, you've got to be willing to make eight bets of similar size. Further, you've got to be willing to lose money on 87.5% of your investments and hope that one deal is at least a ten-bagger! Unless you're incredibly rich, good luck feeling comfortable enough investing with those odds.

   The best VC firms get all the first looks. They have some of the brightest people spending fifty-plus hours a week reviewing company after company. Oftentimes they see information about competitor companies that enables them to evaluate who will likely come out ahead. They also talk to their VC industry colleagues about what other companies and other VCs are doing. In comparison, you and I get no looks. Instead,

---

* The internal rate of return (IRR) is the discount rate that makes the net present value (NPV) of a project zero. In other words, it is the expected compound annual rate of return that will be earned on a project or investment.

individual angel investors get only the companies that have been rejected by the VCs. Talk about an unfair advantage.

2. **Your money is more sacred than other people's money.** Being a VC is one of the best jobs ever because you get to make $250,000 to $1 million a year in salary and make investments using *other people's* money. If your investments turn sour, you're not negatively affected. You still get paid your base salary for the eight- to ten-year life of the fund. If your investments do well, you get to earn even more money off other people's money in the form of carry.

   As an angel investor, you're putting your own money on the line. In order for me to follow Sequoia's model, I would have to personally make an investment total of $480,000 at $60,000 each in eight unproven companies. Other VCs with worse returns have a 1:9 win-loss target. In other words, I'd have to make a $600,000 investment to try to make money. Even if we're allowed to invest only $25,000 per deal, most of us wouldn't be willing to risk $250,000 in venture capital.

3. **Your stake will be diluted away.** As a minority investor, you have no say in management decisions or funding rounds. If the company starts getting desperate for cash, it may offer sweetheart deals to future investors at your expense. One such sweetheart deal is called liquidation preferences.

   For example, assume a venture capital company has a 2X liquidation preference after investing $1 million for a 50% stake in the company. The founders own 30%, and you, the angel investor, own 20% after investing $100,000. If the company is sold for $2 million, you might think you'd be getting $400,000 back. In reality, you'd get $0 back because the VC gets paid 2X their initial $1 million investment during the liquidity event. Meanwhile, the founders get $0 back as well!

   Just realize that whenever your private company raises a new round of funding, your stake will get diluted by 20% on average.

4. **You have zero liquidity.** Goodness forbid you need the money to cover an emergency during a typical eight- to ten-year holding period. So sorry! You will never get your money back unless there is a sale or an IPO. And given that ~90% of companies fail, and 9% of companies end up barely staying alive, you will likely never get your money back even if you wait fifty years.

5. **The returns aren't even that great.** For all the sexy talk about angel and venture capital investing, for the typical VC and angel investor, the return is truly dismal. We're talking median 0% to 2% returns a year from 2001 until now. The mean (arithmetic

average), however, was more like 8% during the same period due to the massive success of the top VC firms. That's nothing special compared with the S&P 500 return.

If you absolutely want to invest in early-stage start-ups, try to invest with top-tier VC funds like Andreessen Horowitz, Sequoia, Kleiner Perkins, Benchmark, and so forth. The difficulty will be getting an allocation through a friends-and-family round. These folks have much better track records and much better access to capital.

I characterize angel investing in the alternative investment bucket. My net worth allocation framework has allocations between 0% and 20% of net worth in alternatives. When it comes to angel investing, invest only the money you are willing to 100% lose.

Alternative investments are a booming asset class. However, we should also realize that we don't have the same edge as ultrahigh-net-worth individuals, endowment funds, and institutional funds. Therefore, the 70/30 move is to invest your alternative investment capital with those who are connected. Yes, you will have to pay a much higher fee than if you owned an index fund—a 1% to 2% annual fee based on your capital commitment and up to 20% of your profits. However, if the returns far surpass an index fund alternative, you won't mind.

Personally, I'm always hunting for unicorns, moon shots, multibagger investments. I will always try to allocate roughly 5% of my investment capital in the most speculative investments. This includes cryptocurrencies. The percentage is high enough to experience the euphoria and benefits of meaningful returns. One of the worst feelings is getting left behind on a trend. However, allocating up to 5% to moon shots is not enough to derail your financial destiny.

THE FINANCIAL SAMURAI WAY

- Practice tax-efficient investing, which is to invest in tax-efficient investments in taxable accounts and less tax-efficient investments in tax-advantaged accounts.

- Max out your tax-advantaged accounts while you have a chance. This includes your 401(k) and Roth IRA. If you end up much wealthier than expected in retirement, your Roth IRA and Roth 401(k) will be welcome tax diversification.

- Invest 80% or more of your public investment portfolio (stocks and bonds) in passive index funds or ETFs. The vast majority of active fund managers cannot outperform their respective indices over a ten-year period. Depending on your level of interest and conviction, invest up to 20% of your portfolio in individual securities, active funds, and alternative investments. This is the Index Plus strategy for your attempt to outperform the masses who invest only in index ETFs or funds.

- To increase your chances of building a larger financial nut quicker, invest mostly in growth stocks while you are young (<40) and gradually shift toward dividend stocks as you get older and desire income. Not only are you investing more tax-efficiently, but you are also mirroring your investments to your personal stage of growth.

- Just say no to angel investing. Instead, if you want to invest in early-stage companies, invest in angel funds managed by people who have an edge.

- Multibagger investments happen all the time. Therefore, you may want to allocate up to 5% of your investment capital in the most speculative ideas.

Chapter 7

Understand Real Estate Fundamentals

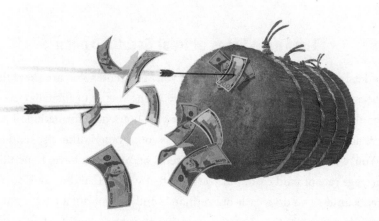

There is enough to say about real estate to fill an entire book, but remember, we have a goal here: financial freedom soon(ish). The next few chapters look at real estate through the specific lens of helping you build wealth. It's not all about the money, of course. We're talking about optimal decisions, and usually the optimal choice in real estate is not the one with the prettiest bottom line. The optimal decision is the one that will let you live a good life now while keeping you on a path toward financial freedom.

That said, we're starting with the money side of real estate because it's so easy to get this part wrong and steer yourself into a financial ditch. This is true whether you're renting or buying. Emotions cloud our judgment about what we can truly afford; loans look more appealing—or scarier—than they actually are; and choices like whether or not to refinance an existing mortgage have a bigger impact on our wealth than we often realize.

This chapter will guide you through the journey of money choices you'll need to make from the moment you start paying to live somewhere. These decisions are a big deal, since real estate affects your wealth even if you're a long way from buying your first home. Because, well, we all have to live somewhere. Inflation's impact on rent, for example, touches everyone except perhaps those who live for free with Mom and Dad. Whether or not it helps or hurts us depends on where we fall in the homeownership equation.

I recommend that everyone try to have a portion of their net worth in real estate by the time they're thirty years old, if not sooner. I hope you'll at least own your primary residence, even if you never aspire to be a landlord.

The Three Types of Real Estate Exposure

Please understand this important concept: If you are a renter, you are *short* the real estate market because you are a price taker. You are at the mercy of (usually) ever-rising rent prices, thanks to inflation, job growth, and growing household formation. If you own your primary residence, you are *neutral* real estate, as your home's value rises and falls with the market. You're not being affected by rising rents because you have, hopefully, locked in your mortgage rate or paid cash. But you can't really monetize the value of any rising equity or rents unless you do a cash-out refinance and/or rent out a portion of your house. Only when you buy more than one property are you *long* real estate. This is when you can benefit by raising rent and selling your investment property for gains if you wish.

Renting is absolutely fine for the short term. You just graduated from college and need a temporary place to stay while you work at a new job? It's good to keep your options open as you try to maximize your career, which may include relocating to another city for a better job opportunity. However, once you see yourself living in one spot for five years or longer, I recommend you try to get neutral real estate by owning your own residence. Just as shorting the S&P 500 over the long term is a suboptimal financial decision, so is shorting the real estate market by renting over the long term.

Let's get started on how to buy your first property using my three rules, cumulatively called my **30/30/3 home-buying rule**.

Understand How Much Mortgage You Can Truly Afford: My 30/30/3 Home-Buying Rule

Buying your first house will likely be one of the most nerve-racking experiences ever, perhaps second only to preparing for the delivery of your first child. From fear to hope, you will feel it all when spending money on what will likely be the biggest purchase of your life. Therefore, it's important to have a home-buying system to follow so your emotions don't overwhelm you.

Well-intentioned buyers usually try to follow some kind of guideline to figure out what they can afford. But they often fail to capture the full scope of their finances. They tend to focus on just a portion of the equation, like saving up a down payment or making sure the monthly mortgage payment is equal to or less than what they were paying in rent. This is a good start—but it's important to consider every facet of your finances, and the cost of the home, when calculating what you can afford.

Prior to 2008, before the global financial crisis, potential home buyers were letting their emotions dictate how much home they should buy. Home buyers thought prices could only go up. Meanwhile, they didn't crunch the numbers as carefully as they should have because they felt like they deserved to own a particular property, even though their finances said otherwise. Meanwhile, banks were handing out money like candy on Halloween. It was a toxic mix that ultimately led to a deep housing downturn that negatively affected millions of lives.

I created my 30/30/3 home-buying rule in 2009 to help people stay disciplined when buying property. It's a basic framework to help you make sure you don't overspend on real estate, no matter what your circumstances may be. Even if you're not ready to buy, my 30/30/3 rule will help you set smart saving and earning targets so you can reach your home-buying goals with a strong financial cushion.

The last thing you want to do is buy property and not be able to sleep soundly at night because you're always worried about your finances. That would be counterproductive! There are plenty of programs to help first-time buyers get into the housing market, such as FHA loans, VA loans, DPA grants, and more. However, please be aware of the risks of making a minimal down payment, paying private mortgage insurance (PMI), and paying a higher interest rate.

I've received some backlash from folks saying my 30/30/3 rule is too strict. But that's partly the point. Financial discipline is a must when you're buying something expensive for the first time with debt. If you follow these rules—at least two out of the three, but ideally all three—there is a 70%+ chance you'll be able to enjoy your property without financial stress. You're also likely to weather a financial downturn without losing your home. If you feel these rules are too intense, you probably need to keep saving and work on earning more money before you buy.

So as you consider real estate as part of your wealth-building strategy—whether you plan to buy now or are still in the saving stage—let these three rules guide you.

Rule #1: Spend No More Than 30% of Your Gross Income on a Monthly Mortgage Payment

I'm referring here to mortgage principal, interest, taxes, and insurance. You may choose to bake in potential maintenance and other expenses as well.

Traditional industry advice is to spend no more than 28% of your gross income on your monthly mortgage payment. So my first rule is pretty conventional, and 30% is easier to remember and calculate than 28%. For example, if you make $10,000 a month gross, your maximum mortgage payment should be $3,000. The 30% rule will also be dictated by how much a lender will lend you. It may cap you out at 28% or it may lend you much more than 30% of gross income. Stay disciplined.

The good news is that today's low interest rates allow you to follow this rule and buy more home than you normally could when interest rates are higher. Lower interest = lower monthly payment = more cash to put toward the price of the home. But it's important to limit your payment at 30% of your monthly gross income, and rule #3 further explains why this is such a big deal.

Middle- to lower-income people are especially at risk if they break this rule because it leaves them with less cash to survive. If your monthly gross income is $50,000, spending 40% of it on a mortgage still leaves you with $30,000 in gross income. You'll likely be okay unless your spending elsewhere is very high. However, spending 40% of your monthly $5,000 gross income thanks to an aggressive lender leaves you with a much smaller $3,000 cushion. You must be able to take care of your basic needs and any unforeseen emergencies with the remaining money. Therefore, the smaller your income, the more important it is to spend a smaller percentage of your monthly gross income on a mortgage, *not* the reverse.

Rule #2: Have at Least 30% of the Home Value Saved Up in Cash or Semiliquid Assets

This 30% rule has two parts: (1) guidance for determining how much to save for a down payment, and (2) guidance for making sure you have enough money for emergency situations, whatever those may be.

Of the 30% of the home value that you have saved, the first 20% is for your down payment so you can get the lowest possible mortgage rate and avoid paying private mortgage insurance. The other 10% is for a healthy cash buffer in case you run into financial trouble. Ideally, you'd have 10% of the home price in cash or semiliquid assets strictly for home emergencies. And even better, that's in addition to a six-month emergency fund you should have on hand to cover a job loss or similar financial surprises. If that's just not possible, at least have the 10% saved.

For example, if you want to buy a $500,000 house, aim to have $100,000 in cash for a down payment and $50,000 in cash and liquid securities earmarked for your buffer. You want to feel great about your purchase, not dread that you stretched too thin.

I realize there are mortgage programs that allow you to make a down payment that's less than 20%. Please avoid the temptation. The homeowners who got blown out the quickest during previous recessions had minimal down payments and no savings buffer.

Imagine putting down only 10% on the $500,000 home because that's all you could afford. Then the housing market takes a dive and your home price declines by 20% to $400,000. And then you lose your job as well. It's bad enough that your $50,000 in equity (down payment) has now turned into a $50,000 loss. You're likely stuck underwater in your home for years while feeling depressed about having stretched so much. If only you had waited to save up for a 20% down payment. Maybe while you were saving, home prices might have come down, so you would have saved yourself from buying at the top. And even if you had still ended up buying at the top, you could afford to hold on.

Of course, the opposite could happen. Your 10% down payment could grow tremendously during a housing bull market. Then greed might take over and you would start wishing you had gotten an even bigger mortgage to buy a larger house. This is human nature. However, when buying your first property or a principal residence, your main purpose should be to buy responsibly in order to live as carefree as possible.

With minimal equity, the temptation to walk away from a mortgage is much greater. The thousands who did between 2008 and 2012 subsequently missed out on one of the largest real estate recoveries ever. With a 20% down payment or greater, you are much more committed to the property. As a result, you will tend to have a greater chance of riding out the downturns because you don't want to lose all of your equity. Eventually, prices tend to come back and reach new highs. The longer you can hold on to your property, the greater the chance you will experience appreciation.

Furthermore, your equity will likely grow as you hold on, thanks to leverage and the fact that you've been paying down principal with your amortizing mortgage. A mortgage as a forced savings account is great for the average person. When you add home price appreciation over the long term, owning a primary residence is usually a winner over renting for the same duration. Many people argue that renters can simply save and invest the difference to earn greater returns. However, the net worth data differential between renters and homeowners shows otherwise—the average net worth of a homeowner is nearly 40X greater than that of a renter ($250,000 versus $6,500, according to the 2019 Survey of Consumer Finances).

Keep at least the 20% down payment in cash if you plan to buy a home within the next six months. It is unwise to invest your down payment in stocks and other risk assets if your home-buying time horizon is so short.

Rule #3: Limit the Value of Your Home to No More Than 3X Your Annual Household Gross Income

This rule helps you achieve two things: First, like rule #1, it helps keep your monthly cash flow in check. If you gross $100,000 a year ($8,333 per month), limiting your home purchase to $300,000 will keep your monthly payment within your means. After 20% down, your $240,000 mortgage at 3.25% will cost $1,044 per month for thirty years. For fifteen years at 3.25%, it would cost $1,686 per month. That's well within the rule #1 limit of 30% of your income. Again, this is where interest rates play a big role. The lower the rate, the more home you can buy.

You can push the limit to 5X your annual household income to expand your search in a low-interest-rate environment. However, you should go forward with 5X only if you are following the other two rules *and* you are bullish on your future earning potential.

Home affordability is a function of the price you pay for the home. Buying a home that's 5X or more your annual salary means not only more absolute debt but also higher expenditures for property taxes, maintenance, cleaning, gardening, heating and electricity, wi-fi extenders, and so forth. If you follow the 3X salary limit (5X max), there's a good chance all the other expenses will align with your budget. Please don't think only about the price of a home. You must always calculate the estimated ongoing carrying costs.

Property taxes in particular can play a big role in your home's affordability if you live in a state with a high tax rate. On the low end, states like Hawaii and Alabama have a tax rate of around 0.3% of a home's assessed value. On the high end, homeowners in New Jersey and Illinois pay over 2%. States like Texas, with no state income taxes, sound great. But these states inevitably have to raise revenue somehow, which they often end up doing in the form of property taxes.

My 30/30/3 rule applies to every home purchase you make. So if you own your primary residence and want to buy an investment property next, 30/30/3 applies all over again. Once you rent out one property, you should hopefully be able to cancel out all costs and ideally generate positive cash flow. The second property's mortgage shouldn't cost more than 30% of your gross monthly income either. You should have 30% of the property's value saved in cash, and the 10% that will be your home emergency fund should be a *new* pool of cash specifically for the new property. And as with your first purchase, don't buy a property that costs more than 3X to 5X your annual gross income.

Therefore, if you want to buy more properties, you must make more money and/or find renters who will cover at least 130% of the annual cost of owning the property. Your renters must cover more than 100% of the annual cost of ownership to account for potential tenant vacancies. Even then, you might get unlucky. Further, banks will generally take into consideration 70% or less of any rental income you do generate when considering you for a rental property mortgage.

Below is my home buyers guide. It provides recommendations for how much income you should have and what your net worth should be before buying a home at various price points. Ideally, a home buyer spends no more than 3X their gross income on a home. However, spending up to 5X gross income is doable under certain conditions.

With regards to net worth, ideally, the home price is no more than 30% of a buyer's net worth; 30% of net worth is more of an aspirational percentage to shoot for as you diversify your net worth. Given that 30% is likely impossible for most first-time home buyers, I've included a minimum net worth column necessary before purchase. The column suggests you can spend 3.3X your net worth for a home at most. But I don't recommend it.

Any income and net worth combination should work. However, clearly, the riskiest combination is buying a home with a minimum income and minimum net worth.

INCOME AND NET WORTH NECESSARY TO BUY A HOME BASED ON THE 30/30/3 AND NET WORTH RULE

Home Price	Minimum Income Required	Reasonable Income	Ideal Income	Minimum Net Worth Required	Reasonable Net Worth	Ideal Net Worth
$200,000	$40,000	$50,000	$66,667	$60,000	$100,000	$666,667
$300,000	$60,000	$75,000	$100,000	$90,000	$150,000	$1,000,000
$400,000	$80,000	$100,000	$133,333	$120,000	$200,000	$1,333,333
$500,000	$100,000	$125,000	$166,667	$150,000	$250,000	$1,666,667
$750,000	$150,000	$187,500	$250,000	$225,000	$375,000	$2,500,000
$1,000,000	$200,000	$250,000	$333,333	$300,000	$500,000	$3,333,333
$1,500,000	$300,000	$375,000	$500,000	$450,000	$1,050,000	$5,000,000
$2,000,000	$400,000	$500,000	$666,667	$600,000	$1,400,000	$6,666,667
$2,500,000	$500,000	$625,000	$833,333	$750,000	$1,750,000	$8,333,333
$3,000,000	$600,000	$750,000	$1,000,000	$900,000	$3,000,000	$10,000,000

Home Price	Minimum Income Required	Reasonable Income	Ideal Income	Minimum Net Worth Required	Reasonable Net Worth	Ideal Net Worth
$3,500,000	$700,000	$875,000	$1,166,667	$1,050,000	$3,500,000	$11,666,667
$4,000,000	$800,000	$1,000,000	$1,333,333	$1,200,000	$4,000,000	$13,333,333
$4,500,000	$900,000	$1,125,000	$1,500,000	$1,350,000	$4,500,000	$15,000,000
$5,000,000	$1,000,000	$1,250,000	$1,666,667	$1,500,000	$5,000,000	$16,666,667
$6,000,000	$1,200,000	$1,500,000	$2,000,000	$1,800,000	$9,000,000	$20,000,000
$7,000,000	$1,400,000	$1,750,000	$2,333,333	$2,100,000	$10,500,000	$23,333,333
$8,000,000	$1,600,000	$2,000,000	$2,666,667	$2,400,000	$12,000,000	$26,666,667
$9,000,000	$1,800,000	$2,250,000	$3,000,000	$2,700,000	$13,500,000	$30,000,000
$10,000,000	$2,000,000	$2,500,000	$3,333,333	$3,000,000	$15,000,000	$33,333,333
$15,000,000	$3,000,000	$3,750,000	$5,000,000	$4,500,000	$30,000,000	$50,000,000
$20,000,000	$4,000,000	$5,000,000	$6,666,667	$6,000,000	$40,000,000	$66,666,667
$25,000,000	$5,000,000	$6,250,000	$8,333,333	$7,500,000	$50,000,000	$83,333,333
$30,000,000	$6,000,000	$7,500,000	$10,000,000	$9,000,000	$60,000,000	$100,000,000
$35,000,000	$7,000,000	$8,750,000	$11,666,667	$10,500,000	$70,000,000	$116,666,667
$40,000,000	$8,000,000	$10,000,000	$13,333,333	$12,000,000	$80,000,000	$133,333,333
$50,000,000	$10,000,000	$12,500,000	$16,666,667	$15,000,000	$100,000,000	$166,666,667

Minimum income required = ⅕ price of home. Ideal income = ⅓ price of home.

Minimum net worth required = 30% price of home. Ideal net worth = 3.34X price of home.

Source: FinancialSamurai.com

30/30/3 Rule in Action

Let's explore a few examples of what it looks like to follow, or closely follow, the 30/30/3 rule.

Scenario 1—A Solid Purchase: You make $100,000 a year and have $120,000 in cash saved. You desire to buy a $300,000 home. After putting 20% down, you have a $240,000 mortgage with a 4% interest rate on a thirty-year fixed mortgage. The monthly payment is $1,146 or 13.8% of your monthly gross income ($1,146 ÷ $8,333). With a $60,000 cash buffer left after putting $60,000 down, you have about four years and four months of mortgage expenses covered.

But look at what happens when nothing here changes except the interest rate. If you have excellent credit and manage to buy when mortgage rates are low, you can lock in a rate around 3% for thirty years. A $240,000 mortgage in that scenario would have a $1,012 monthly payment. That's a very reasonable 12.1% of your monthly income—well within the 30/30/3 rule.

Scenario 2—A More Aggressive Purchase: With the same income and cash savings, you decide to live it up and buy a $400,000 home. After putting 20% down, you have a $320,000 mortgage and a $40,000 cash buffer after putting $80,000 down. You've *just* made it within rule #2 of keeping 10% of the home value in cash or semiliquid securities as a buffer. Even with a 5% mortgage rate, your monthly payment is $1,718. That's 20.6% of your $8,333 monthly income—still looking great.

If you buy when mortgage rates are near all-time lows and you have excellent credit, a 3% mortgage rate on that same $320,000 loan would put your monthly payment at $1,349. That's a significant $369 a month less than if you took out a mortgage rate at 5%. Is there any wonder why demand for real estate goes up when mortgage rates go down?

If you want to stretch to 5X your household income and buy a $500,000 home, you would need to save up $150,000 of the home's value in cash or semiliquid securities (30%). However, since you only have $120,000, you need to save another $30,000 to satisfy the second part of the 30/30/3 home-buying rule.

Now let's see how easy it is to fall away from the 30/30/3 home-buying rule.

Scenario 3—An Irresponsible Purchase: You make $120,000 a year and have $100,000 in cash saved at thirty-two years old. Pretty good! However, you're also salivating for an $850,000 home, which equates to 7X your annual income.

You can't put 20% down (you're $70,000 short), so you put only 10% down ($85,000). This leaves you with only a $15,000 cash buffer and a $765,000 mortgage.

Due to a lower down payment, the best mortgage rate you can get is 4.25%, despite your excellent credit. This is still low by historical standards. However, your monthly payment of $3,763 is 37.6% of your $10,000 monthly gross income. It's probably closer to 40% due to private mortgage insurance. You have now violated all three of my home-buying rules.

If you lose your job, your $3,763 mortgage alone will eat up your $15,000 remaining cash in four months. You may manage to hold on a little longer with government unemployment benefits, but think about how stressed you will be. Because don't forget, besides the mortgage, you've got to come up with more than $10,000 a year in property taxes in most states on an $850,000 home. If a tree then happens to crush a section of your roof, it might be game over.

If you're just dead set on having an $850,000 home, save up another $155,000 to get to $255,000 in cash and semiliquid investments. With 30% of the home price saved, you can put down 20% and have a nice $85,000 cash cushion. Further, your mortgage will decline to $680,000. At a 0.25% lower 4% mortgage rate (now lower partly because you put 20% down), your mortgage payment would be $3,246, or 32.46% of your monthly gross income. You're so close to getting under 30%! You just need to make $130,000 a year, or $10,000 more than you're making now, to get the mortgage rate under 30% of your income. Go get that raise! Or you can wait until you get a 3.3% mortgage rate or lower.

At a $130,000 annual income, you'd still be violating rule #3 by buying a home that's 5X more than your annual income. I don't recommend this, but if you are confident in your future earning power and can cover the rest of your living expenses, it's passable since you're still following two out of three rules.

Rent or Buy?

Just as my 30/30/3 rule applies to anyone considering real estate, the question "rent or buy?" is universal. Even if you already own your primary residence, it's a good exercise to regularly question whether living there is the optimal move for maximizing your lifestyle and your net worth.

Taking on debt to buy a risk asset is always a gamble. Your goal is to use the debt to live a nicer life than you could have afforded to if you had to pay cash. The initial years after taking out debt to buy a home are generally the riskiest. My goal is to help you sail through that period unscathed and, hopefully, richer as well.

In contrast, the return on the rent you pay is always –100%. Yes, in exchange for paying rent, you get a place to stay. But you have *no chance* of building equity through your home at the end of your stay.

For the first five to ten years out of school, the decision to rent or buy might be a coin flip (fifty-fifty) as you figure out what you want to do and where you want to live. You might even take the scenic route to financial freedom by going to graduate school. Renting provides maximum flexibility, which is extremely important for optimizing your career—your number one moneymaker in the beginning. What a shame not to take a great job offer across the country or the world just because you own a home you don't want to sell in an iffy market.

However, after about ten years, the calculation starts to strongly shift beyond fifty-fifty in favor of buying. By the time you're in your early thirties, you should have a good idea of what you want to do. After all, your life is likely a third over! If you take on a thirty-year fixed-rate mortgage, it would be nice to pay it off by the time you're in your early sixties, if not earlier. If you want to start a family, establishing some roots and getting neutral real estate by owning your primary residence is the 70/30 decision. At the end of the day, we are governed by time.

In an inflationary environment, as a homeowner, the real cost of your mortgage debt gets inflated away while the value of your asset appreciates. As a renter, your rent will likely continue to go up while you miss out on real estate appreciation.

According to the National Association of Realtors, the median age for first-time home buyers in 2019 was thirty-three. The sooner you can figure out what you want to do with your life, the sooner you can own your first primary residence. When it comes to investing, time in the market is your greatest friend.

Now let's move on to investing in real estate by going long. Remember, you are not really long real estate until you own more than one property. It is that second, third, fourth, etc. property that will build you passive income and capital gains.

BURL: The Real Estate Investing Rule to Follow

As a real estate investor, consider following the rule "buy utility, rent luxury"—or BURL for short.

BURL helps you maximize how your real estate dollars are spent. Utility can be defined as something you need, with very little unused space. Luxury can be defined as something beyond what you need, such as a third empty bedroom and an infinity pool with a tunnel that leads to a hidden hot tub.

BURL helps us see that the true cost of living in a home that we own isn't just the money we spend to live there. *It is the opportunity cost of not renting it out at market rate.*

Let's take a look at a Financial Samurai case study in expensive San Francisco. A homeowner decided to buy a smaller house because his existing home could have rented out for $7,500 a month. His existing house was a four-bedroom, three-and-a-half-bathroom house across 2,600 square feet for just him and his wife.

He discovered that rents had risen by 50% over the years since he purchased his existing house. Given that he wasn't willing to let $7,500 a month pass him by, he rationally decided to rent out his house to another party and downsize. The new house was 40% cheaper, had one less bedroom, and one and a half less bathrooms. By buying a smaller house, which could have rented out for $4,500 a month, he went from luxury to utility and boosted his monthly cash flow by $3,000 ($7,500 – $4,500). No longer did he feel like he was driving a bus to work with forty empty seats when all he needed was a motorcycle.

Conduct the same exercise if you own your existing home. If you haven't rented in a while, you may be surprised by how much rent your primary residence could command on the open market. Over the course of 2021, for example, the national median rent went up by more than 10%. Thanks to inflation, rent will likely continue to go up indefinitely.

BURL gets to the heart of the question "Rent or buy?" because the math on market prices—whether we're buying or renting—shows us that it's much more economical from a cash-flow perspective to *rent* a luxury property than it is to own one. And it makes better sense financially to *own* a utility property. Here's why.

Savvy real estate investors often follow the rule of paying no more than 100X the monthly rent to purchase a property. In the case of the house in San Francisco highlighted above, an investor following the 100X monthly rent rule wouldn't pay more than $750,000 because the market rent was $7,500 a month.

The challenge is that it's impossible to follow that rule when buying in expensive cities such as New York, San Diego, Los Angeles, or San Francisco (which can be considered "luxury markets"). Yet almost half the U.S. population lives in an expensive coastal city.

Even finding properties priced at 150X to 200X monthly rent is difficult in luxury markets because there is excess demand for buying property for *lifestyle* and *capital appreciation*. Housing becomes more than a roof over one's head—it becomes a *luxury option*. Further, many coastal city markets face not only a domestic demand curve but an international demand curve looking to buy up the American dream.

A Honda Civic takes you around just fine, but some people like to drive Ferraris. BURL says to buy the Honda Civic and rent the Ferrari on weekends.

Spending $7,500 per month ($90,000 a year) on rent may sound expensive. But *paying $7,500 a month in rent is actually a relatively good value*, since you would have needed to spend roughly 360X the monthly rent to buy that house at its market price of ~$2.7 million at the time.

In other words, the 100X to 200X monthly rent rule investors seek to follow to buy a primary residence or rental property doesn't work in this case. Conversely, paying $2.7 million for the house is not good value from a cash-flow perspective. However, if the house continues to appreciate in value, as is often the case with international cities, it may be.

Let's break down the reality of buying this house for $2.7 million with a 26% down payment, $2 million mortgage, and 3.5% interest rate. The annual costs of owning the home would be:

$70,000 mortgage interest

$33,750 property taxes ($2.7 million × 1.25% estimated California property tax rate)

$2,500 insurance

$5,000 maintenance

= $111,250 annual costs

Meanwhile, that $700,000 down payment could have earned at least a 2.5% annual rate of return risk-free (ten-year bond yield at the time), which comes to $17,500. When we bake that into the $111,250 annual expenses, the total gross cost of ownership goes up: $111,250 + $17,500 = $128,750.

Renting for "only" $90,000 a year is the financially cheaper option than owning for $128,750 a year. The only way the owner comes out ahead is through principal appreciation and tax deductions, which are not to be dismissed. The challenge for many people is coming up with the down payment.

The question of rent versus buy boils down to this: if you have the cash for a down payment on a "luxury home" and want to avoid economic waste, buy and live in a property only if you'd be willing to pay its fair market rent. If you want to go luxury but don't have the down payment, you can rest easy as a renter knowing that you're actually getting a better deal on your rented home or apartment than its owner is.

Now let's look at the other side of BURL. In the Midwest, there are occasionally properties available to purchase for around $200,000 that *could* rent for $2,000 per month based on the 100X monthly rent rule. Amazing value for investors but not so much for renters, even if the absolute dollar amount for rent is low. If you were to buy such a home with a $40,000 down payment, $160,000 mortgage, and 3.5% interest rate, the annual costs of ownership would be about:

$5,600 mortgage interest

$2,400 property taxes

$1,200 insurance

$3,000 maintenance

= $12,200 annual costs

Add $800 a year in opportunity cost for not earning a 2% risk-free return on the $40,000 down payment, and it costs only $13,000 per year to own compared with $24,000 a year to rent. Even if the owner could only charge $1,200 a month in rent, bringing the $200,000 property purchase equal to 167X monthly rent, owning is still a better value proposition, especially if the property continues to appreciate. After all, $14,400 in annual rent is greater than the estimated $12,200 annual cost to own the property.

Therefore, if the area in which you live, or would like to live, has market prices that look like this, you should buy rather than rent, since you could get cash-flow positive immediately if you were to one day rent the property out. You should own your primary residence and buy as many rental properties in this area as you can comfortably afford and manage. With the growing acceptance of working from home, such properties are increasingly in demand.

Ultimately, where we choose to live is a very personal decision. The definitions of luxury and utility are subjective. Fundamentally, we all want to live close to good friends and loving family members. We'd also all love to live in an area with great food, wonderful entertainment, and pleasant weather. However, we can't have it all! But what we can do is choose the best options with the money we have.

Take Out an Adjustable-Rate Mortgage or a Fixed-Rate Mortgage?

Once you are ready to buy, the kind of mortgage you choose will have an important impact on your finances. You have two main options: an adjustable-rate mortgage (ARM) or a fixed-rate mortgage.

CONDUCT REAL ESTATE ARBITRAGE WITH BURL

If you live in an amazing city with expensive luxury housing, consider renting and buying real estate in less expensive cities around the country for greater income. This way, you could eventually have your rental property cash flow pay for the place you are currently renting.

Let's say you're renting a luxury apartment for $80,000 a year in New York City. Using a 2.5% cap rate, the home would cost about $3.2 million to buy. Instead of spending $3.2 million on your luxury apartment, you could BURL by buying $3.2 million in real estate in Des Moines at an 8% cap rate. In other words, you could potentially earn $256,000 in Des Moines rent that could easily pay for your $80,000-a-year luxury apartment in New York City, with $176,000 left over. (For more on cap rates, see chapter 9.)

The BURL mindset helps real estate investors always think about how to best optimize their lifestyle and capital.

Their names give away their meaning. An ARM has an adjustable interest rate. It starts off with a fixed rate for a set number of years; then the rate varies in the years that follow depending on the loan's terms. For example, a 5/1 ARM has a set rate for the mortgage's initial five years. Then the rate resets every year. A fixed-rate mortgage, on the other hand, has the same rate for the life of the loan. Typically, the shorter the loan duration, the lower the interest rate. Both an ARM and a thirty-year fixed-rate mortgage tend to be on a thirty-year amortizing schedule.

Since 2009, I have argued that adjustable-rate mortgages are the most cost-effective option because I believe interest rates will continue to decline or stay low. Therefore, paying a higher mortgage rate with a thirty-year fixed is suboptimal. The average ARM rate is lower than the average thirty-year fixed rate due to the time value of money. Due to inflation, lenders of longer-term loans require a higher interest rate to account for higher risk and for inflation eating away at money's buying power. But if you needed to borrow $10 from your friend for a day, he'd probably charge you nothing because he knows you're good for it, and $10 will still buy the same amount of goods tomorrow.

Further, it is more efficient to match the fixed duration of the mortgage interest rate with your planned length of ownership.

Back in 2009, the average U.S. homeownership tenure was about four years, according to ATTOM Data Solutions. Therefore, taking out a 5/1 ARM in a declining-interest-rate environment made sense. By the time the ARM adjusted in the sixth year of a 5/1 ARM, the average U.S. homeowner had sold the home. Therefore, it wouldn't matter if the rate went up in an ARM reset. However, when ARMs reset, many of the rates stayed the same or went down.

Today the average U.S. homeownership tenure has more than doubled. Although interest rates have continued to stay low, homeowners may want to get a 7/1 to 10/1 ARM to match their likely homeownership tenure, just in case mortgage rates do go up in the future. However, the most likely scenario is a continued low-interest-rate environment for the rest of our lifetimes due to globalization, technology, productivity, and better central banking decisions.

Most people avoid ARMs because they fear their mortgage rate will skyrocket once their rate resets. Lenders also love to talk borrowers into a thirty-year fixed mortgage (the most profitable for lenders) by convincing borrowers they'd be at risk of financial hardship when their ARM inevitably resets to a higher rate. The truth is, in our likely permanently low-interest-rate environment, when an ARM resets, there's a good chance it resets to a similar rate.

The Beauty of the Fifteen-Year Fixed

Let's return to the fifteen-year fixed mortgage because it is a mortgage I've found more appealing the older and wealthier I've gotten. Given that we'll all eventually run out of time, taking out a fifteen-year fixed psychologically feels better because it improves your chances of paying off your mortgage sooner. If you're forty-five years old and planning to retire at age sixty, a fifteen-year feels better than a thirty-year that won't be paid off until you are seventy-five if you don't pay extra principal.

As Willy Loman said in *Death of a Salesman*, "Work a lifetime to pay off a house. You finally own it, and there's nobody to live in it." Ideally, you want to pay off your mortgage before you retire. This way, there are no loose ends and you can give your home in full to someone you care about with fewer complications.

But psychological reasons aside, there is a strong mathematical reason why a fifteen-year mortgage is superior, if you can afford the higher monthly payments. The average fifteen-year mortgage rate is almost always lower than the average thirty-year fixed mortgage rate. And because it amortizes over fifteen years instead of thirty years, you end up paying less interest overall. Now imagine if you could get a fifteen-year mortgage rate for less than the average 5/1 ARM mortgage rate. Then you've really hit the jackpot.

An average fifteen-year fixed-rate mortgage lower than an average 5/1 ARM won't always occur. But when it does, you should take advantage if the monthly payment plus taxes and insurance are still 30% or less of your gross monthly income. If they're not, and you can still qualify for a loan, I'd probably still go with a fifteen-year fixed-rate mortgage if the percentage is under 40%. Your liquidity risk goes up due to lower cash flow. However, each payment you get through brings you one step closer to a paid-off house.

The combination of a lower rate, a longer fixed-rate period, and a shorter amortization period results in much less in total interest payments. To prove it, let's look at the following total interest paid over the life of a $1 million mortgage with three types of terms:

thirty-year mortgage at 3%: $517,777 in total interest paid
fifteen-year mortgage at 2.3%: $183,347 in total interest paid
fifteen-year mortgage at 5%: $423,428 in total interest paid

Even if you took out a fifteen-year mortgage with an interest rate that was 2% higher than a thirty-year mortgage rate, you would still end up paying *$94,349 less* in interest during the duration of the loan. The power of compounding works both ways.

Another big advantage of a fifteen-year mortgage is that it forces you to rapidly save your money. Forced savings is one of the reasons the average net worth of a homeowner is so much greater than the average net worth of a renter.

Given the shorter amortization period, the monthly payment on a fifteen-year mortgage is much higher than that of a 5/1 ARM amortizing over thirty years or a thirty-year fixed-rate mortgage. In addition, if you take out a fifteen-year mortgage, a greater percentage of your payment will go toward paying down principal.

You need to have the cash flow for a fifteen-year mortgage. A $1 million, fifteen-year mortgage at 3% has a $6,906 monthly payment versus a $4,216 monthly payment for a thirty-year mortgage at the same rate.

This brings us to the disadvantages of a fifteen-year fixed mortgage:

1. **Less affordability.**
2. **Less money going toward savings or other investments.**

A fifteen-year fixed mortgage is ideal for paying off your loan fast and saving on interest, but only if the math works with your income. If it doesn't, an ARM is the next-best choice. Once you've built up some home equity and grown your savings, you can try refinancing to a fifteen-year mortgage or taking out a fifteen-year mortgage for your next home.

Fifteen years goes by pretty quickly. Let's say you bought your second primary residence, a forever home, at age thirty-two. Having a fully paid-off home by forty-seven without paying extra principal is pretty sweet. You now have plenty of cash flow to invest or spend as you wish.

CASH IS KING . . . BUT WHAT IF YOU DON'T HAVE ENOUGH?

To get the best deal possible, try to pay cash. Savvy buyers know this: data from Redfin shows that 30% of home purchases in the first half of 2021 were made in cash. Here are the main benefits of paying cash:

- Positive signaling that you are a serious buyer
- A lower chance the deal falls through during escrow
- A faster close

But of course, not everybody is able to buy with all cash. In such a scenario, you can try to get approved for a no-financing contingency loan where the bank basically promises to lend you the full amount of the purchase price. In order to qualify, you have to go through a rigorous underwriting process before finding your desired property. Then you need to find your desired property, with a purchase price up to the no-financing contingency loan amount, within a short period, usually two months. After two months, your lender will likely require updated financial documents because so much can change within that time frame.

From the seller's point of view, a no-financing-contingency offer sounds almost as good as an all-cash offer. And if the bank lending the money is a large, reputable bank, even better.

Taking out a mortgage in a low-interest-rate, high-inflationary environment is attractive. However, the more you want the house and the more competitive the situation is, the higher your down payment should be. As an expert negotiator, the number one thing you need to care about is what the other side cares about.

Refinance Your Mortgage or Keep Your Current Loan?

One of the good things about mortgages is that you can always look for a better one. And in a low-interest-rate environment, often a better one is out there. So if you go for that thirty-year fixed and your income grows, you can shift to a fifteen-year fixed or an ARM. Always keep your eye on interest rates, even if your income hasn't changed and even if you recently closed on a new mortgage.

Refinancing is usually a good idea even with all of the associated fees. As a rule of thumb, it is worth the cost to refinance if the resulting savings will cover the cost within eighteen months. The shorter the breakeven period, the better. For example, if your refinance costs $3,000, your monthly interest savings should be at least $167. Every month you own your home after the break-even period, you're saving.

The longer you plan to live in or own your home, the more you can afford to violate the eighteen-month-breakeven rule. I recommend sticking to a maximum twenty-four months to break even, given that the average homeowner lives in their home for only about ten years. You might think you'll own and stay in your home forever, but things change all the time.

No question, refinancing is a hassle. You'll have to provide your last two years of tax returns, your last two months of pay stubs, and endless amounts of other financial documents to the bank during the underwriting process. Then you'll need to sign a binder full of documents and set up new autopayments. But if you can cover your refinance cost within eighteen months, then it behooves you to put in the effort to refinance.

Another alternative is to do a "no-cost refinance," where the bank covers all the fees. In return, the bank charges you a higher interest rate. If you can refinance your mortgage with no out-of-pocket fees and instantly lower your monthly payments, you can't lose. The only thing you need to be aware of is that your amortization period will usually reset back to thirty years after each refinance. Therefore, a lower percentage of your payment will be going to pay down principal.

On the next page is a snapshot of my final mortgage refinance statement. You can see in the debits column all the fees the bank covered. At the end of the transaction, the bank actually ended up sending me a check for $220.

Always Refinance Before Kissing Your W-2 Income Goodbye

I always recommend that people refinance their mortgage before quitting their job, retiring, negotiating a severance, or simply taking an extended leave of absence. Once a bank sees your main source of income is gone, you become dead to them. You're like the ex–love interest who suddenly got dumped because you ran out of money. Banks are unlikely to let you refinance with them because you are perceived as higher-risk.

No underwriter is going to approve your mortgage if they don't see evidence that you have steady income, usually in the form of a paycheck. The longer you've had your steady paycheck, the more comfortable they will feel. Banks generally want to see at least one year of employment with one firm before giving you a loan. The longer the better.

	$ DEBITS	$ CREDITS
FINANCIAL CONSIDERATION		
Loan Amount		700,711.00
NEW LOAN CHARGES - Wells Fargo Bank, N.A.		
Total Loan Charges: ($1,538.52)		
Processing　Wells Fargo Bank, N.A.	1,350.00	
Relock at Market Rate　Wells Fargo Bank, N.A.	875.89	
Tax Service　Wells Fargo Bank, N.A.	80.00	
Rate Lock Extension　Wells Fargo Bank, N.A.	875.89	
Appraisal Fee　Corelogic Valuation Solutions		
$620.00 paid outside closing by Borrower		
Credit Report Fee　Corelogic Credco, LLC		
$15.43 paid outside closing by Borrower		
Prepaid Interest	1,410.92	
$50.39 per day from 10/04/19 to 11/01/19		
Wells Fargo Bank, N.A.		
Lender Credits		6,131.22
TITLE & ESCROW CHARGES		
Title - ALTA 6-06 - Variable Rate (CLTA 111.5-06)　Fidelity National Title Company	0.00	
Title - ALTA 8.1-06 - Environmental Protection Lien (CLTA 110.9-06)　Fidelity National Title Company	25.00	
Title - Escrow Fee　Fidelity National Title Company	475.00	
Title - Lender's Title Insurance　Fidelity National Title Company	635.00	
Title - Mobile Signing Fee　Notaries Express, LLC	150.00	
Title - Recording Service Fee　SimpliFile	14.00	
Policies to be issued:		
Loan Policy		
Coverage: $700,711.00　Premium: $635.00　Version: ALTA Loan Policy 2006		
GOVERNMENT CHARGES		
Recording Fees　Fidelity National Title Company	155.00	
PAYOFFS		
Payoff of First Mortgage Loan ($704,419.64)　Central Loan Administration & Reporting		
Principal Balance	700,711.64	
Additional Interest (From 09/01/19 To 10/11/19 @ $86.600000 Per Diem)	3,464.00	
Demand Fee	60.00	
Recording Fee	184.00	
MISCELLANEOUS CHARGES		
Homeowner's Insurance Premium　USAA	1,267.05	
Buyer's funds to close		5,111.17
Subtotals	711,733.39	711,953.39
Balance Due TO Borrower	**220.00**	
TOTALS	711,953.39	711,953.39

If you decide to become an entrepreneur or freelancer, getting a mortgage or doing a refinance will not be easy, maybe not even possible. Banks usually want to see at least two years of steady income before they consider you for a loan. From the bank's perspective, entrepreneurs and freelancers are categorized as higher-risk borrowers who have unpredictable income. Therefore, an entrepreneur's or freelancer's mortgage rate might be higher as well, if they do actually qualify for a mortgage.

The exception to the rule is if you have a significant amount of other assets as collateral and you have a large enough recurring stream of investment income and/or freelance income that has been established for many years. Collateral-based mortgage pricing is common for wealthier individuals who might not have strong incomes.

It doesn't matter how high your credit score is, how loyal you have been to the bank, or that you have a baseball card collection worth more than your mortgage itself. If you no longer have a job, it is almost impossible to get or refinance a mortgage.

When to Pay Down Your Mortgage—Hybrid FS DAIR

Finally, if you're wondering whether to pay down extra principal to pay off your mortgage early, there's a mathematical *and* an emotional component to this decision.

If the interest rate on your mortgage is equal to or lower than the risk-free rate of return (ten-year bond yield), then not paying down extra principal is the financially optimal decision. You are borrowing free money, so keep on borrowing as much as you can for as long as possible. However, this scenario is rare because lenders need to charge a real rate to make a profit.

When the inflation rate is higher than your mortgage rate, even if the mortgage rate is higher than the risk-free rate of return, this is another time when you shouldn't be in a rush to pay down your mortgage. For example, if the inflation rate is 7% and your mortgage rate is 3%, you have a real negative mortgage rate of 4% (3% − 7%). Inflation is reducing your borrowing cost. However, be careful not to hold on to too much cash because inflation also reduces your cash's purchasing power.

Finally, when the interest rate of your mortgage is greater than the risk-free rate of return and lower than the inflation rate, you should strongly consider implementing my FS DAIR framework or at least a hybrid version. The hybrid version takes the existing mortgage interest rate minus the risk-free rate of return and multiplies it by ten to figure out what percentage of your cash flow you should use to pay down extra debt each month.

For example, let's say the risk-free rate is 2% and your mortgage rate is 3.5%. Using the hybrid FS DAIR model: $(3.5\% - 2\%) \times 10 = 15\%$. Consider using 15% of your cash flow to pay down extra principal each month, and invest the remaining 85%. Of course, you can always use the regular FS DAIR model and utilize 35% of your cash flow to pay down extra principal.

Personally, I've never regretted paying off debt, even if I could have made more in an investment. Sure, taking on debt to make more money feels amazing, but so does paying down your debt. Once a debt is paid off, it almost feels like you got away with something for free if your property also went up in value. This is the emotional component to paying off debt that only you can decide.

In the end, ideally, we pay down all debt when we are unwilling or unable to work.

THE FINANCIAL SAMURAI WAY

- By your thirties, you should strongly consider getting neutral real estate by owning your primary residence. Only when you own more than one property are you truly long real estate.

- The 30/30/3 home-buying rule will help you buy responsibly. In a low-interest-rate environment, you can stretch to buy a home up to 5X your household income if you meet the other two conditions.

- BURL is a real estate investing rule that encourages you to allocate your capital more efficiently for maximum returns. It makes you consider the true opportunity cost of living in your home, rather than what you are currently paying.

- Refinance your mortgage if you can break even within eighteen months or less. Consider a no-cost refinance, even if the mortgage rate is higher, so you can immediately start saving.

- Match your mortgage's fixed-rate duration with the estimated length of time you plan to own your home. Given that the average homeownership tenure is roughly ten years, a 7/1 to 10/1 ARM makes the most sense, not a thirty-year fixed. If you can afford the higher payments of a fifteen-year fixed, choose this option, especially if the rate is lower than the one you can get with an ARM.

- Aim to be mortgage free and certainly debt free by the time you no longer want to work. Although you should have recurring passive investment income, in retirement it's better to minimize financial liabilities in order to simplify life.

Chapter 8

Choose Where to Live for Maximum Wealth Potential

Figuring out how much home you can afford is an important first step to owning real estate. But there's a lot more to consider if you want your home purchase to help set you up for financial freedom. Your choice of *where to live* can have a huge impact on your future wealth. And determining your *where* comes with its own set of options.

When choosing a location, a true Financial Samurai will factor in variables like career opportunities, type of home, neighborhood, and how long they plan to stay. Even if you already have a good idea of what you want your next few years to look like, it's easy to overlook the real estate choices that can affect your wealth in big ways.

This chapter will help you buy real estate to get the best probability of making a positive return while also building your career income. As you consider what to buy and where, I'll help you look at those choices through the lens of maximizing your wealth potential now and in the future.

We'll touch on rental properties here, but chapter 9 is where I will discuss real estate as an investment in full detail.

First, you need to make optimal choices for where you lay your head at night.

Live in an Expensive Coastal City or an Affordable City in the Heartland?

Let's start with geography.

If you live and work in the U.S., the disparity between the cost of living in coastal cities versus the heartland of America is enormous, and worth considering in our remote-work environment. This is important for renters and buyers alike. A property's price tag and associated cost of living are not the most important factors in deciding where to live. At least, not at first.

When you're starting out on your journey to financial independence, your priority should be your career. Your career is your main moneymaker. **Hence, you must go where your career opportunity takes you. This is your 70/30 move.** It doesn't matter if you have to go to Williston, North Dakota, in the middle of winter. If the fracking company is going to give you a big raise and a promotion, you should strongly consider taking the job.

Even if your career sends you to a city with a higher cost of living, don't fret. Rejoice! Expensive cities are often where there is the most opportunity. You will have a greater chance of making a higher income throughout the course of your career. After all, job growth and salaries are mainly what drive a city's cost of living, not the other way around. This is what the media and various pundits who rail against high-cost cities miss. Cities are expensive because incomes are high! Not only are salaries greater in more expensive cities, but so are the opportunities you can't even foresee due to a higher density of people. We call this the network effect.

When I landed a job with Goldman Sachs in New York City in 1999, I was thrilled. I was finally going to be able to afford to take my girlfriend out to a nice dinner after a movie. Goodbye, late-night trips to McDonald's! Of course, I gladly relocated to one of the most expensive cities in America for the job. However, I quickly realized that a $40,000 base salary didn't go very far in Manhattan. But what I banked on was a strong year-end bonus and a career upside from working in the financial capital of the world.

Since I had to get in, bleary-eyed, at 5:30 a.m., long before the markets opened at 9:30 a.m., I had to live close to One New York Plaza, where I worked on the forty-ninth floor.

As a result, I rented a studio apartment at Forty-five Wall Street for $1,800 a month. It was the cheapest place I could find close by.

But because New York City apartments require someone to earn at least 40X the monthly rent, I found a high school friend to live with me. It was like we were both back in college, sharing a dorm room. With my rent split at a more affordable $900 a month, I could now save and invest more money. I was hardly ever at home enough to care that I still shared a room.

To the best of my recollection, here was my budget from 1999 to 2000. At the time, my main goal was maxing out my 401(k) contribution and investing whatever cash flow was left.

SURVIVING ON $40,000 A YEAR IN MANHATTAN WHILE SAVING FOR RETIREMENT

Gross Income	Annual $40,000	Monthly $3,333
401(k) contribution	$10,500	$875
Tax (25% effective federal + NY state + city + FICA)	$10,000	$833
Income after 401(k) and tax	$19,500	$1,625
Tax refund	$500	$42
Net income	**$20,000**	**$1,667**
Expenses	Annual	Monthly
Rent (shared studio at 45 Wall St. with high school friend)	$10,800	$900
Utilities	$240	$20
Food & drinks (stay past 7 p.m., eat for free at office cafeteria)	$3,600	$300
Clothes, shoes, accessories (formal work clothes)	$600	$50
Health insurance premiums	$840	$70
Transportation (NYC subway pass, taxis, bus, train)	$960	$80
Personal care products (soap, shaver, shampoo, etc.)	$120	$10
Vacation (all staycations in NYC for two years)	$600	$50
Cable, internet	$0	$0
Mobile phone (company-provided BlackBerry device)	$0	$0
Health club (small gym in building)	$0	$0
Gas, maintenance, auto insurance (did not have car)	$0	$0
Life insurance (company-provided, 4X salary)	$0	$0
Total expenses	**$17,760**	**$1,480**
Leftover cash flow for misc.	**$2,240**	**$187**

Source: FinancialSamurai.com

Although New York City was incredibly expensive, it also gave me the opportunity to make more money in a way I could not have anticipated. During the height of the dot-com bubble in 2000, I got lucky and turned a $3,000 investment in a Chinese internet company called VCSY into ~$150,000. I did so because I sat on the international equities floor at a major investment bank. I saw an investment idea and I pounced. Then I shared my idea with my friends, who then told their friends on the trading floors of other banks. I was at ground zero for how manias started back then. Now ground zero seems to be Reddit message boards.

If I had taken a job at a consulting company like Deloitte or PricewaterhouseCoopers in Washington, DC, I would have lived a more comfortable life due to more humane work hours and a lower cost of living. The starting salaries were similar. But I doubt I would have been able to find the multibagger investment idea that gave me enough for a down payment when I wanted to buy a home a few years later.

On the next page is a sample budget for a first-year consulting analyst making a $75,000 base salary in Washington, DC. After maxing out their 401(k) and paying all expenses, the analyst has $6,690 in cash left over a year before any year-end bonus. However, the new college graduate earns an extra $500 a month in side-hustle income, all of which they put in their taxable investment accounts.

Live where you have the best opportunity to make the greatest amount of money, regardless of geography. Once you've made your fortune, relocate to save money if you want to. Or stay because you've made a fortune and can now afford the costs and have built a deep network of friends.

Once you've found the job that suits you, if you see yourself in the area for at least five years, then it's smart to try getting neutral real estate by buying a home you love. The ultimate combination for wealth creation is to move to an area you love that helps you make the most money while *also* investing in a property that appreciates in value. After all, if the place attracted you to work, it must also be attracting others. This one-two combination will benefit you later if you decide to sell the home or rent it out as you move to another place you love.

If you are stuck in an expensive coastal city to maximize your earnings, consider also investing in real estate in the heartland or eighteen-hour cities. This way, you can get the best of both worlds by following my BURL investing strategy (see chapter 7). I've been investing in the heartland since 2016 and plan to continue doing so for decades to come. I'll show you how to do this in chapter 9.

MAXING OUT YOUR 401(K) ON A REGULAR SINGLE INCOME
(WASHINGTON, DC, AREA)

Gross Income	Annual $75,000	Monthly $6,250
401(k) contribution	$20,500	$1,708
Tax (18% effective federal + Virginia state + FICA)	$13,500	$1,125
Income after 401(k) and tax	$41,000	$3,417
Tax refund	$850	$71
Net income	**$41,850**	**$3,488**
Expenses	Annual	Monthly
Rent (share nice two-bedroom apartment with roommate)	$18,000	$1,500
Utilities (split two ways)	$720	$60
Food and drinks	$8,400	$700
Clothes, shoes, accessories (business casual)	$600	$50
Health insurance premiums	$2,400	$200
Transportation (monthly Metrorail pass, rideshare)	$1,440	$120
Personal care products (soap, shaver, shampoo, etc.)	$360	$30
Vacation	$1,800	$150
Cable, internet, streaming services (split two ways)	$720	$60
Mobile phone	$720	$60
Health club (run outside, push-ups and resistance bands inside)	$0	$0
Gas, maintenance, car insurance (don't have car)	$0	$0
Life insurance (company-provided, 5X base salary)	$0	$0
Total expenses	**$35,160**	**$2,930**
Leftover cash flow for misc.	**$6,690**	**$558**
Side-hustle income (5 hours a week freelance work)	$6,000	$500
Total income left over	**$12,690**	**$1,058**

Source: FinancialSamurai.com

One day over tennis, I asked Jeremy Stoppelman, CEO and cofounder of Yelp, what he thought was the main reason why he was able to build a successful company. He immediately said, "Moving to San Francisco and a lot of luck."

Like me, Jeremy came from a middle-class background. He went to my rival public high school, Langley High, and then attended the University of Illinois Urbana-Champaign, another public school. He could have gotten a job as an engineer back in northern Virginia, like some of his old classmates. However, he decided to accept a job in the Bay Area at @Home Network because that's where the action was.

Jeremy eventually landed a job as an engineer at X.com, which eventually became PayPal. There he worked with people like Max Levchin, Elon Musk, Reid Hoffman, Steve Chen, Keith Rabois, and a number of other successful founders. Max helped seed his company with $1 million in 2004. Eight years later, Yelp successfully went public.

Making the Numbers Work in an Expensive City

If your job brings you to an expensive city like San Francisco or New York City, more sacrifices need to be made in order to save. Besides sharing a studio for two years with a friend, another sacrifice I made was working fourteen hour days so I could qualify for free dinner in the all-you-can-eat cafeteria at Eighty-five Broad Street. After stuffing my face, I would often pack some fruits and cereal in my bag to save for weekend breakfasts.

The goal for the first two to three years in an expensive city is to survive until your income finally starts reaching levels where you can breathe more easily. For example, after my first year was over, Goldman bumped second-year financial analyst salaries up from $50,000 to $65,000. Third-year financial analyst salaries climbed to $75,000 and first-year associate salaries grew to $85,000. Once you added on a year-end bonus, saving and investing got much easier. The key is surviving the initial price shock.

As I mentioned back in chapter 1, if you and your partner want to raise two kids in an expensive city, I believe you'll need to generate around $300,000 to $350,000 in annual income to live a comfortable, middle-class existence. Therefore, if you're moving from a lower-cost city, you need to find jobs with this target income and trajectory in mind. Nowadays, first-year graduates working in big tech, banking, and management consulting often earn \$150,000+ a year. So by the time these types of workers get married, they should be able to clear \$300,000 without a problem.

For those of you who can't or don't want to join these target industries that pay higher salaries, keeping housing costs low, especially during the initial years of a relocation, is vital. You may have to live in a cheaper neighborhood and/or share an apartment with multiple roommates as you work to build your income and savings. The key is to last until better opportunities arise.

On the next page is a realistic \$400,000 household income budget for a family of four. Sure, there is some fat to cut here and there. Yes, the family is saving for retirement, contributing to 529 plans, and building equity in their home. But it's not like they are popping Cristal off a yacht in the South of France.

Always crunch the numbers. And please don't pretend like you'll be a monk on a shoestring budget. Be realistic with your expenses.

Again, the main reason coastal cities are so expensive is high wages. Therefore, move to an expensive city with a high-income job offer intact. Then live frugally for as long as possible as you maximize the gap between your income and your expenses. The more you can widen this gap, the more you'll have to invest. If you move to a low-cost city, growing the gap may be harder because your income upside may be more limited.

If you plan to risk moving to an expensive city without a high-paying job, then set a three-year time limit for finding one before you have to move on. Staying in an expensive city with a low-paying job for an extended period of time will dramatically elongate your time to financial freedom. Therefore, you've got to eventually face the music.

Relocate to Save

All this said, if you can make a salary that is comparable to what you'd make in an expensive city while living elsewhere, do it. This generally can be done *after* you've gained several years of experience and the trust of your managers.

You can make huge strides toward achieving financial freedom through geoarbitrage—that is, moving somewhere with a lower cost of living while maintaining an income that is higher than the typical salary range for your location.

Postpandemic, opportunities are more decentralized. Geoarbitrage is more feasible than ever, since both technology and many company cultures now allow us to be untethered from an office. If you have the flexibility, there is no reason to live in a city where you have to pay over \$5,000 a month for a two-bedroom apartment if you can be happy in a

FAMILY OF FOUR WITH A $400,000 HOUSEHOLD INCOME
LIVING IN AN EXPENSIVE METROPOLITAN AREA

Gross Income	Annual $400,000	Monthly $33,333
401(k) contribution (two working parents)	$41,000	$3,417
Taxable income after 401(k) contributions	$359,000	$29,917
Taxable income after $25,900 standard deduction and 401(k) contributions	$333,100	$27,758
Tax bill (30% effective tax rate, includes state and FICA)	$99,930	$8,328
Net income + $4K child tax credit + noncash standard deduction	$263,070	$21,923
Expenses	Annual	Monthly
Daycare (7:00 a.m.–6:00 p.m., as both parents work)	$26,400	$2,200
Preschool (8:15 a.m.–5:00 p.m.)	$30,000	$2,500
Food for four ($65/day on average, includes regular food delivery)	$24,000	$2,000
529 plan (K–12 + college for two kids)	$18,000	$1,500
Mortgage (3% rate on $1.6 million mortgage after putting 20% down)	$80,952	$6,746
Property tax (1.24% rate on $2 million home with 4 bedrooms/2 bathrooms)	$24,804	$2,067
Property insurance (through Policygenius)	$1,560	$130
Property maintenance	$3,600	$300
Utilities (electricity, water, trash)	$4,200	$350
Life insurance ($2M term to cover all liabilities+)	$1,440	$120
Umbrella policy ($2M)	$600	$50
Health care (employer subsidizes 70% of total cost)	$9,000	$750
Baby & toddler items (diapers, toys, crib, stroller, playpen, etc.)	$1,800	$150
Three weeks of vacation per year (two staycations, one road trip)	$8,400	$700
Entertainment (Netflix, Disney+, museums, zoo, weekend getaways)	$3,600	$300
Car payment (Honda Passport, not Mercedes-Benz G 550)	$4,200	$350
Car insurance and maintenance	$2,400	$200
Gas (regular)	$4,200	$350
Mobile phone (family plan w/20 GB of data)	$1,800	$150
Clothes for four (Banana Republic, not Prada)	$2,400	$200
Personal care products	$1,440	$120
Charity (foster care, nystagmus vision research, UNICEF)	$3,000	$250
No student loans	$0	$0
Total expenses	$257,796	$21,483
Cash flow after expenses to pay for miscellaneous	$5,274	$440

Relevant cities: San Francisco, NYC, Boston, LA, San Diego, Seattle, DC, Miami, Denver, Honolulu, Vancouver, Toronto, Hong Kong, Tokyo, London, Paris, Sydney

Source: FinancialSamurai.com

similar home elsewhere for less than half the monthly cost and make a similar amount of money. Just make sure you're not sacrificing your happiness to live somewhere cheaper.

Before making a big move, I highly suggest you "try before you buy" by taking a two-week vacation to your potential new city. You might find the weather, the politics, the people, the laws, or the culture just rub you the wrong way. Even if you like what you experienced on vacation, I would go back one last time just to make sure.

I have a friend who decided to relocate from San Francisco to a conservative suburb on the east coast after selling his software company because he wanted to live closer to his in-laws. Both my friend and his wife are white, but his adopted children are Black. After eight short months, my friend relocated back to San Francisco. He said his kids were teased one too many times, and the culture was just too different from what his family was used to in San Francisco, so they decided to return "home." Selling his house, buying a new house, selling his new house, buying another house, and getting his four children in and out of school was a massive ordeal.

Always try before you buy, folks.

Ultimately, there are plenty of great places to live in America, and in the end, the best place may simply be where you have the most family and friends.

Buy Your Forever Home or a Temporary Home?

Once you decide *where to buy*, you need to figure out *what to buy*. This is a rare time when the optimal choice for most people will be universal: buy your forever home. There's just one caveat: buy your forever home, and understand that it will likely be . . . temporary.

Here's why: just as with the S&P 500, the ideal holding period for real estate is forever. The longer you can hold on to your investments, the more time you give them to compound.

A fantastic way to build wealth is to buy a great property, live in it for several years, and then rent it out. In a normal life span, it's feasible to go through this process three to five times to build wealth and passive income. So even if you may not live in the home forever, you'd ideally buy with the intention of owning it forever for passive-income purposes.

After five or more years, you will have enjoyed your home and most likely built some equity and grown your net worth. Further, because you enjoyed your home, future people, in the form of renters, will likely enjoy it as well. You've tested your product before you put it out to generate passive rental income.

Another reason to buy and hold forever—or as close to forever as you can—is that selling a property creates economic loss. With commissions, taxes, and fees, it can easily cost anywhere from 4% to 8% of the value of a home to sell it. The math may work in your favor if you buy in a downturn and sell when the housing market is high, but it's hard to plan for that. Assuming the market remains steady, buying a home and then selling in just a few years usually doesn't give you enough time to build up principal appreciation.

So buy with the intention of staying long term. Then embrace the fact that you'll probably move eventually, because the one constant in life is that it's always changing. Just when you think you've got a great groove going, something tends to come up.

The Forever Home That Wasn't Meant to Be

In 2005, at age twenty-eight, I thought I had found a forever home. Little did I know how different my life would turn out to be over the next ten years. It was a four-bedroom, two-bathroom home of 2,070 square feet. It took all the money I had to buy it. I had just gotten promoted to VP and thought my income would keep going up. But I had violated my 30/30/3 rule (which had not been born yet). And I tell you, I was sweating bullets owning the home during the financial crisis. If I had lost my job, I likely would have had to sell the home and take a big loss.

I thought that over the next ten years, we might start a family and grow into the home. But our baby never came. So in 2014 we bought a smaller home in a quiet part of San Francisco and rented out our larger home in true BURL style. The new house cost about 60% less than our budget based on my 30/30/3 home-buying rule. It was a three-bedroom, two-bathroom home with an office facing the ocean in a cheaper neighborhood. When we moved in, it was a more suitable 1,720 square feet. Ah, not feeling the financial stress of owning too much home felt great! This would be our new forever home as a couple. My wife was in the process of engineering her layoff and ultimately did in 2015.

We thought we were destined not to have kids due to biology. We certainly tried. It was just as well, since neither of us had a day job anymore. But three years later, our son finally came. Hooray! But . . . oops. In retrospect, we should have stayed in our larger old home that could accommodate much-needed help from family. But now it had renters, and I no longer wanted to manage it. So in the end, I sold the home and reinvested the proceeds in passive investments to simplify life.

We made the most of our cozy home until our daughter joined us two and a half years later, in December 2019. Then, in April 2020, a month after the beginning of lockdown, we decided to buy our next forever home because we wanted more space. We saw an opportunity and we took it. There should be no problem living here until our kids become adults, but based on my track record, I have my doubts.

Besides unexpected life changes, forever homes are also rarely forever because our growing wealth causes our desires to change. In ten years, I'm certain the majority of us will be much wealthier than we are today. After all, we are Financial Samurais!

If you currently own a home with a mortgage, the cost of owning that home will eventually feel minuscule thanks to the beautiful cocktail of inflation, relatively fixed expenses, and your higher net worth. So even if you think you own your forever home now, you may want something different in a decade or so. And that's fine, because there is no point in working, saving, and investing if we don't consistently utilize our money to live our best lives as often as possible.

THE BEST TIME TO OWN THE NICEST HOME YOU CAN AFFORD

With all this talk of buying a forever home while also being disciplined in how we buy, you might be wondering when is the best time to spend up on a great house.

The answer is simple. If you have kids or plan to have kids, the best time to own that dream house is during the time your kids are living with you. This way, your home is being utilized by more heartbeats and the cost is spread out as well.

Once your kids become adults, unless you plan to have them live with you forever, it's unlikely you will want to upgrade to a larger house. Instead, you may want to downsize. You could certainly spend more money on a nicer house on the beach or buy a condo with great amenities. But you more than likely won't want to buy a bigger house when you have fewer people to live in it. That would feel lonely and wasteful. Therefore, if you want to stretch to the top of your budget, you have about a twenty-year window to do so.

The Optimal Way to Buy a Forever Home

Some buyers use the excuse of buying a forever home to pay more than they should. They tell themselves and others that because they plan to live in the home for decades, stretching to overpay is fine. The situation is akin to someone justifying buying a fancier car because they plan to drive it for 200,000+ miles. The reality is that this seldom ever happens. The data says the average homeownership tenure is now about ten years. Just look at your own historical living tenure to see if living in one place forever is realistic.

The best way to buy a forever home is to get the nicest home you can afford up to 5X your household income as long as you stay within the *rest* of my 30/30/3 home-buying rule. Make no mistake about it: buying a home up to 5X your household income is aggressive. Remember that my 30/30/3 rule advocates for a home no more than 3X your income, but as long as interest rates remain low, stretching to 5X provides a similar level of affordability as when interest rates were 2X to 3X higher.

After you've purchased your forever home, aim to live in it for at least five years, if not ten-plus years. Five to ten years is long enough to:

- Enjoy your home and get the most out of your initial down payment. The first two years will be filled with excitement as you get comfortable with your home and the neighborhood. Once you're settled in, you can enjoy entrenching yourself in your community to the extent that you'd like to do so.
- Accumulate a significant amount of additional capital. Perhaps after paying 5X your household income, you are left with a small financial buffer. You want to rebuild your cash hoard to gain back some financial peace of mind. Over the duration of your ownership, aim to get your primary residence equivalent to 30% or less of your overall net worth. After ten years, hopefully you'll have a big enough financial buffer to afford a new forever home if you want one.

After a decade of ownership, you will likely have a clear sense of whether your home is truly the one. If it is, congratulations! Having to find a new home and move can be a real pain. But if you create enough wealth during this time period, and you want to move, then go for it, and keep living your best life.

Buy in a Prime Location or in an Up-and-Coming Location?

Even once you've figured out the optimal city in which to buy your forever home, there are more key moves you can make to maximize your wealth potential. A smart strategy is to explore relatively unloved or unknown neighborhoods that have a good chance of becoming more popular. If you want to accelerate your path to financial freedom, you've got to squash your ego-driven desire for that fancy house or apartment in a prime neighborhood.

Moving out of our single-family home in the north end of San Francisco in 2014, renting it out, and buying a single-family home just three miles west enabled us to save roughly $4,200 a month, or 50%. Not bad for being able to still breathe the same fresh air!

Lowering our housing expenses by 50% since 2014 while concurrently growing our passive income by 50% in the same time period has really helped increase my family's financial security. Our monthly housing cost has now plummeted to well below 10% of our gross income as a result.

If you want to achieve financial freedom, I recommend keeping your housing expenses to no more than 20% of your monthly gross income. Ideally, you do so by growing your income.

HOUSING EXPENSE GUIDELINE TO ACHIEVE FINANCIAL INDEPENDENCE

Housing Expense as a Percentage of Gross Income	Comments
50%+	You will never be free. Permanent rat-race misery.
40%	You're not sacrificing enough, even though you know you should.
30%	Not bad, but you're running in place like the masses.
20%	Great work! You're finally feeling financial momentum pick up steam.
<10%	Congratulations! Financial independence is an inevitability.

Growing this gap between income and expenses is fundamental for financial freedom. Housing is consistently one of our biggest expenses. Therefore, if you can prevent housing and other expenses from rising as fast as your income, you will accelerate your path to financial freedom if you diligently save and invest the difference.

Please spend some time looking at different neighborhoods in your city. Don't be wedded to the most popular ones where all the cool kids live.

Once we moved to the less-dense west side of San Francisco, we got excited again. There were new parks and museums to enjoy. New restaurants to explore. New types of people to meet.

Finally, if your company is cutting pay for those who move away, moving to a cheaper location *within your city* will not only save you money but also enable you to keep making your maximum salary.

Buying in the best location possible is the most often-cited home-buying rule. But the thing is, prime locations are expensive. If you can't afford a property in a prime location, then look for property in an "undiscovered" or "up-and-coming" location that you think will be in high demand. The key is to estimate a discovery period of no longer than about ten years. You don't want to be stuck waiting twenty years for your neighborhood to improve. Your life may be completely different by then.

Signs of a potential neighborhood boom include new restaurants, supermarkets, and convenience stores opening up. For example, if a Walgreens is opening up in your neighborhood, it must mean that demand is there. You can bet your bottom dollar that the suits at Walgreens have done a feasibility study before sinking millions into building or renovating a store.

Another key sign that a neighborhood is up-and-coming is new companies establishing offices in or near it. For example, when Apple decided to build a $5 billion campus in Cupertino, California, home prices in the area began to rapidly increase. Before you buy a property, definitely do your research on new companies potentially moving into your desired area of purchase. These can make all the difference.

Additionally, ridesharing, self-driving cars, and working from home will only increase. City centers can and will change out of necessity. As a real estate investor looking to maximize returns, buying in an up-and-coming neighborhood will likely provide higher-percentage returns.

KNOW THE FRENZY ZONE

In every city, there is a pricing sweet spot where demand will be strongest. This is what I call the Frenzy Zone because the greatest number of people can afford this price range. It's hard to get a deal if you buy a property priced in the Frenzy Zone. But if you do, you have a greater chance of moving up with the overall prosperity of the city. At the same time, you will likely not lose as much during a downturn either.

The Frenzy Zone is more or less the median-priced property in your city +/− 20%. For example, if the median-priced property is $500,000, the Frenzy Zone is $400,000 to $600,000. If the median-priced property is $1,800,000, then the Frenzy Zone is $1,440,000 to $2,160,000 and so forth. The Frenzy Zone should increase by at least the rate of inflation over time.

If you can afford it, one strategy you should consider is buying slightly above the Frenzy Zone, 21% to 30% above the median-priced property. At this price level, demand tends to drop off, which may provide you a better chance of snagging a deal.

Buy a Home with Expansion Potential

Besides buying in a promising location, an equally important—and often overlooked—rule is to buy a home with expansion potential. In other words, buy a home where there's enough land to expand outward for more livable square feet. Alternatively, buy a home where you can convert wasted space into livable space. The more livable square feet, the more valuable your home.

A lot of people get carried away with the cosmetics of a home. They get fooled by the fancy staging, nice floors, and brushed nickel. But if you've ever remodeled a home, you know that everything is replaceable. Most home remodels don't recoup the cost of the remodel. It's only when you've remodeled a total fixer that you tend to see a nicer return on your investment. Meanwhile, some people remodel to fit their unique tastes, when they should remodel to appeal to as many people as possible.

The sweet spot for maximum real estate profits is if you can buy property with expansion potential in the most expensive neighborhood you can afford. If you're willing to build out and/or renovate your home at a lower cost per square foot than the selling price per square foot, you will create tremendous value.

Do an Expansion or Buy a Completely Done Home?

If you're still young, putting in the "sweat equity" to expand or remodel your home is worth it. Your hourly salary will likely be lower than when you're older, and you will have more patience and time to remodel. After doing four remodels, I swear I am never doing another one. My time is simply more valuable than it was when I was younger because I have less of it.

If you're open to expanding your home to increase its value, focus on the differential between the selling price per square foot and the remodel cost per square foot. The larger the gap, the larger your profits. Look for underdeveloped lots and much larger neighbors that provide precedent for you to build.

Spend hours researching the average selling price per square foot in your neighborhood, down to your very block. The closer the comparable, the better. Once you've done your research, calculate the realistic selling price per square foot minus the realistic building cost per square foot. This is your instant profit.

Although living in an expensive part of the country can be painful, the great thing is that construction and remodeling costs don't usually jump as high as the cost of housing.

For example, a refrigerator should cost about the same in Little Rock as it does in Los Angeles. Lumber and steel prices are also largely the same around the country. The biggest fluctuation in construction and remodeling costs is labor costs.

When it comes to real estate development, returns will usually be much greater in places like San Francisco, Washington, DC, and New York City than in less expensive places like Houston, Portland, or Orlando.

Expanding does have downsides, like higher property taxes once your property is reassessed. However, given that the cost of expanding or remodeling is almost always lower than the cost of buying, your property tax bill will be lower than if you paid for a fully remodeled house. There are also cash-flow risks if you underestimate your project's costs.

When you combine an expansion strategy with geoarbitraging in your own city, you can find that sweet spot between living in the neighborhood you want and maximizing your home's future value.

Just make sure you don't overremodel. For the best bang for your remodeling buck, focus on expanding livable space, then remodeling kitchens and bathrooms, then windows and doors, then decks and landscaping if possible.

Buy a House, a Condo, or a Multiunit?

Mixed in with your decision of *where* and *when* to buy is *what* to buy. This is another choice that can have an especially big impact on your wealth.

From a strictly by-the-numbers perspective, buying a multiunit property with the intention of living in one unit and renting out the other units is likely the most efficient and powerful way to build real estate wealth. But it's great only if the logistics work for you.

Two key factors should drive your choice of what to buy: what you can afford and the lifestyle you're after—in that order. If you plan to rent out the home at any time, rental income is third on the priority list.

My 30/30/3 rule has you covered when figuring out what you can afford, and I'll get into the math of rentals in a moment. So let's take a closer look at lifestyle.

Picture Your Life in a House, Condo, or Multiunit Home

If your focus is on maximizing lifestyle over the next five to ten years, then you may want to buy as much as you can afford so you can grow into the home. A smart way to figure out the ideal home size is to think in square feet per person. I believe the ideal number of square feet per person is about 600 to 800. This means for a family of three, the ideal home size is 1,800 to 2,400 square feet. For a family of four, the ideal home size is 2,400 to 3,200 square feet, and so forth. It's up to you to decide how much space you're most comfortable with. But of course, everybody's preference is different.

If you choose to live in an expensive city, due to high housing costs, you may be forced to adapt to smaller-apartment living. Your choice between a single-family home, a condo, and a multiunit home may also be limited in certain cities based on pricing and availability.

Home maintenance plays a role in lifestyle, too. You may be drawn to a condo over a single-family home if you don't want to think about things like lawn care and snow removal. It's nice when the Homeowners' Association (HOA) maintains all the common areas. Meanwhile, a multiunit means you'd need to maintain at least double everything: rent checks, appliances, toilets, water heaters, electrical grids, and so on.

If you plan to eventually move and rent out the home, put your future-landlord hat on and consider how much work you want to put into managing the property once you're gone. Think deeply, since your answer will change over the years. You may not mind the idea of managing tenants and home maintenance today if you don't have kids or a whole lot of responsibilities tugging at you. But how about in ten years, when you might have two kids, a dog, elderly parents to look after, and a spouse with whom you'd like to spend more time? Buying a multiunit property will mean more rental income, but that also means more work is required to maintain your property.

The ease of maintaining a single-family home or condo compared with a multiunit building is one attraction for small landlords like me, who don't employ property managers. The older and wealthier we get, the less we want to deal with other people and the less we care about maximizing our time.

Then there's the privacy factor. While buying a multiunit property can be an optimal financial move, be sure you're willing to forfeit the privacy of living in a single-family home if you plan to stay in one unit and rent out the other.

However, when you're earlier in your financial journey, the 70/30 decision is to buy a multiunit property. You want to live in a property with no wasted space and extract as much income as possible from your asset. Of course, your finances may not enable you to do so. If you ended up buying a single-family home or multibedroom condo, try to rent out the rooms to maximize utility.

In retrospect, buying a single-family house in 2005 over a multiunit property was a suboptimal financial decision. Our four-bedroom house was highly underutilized for ten years because there was just my wife and me. It would have been much better if we had bought a two-unit property for the same price as our home, each unit with two bedrooms and one bathroom. We could have lived in one and rented out the other to help cover our living expenses. Then, when it was time to expand to a larger living space, we could have rented out our unit for even more passive income.

Let me share some realistic numbers to give you an idea of why owning a multiunit property can make the most sense.

Back in 2014, our single-family home could have rented for $6,000 a month. However, if we had rented out the house, we would have had nowhere to live! But if we had bought a two-unit building for the same price, we could have rented out one unit for $3,500. If we had eventually bought a new place, we could have rented out the top unit, where we lived, for probably around $4,000. In other words, for the same purchase price, we could have received $1,500 more rental income for a two-unit building than for a single-family home. We would have also lived more efficiently, which feels good, too.

From a landlord's perspective, it is most profitable to own multiple smaller rental properties. From a renter's perspective, you get the most bang for your buck renting a larger unit with multiple roommates.

As you decide between a single-family home, condo, and multiunit, keep these factors in mind:

- **Single-family homes** tend to appreciate faster than condos and sometimes multiunit properties. Much of the value in a single-family home is in the land, so look for homes with large, flat lots, views, proximity to good schools and restaurants, and expansion potential. Single-family homes tend to provide their residents with a better lifestyle due to more space and fewer neighbors. Downsides include more hands-on maintenance and a lower rental income yield. Postpandemic, the demand for single-family homes is at an all-time high because everybody wants more separation from others.
- **Condos** are generally cheaper to acquire and tend to provide a higher rental income yield. Those who cannot afford a single-family home or who like spending less time on maintenance should consider a two-bedroom condo. Studios and one-bedroom condos don't appreciate as quickly due to less flexibility and more similar supply. Downsides include HOA fees and HOA regulations that may restrict rental freedom and reduce rental profits. You're the king or queen of your condo, but not king or queen of the common domain. During a downturn, condos tend to get hit harder because more supply comes on the market and there are fewer differentiating factors among condos to make them unique to buyers.

- **Multiunit properties** tend to provide maximum rental income yield and a high amount of tenant-type flexibility (individuals, couples, families, multigenerational). The main downside is potentially higher turnover rates and more active management by the landlord. Also check into rent-control laws. In San Francisco, multiunit properties are under rent control, but single-family houses and condos usually are not. For those who have more energy and more time, multiunit properties are the way to go.

The big picture? Climbing the property ladder takes time. The key is to at least get neutral real estate by owning your primary residence as soon as you see yourself living in a place for five years or longer. Once you're on the property ladder, you have a better chance of improving your living situation over time by accumulating more properties.

THE FINANCIAL SAMURAI WAY

- Move to where you get the best job offer or where the opportunities are the greatest to make the highest income. Moving to a lower-cost city for the main purpose of saving money is the 30/70 move. Instead of focusing on saving money, you need to be focusing on income maximization.

- Buy property with the intention of owning it forever. Ideally, buy your home, live in it for five to ten years, rent it out, and buy another. Over a working lifetime, you could easily end up building a rental portfolio of three to five units to generate passive income. Shoot to keep your housing expenses to no more than 20% of your gross monthly income to increase the gap between your earnings and expenses.

- Due to the proliferation of work from home, investing in up-and-coming neighborhoods or neighborhoods farther from downtown is becoming more appealing.

- For greater living efficiency and higher income, buy a multiunit property. For better living and potentially faster price appreciation, buy a single-family home. Ideally, find a single-family home with expansion potential. Condos provide the easiest way to gain access to the property market due to a lower price point. However, they tend to decline the most in value during a downturn.

- If you build your career in a more expensive city and achieve financial independence, it's easier to relocate to many other cities if so desired.

Chapter 9

Go Long on Real Estate

O nce you've gotten neutral real estate by owning your primary residence, it's time to consider getting long real estate by owning rental properties and/or online real estate. After all, if you own only the place you live, it's hard to monetize it unless you do a cash-out refinance or rent out spare rooms for income, and there are better ways to maximize your real estate returns.

Real estate is my favorite asset class to build wealth because it is a tangible asset that is both offensive and defensive.

On the defensive side, real estate tends to outperform in a downturn because people seek the basics of food, clothing, and shelter. Owning a company stock that produces a gadget we don't need becomes low priority in a bear market. As stocks sell off, bond prices rise and interest rates fall. As a result, even more capital tends to flow to real estate due to lower borrowing costs.

During the 2008–9 financial crisis, although the value of my San Francisco rental properties probably declined by ~15%, my rental income stayed steady because my tenants didn't move. They kept paying the same amount right through the eighteen-month downturn. Today my rental properties are cash cows and their values have risen tremendously.

On the offensive side, real estate benefits in a robust economy due to rising rents and rising property values. If you own real estate, you don't fear inflation, you root for it. Thanks to the use of leverage, the cash-on-cash return for real estate investors can be very robust.

Finally, during times when there is both tremendous fear *and* greed, real estate has proven to be a winning asset class. The pandemic period is a perfect example of the attractiveness of real estate. When stocks were collapsing in March 2020, real estate values stayed steady. There was little panic from properly leveraged real estate investors who ended up spending more time in their homes. As the outlook improved, real estate demand began to quickly take off.

Sure, stocks are a 100% passive investment that has historically generated ~10% returns a year, but the downside to their being so low-maintenance is that you have no control. You are at the mercy of management's decisions and random external variables. With real estate, you are the boss.

If properly acquired, real estate comes as close to the unbeatable "heads you lose, tails I win" unicorn investors so often seek but rarely find. Add any government support through tax breaks or incentives, and it becomes suboptimal not to invest in real estate long term. Real estate has the power to build wealth in ways that no other asset can, and it mostly has to do with risk.

When an asset class is deemed less risky, the returns are usually lower as well. A simple example: stocks versus bonds. Bonds are safer, but the returns are lower. Ironically, even though real estate is considered less risky than stocks, investors can sometimes make more money in real estate.

Why? Confidence. Because real estate investors are confident real estate values won't just go *poof* overnight like stocks can, they are more willing to take on leverage to buy a higher-dollar-value asset. Over time, the absolute returns may end up growing much larger than an investment in stocks or any other risk asset.

How Real Estate Can Make the Average Person More Money Than Stocks

Think back to your latest stock, ETF, or index fund purchase. Now compare that purchase amount to the median home price in America (~$400,000 in 2022), or the purchase price of your actual house if you have one. The difference between the two purchase amounts is likely enormous.

According to the Survey of Consumer Finances, the median stock holdings for all families in 2019 was $40,000 (the median home price in 2019 was ~$327,000). Meanwhile, according to digital wealth adviser Personal Capital, the median balance in its clients' retirement accounts in 2021 was $123,000.

In other words, since the median stock balance is lower, it takes a much greater percentage gain in stocks for the typical American family to match the absolute dollar value gain in a home. For example, if the median home price in 2022 went up by 10%, that would amount to a roughly $40,000 increase. To match a $40,000 increase in stocks would require a 100% increase in the median stock holdings for all families in 2019 and a 32% increase in the median balance in retirement accounts for Personal Capital's clients. It's possible, but unlikely.

The typical person is more comfortable spending much more money buying an individual piece of real estate than an individual stock or index fund. Why? Because real estate is a tangible asset that tends to hold its value better. Your house is not going to suddenly lose 25% of its value in one day after missing earnings estimates by a couple of percentage points, as some stocks do.

Not only does real estate provide shelter, it can also generate tax-efficient income and can appreciate in value. As a result, even if average returns for real estate are lower than stocks, the absolute dollar returns may be much higher.

If you do not have enough confidence to invest in a risk asset, then either you won't invest or you won't invest enough to make a difference. A lack of confidence is why I've come across plenty of readers who've just sat on cash for years. Sure, there are examples where some investors went all in on their favorite multibagger growth stock. But for the average American without a trust fund and with a family to support, buying real estate that serves a purpose is an easier, safer way to build wealth.

So long as you can afford to purchase a home under the 30/30/3 rule, even if it proceeds to decline in value, you aren't being constantly reminded about its depreciation. Instead, you're enjoying the utility your home provides while making wonderful memories. Or you have tenants who are enjoying the home and covering your overhead while you ride out the housing market downturn. This utility is what will make a potential real estate investment loss much more bearable. When it comes to stocks, no amount of ownership joy will make up for a stock loss. Stocks provide zero utility.

Given that real estate is less risky than stocks, it is ironic that the average person can make much more money from real estate. We have the government's support to partially thank for this anomaly, as I covered in chapter 4. But we can also thank our ability to courageously take more calculated risks for potential financial glory.

At the end of the day, the 70/30 move is to invest in both real estate and stocks following my net worth allocation framework in chapter 5. Each has its own benefits. They are not mutually exclusive investments.

The Power of Investing in Real Estate for Historically Marginalized Groups

One day I realized that all my tenants were white. I'd honestly never thought about my tenants' racial makeup until the media began heavily covering racial injustice and the rise in anti-Asian hate crimes from 2020 to 2022.

As an Asian American living in San Francisco, I had been largely shielded from racism, since we are a "minority-majority" city. But the more the media focused on the ills of society, the more I became aware of my status and came to appreciate real estate as an insurance policy.

Perhaps you have a disability that makes it more difficult to get a particular job in your field of interest? Maybe your company's management is entirely made up of people who don't share your gender? Or maybe you simply don't have the connections to get a warm referral? Real estate can be an especially powerful way to build income and wealth for folks who don't have an edge.

It can also act as a security blanket that provides a fundamental feeling of confidence in the face of discrimination. Without getting into the weeds about structural problems, I think it's enough to say that if you are a member of a marginalized group, there may be a greater chance you will have fewer opportunities compared with those who are not. It's just math.

For example, let's say your race makes up 6% of the country's population and you're competing in a political race with someone whose race makes up 61% of the population. Even if you were able to win the hearts of 100% of the 6%, you would still lose to the person who wins the hearts of just 10% of the 61% (6.1% > 6%).

In a winner-takes-all society, it can be easy to give up once you realize the odds are stacked against you. However, a true Financial Samurai never gives up. They find a way to adapt.

I see human nature as the most expansive and encompassing reason why there is inequality. We have a tendency to take care of our own above all else, especially when it comes to our children. Opportunity and access are not equal. Therefore, real estate is a good hedge.

In all, I have three rental properties as part of my passive-income retirement portfolio. My goal as a landlord is to find the best tenants possible, and during my screening process, I focus on financials, length of employment, length at previous residence, references, and character.

Each of my tenants makes between $27,000 and $50,000 a month gross and has a stable job in big tech, the medical field, or a start-up. They could also all be prototypical *Financial Samurai* readers who follow my housing expense guideline of not spending more than 20% of household income on rent. Here's the kicker. There's only a small chance I would ever be able to get hired into any of my tenants' jobs. I know because I've tried.

In early 2012, before I left finance, I submitted dozens of résumés to tech companies like Airbnb, Google, Facebook, and Apple. I either didn't get a response or got rejected by all of them. My streak of rejections continued year after year. In 2013 I was rejected for a journalism fellowship after extensive meetings with professors.

In 2015 I applied to a couple of start-up incubators. One was a straight-up rejection and another had me pitch my idea for an hour. I ended up getting rejected by that one too, but I've seen a couple of different companies execute on my idea with great success.

Darn. I could have made everyone rich, including myself! Oh well. I could go on, but you get the point. Perpetual failure is one of the reasons why I continue to save 50%+ of my passive and online income. Perpetual failure is also a key reason why I've built a rental property portfolio. If you're not constantly failing, you're not constantly trying.

Let me be clear: I *doubt* being a minority was a reason I was rejected by so many places. My lack of experience, or too much experience, were the main reasons. Or maybe I simply didn't give off the true enthusiasm of a typical job seeker. Who knows for sure? But I sure as heck didn't have any connections to provide warm introductions. And let's be honest. The people who landed these fellowships, incubators, and jobs are all extremely smart, with glowing résumés, whereas I'm objectively average. The only above-average trait I possess is high endurance.

It doesn't take a genius to properly analyze a real estate investment opportunity. Real estate can also be a hedge against traits that can prevent you from landing a job or raising funds for your company. Some of these traits include poor social skills, a boring personality, a lack of charisma, or a lack of confidence.

Real estate can also be a particularly beneficial asset if you're excluded from the job market because you have a disability. Roughly 15% of the world's population has some type of disability. Most of us can work on improving things like our technical skills or our confidence. However, it's much harder to overcome individual conditions that are outside of our control. Helping level the playing field for those with a disability is the right thing to do. I hope more companies continue to invest in accessibility initiatives that give people with disabilities a fair shot.

Another very real challenge for marginalized groups is that a lot of getting ahead is about who you know. My tenants all work at high-caliber companies. Once you've worked at a place like Facebook, you can easily job hop to Google, Apple, and so forth. Then, of course, it's much easier for your siblings, friends, and relatives to get into these companies as well, due to referrals and legacy admissions. Although nepotism is frowned upon, it still happens all the time.

For most, there is simply no way to break in. Check out the employee racial profile at Facebook (now Meta), a company that pays at the top end of the pay scale. We're talking ~$180,000 compensation packages for new college graduates and over $600,000 for an E6-level engineer after about seven or eight years of work experience.

If you are a Black or Hispanic person wanting to join Facebook, you may look at the

EMPLOYEE RACIAL PROFILE AT FACEBOOK

	White	Asian	Hispanic	Black	Two or more races	Other
2014	57%	34%	4%	2%	3%	0%
2015	55%	36%	4%	2%	3%	0%
2016	52%	38%	4%	2%	3%	1%
2017	49%	40%	5%	3%	3%	1%
2018	46.6%	41.4%	4.9%	3.5%	3%	0.6%
2019	44.2%	43%	5.2%	3.8%	3.1%	0.7%
2020	41%	44.4%	6.3%	3.9%	4%	0.4%

percentages and not even bother applying. It can feel like there are simply too few people pulling for you. Representation matters to give those who are underrepresented enough *hope to even try.*

Overrepresentation matters, too. As an Asian person, you might look at the percentages at Facebook and think you've got a decent shot at landing a job. However, you might also look at the figures and feel dread. Due to the overrepresentation of Asians at Facebook and other big tech companies, there's a feeling that the competition is too fierce to get in. As a member of an overrepresented minority, you may feel like you are part of the wrong group, which Facebook won't prioritize. Therefore, why bother applying in the first place?

When you are shut out from opportunities or *feel* like you are shut out from opportunities, you tend to *make your own opportunities* instead—and real estate is a way to participate in a booming economy that doesn't evenly enrich all members of society.

Even if you can't get a good job, by owning real estate, you can still benefit from rising rents and property values due to a strengthening economy. Even if you can't join a promising company that plans to go public, real estate should benefit from new liquidity in the local economy. As a real estate investor, you are selling the picks and shovels during a gold rush.

It's important to continually try to predict how things will be in the future because it's not just your opportunities that are at risk; your children's may be as well. The cycle of lost opportunities I've experienced may repeat for my children. Therefore, owning a real estate portfolio provides me some comfort that no matter how much rejection my children may face in their lives and careers, they won't starve. Worst case, they can earn a living as property managers.

Thrive Without Needing Permission

Owning real estate investment properties is a permissionless business. Security for the family is also why you see so many restaurants, nail salons, laundromats, and retail stores owned by members of marginalized groups. All of these businesses can be conducted without gatekeepers. Often only a perfunctory use of English is needed. If you have the capital and the grit, you can start a small business.

While building your business, you can put your kids to work washing dishes, serving food, cleaning, painting walls, and more. With earned income, you can open a Roth IRA for each child. Who knows, with a strong enough work ethic and solid investment returns, your kids might even become millionaires at a young age. And in the event that things don't go well for your kids on their own, they can always come back and work at the family business.

I love running *Financial Samurai* because nobody tells me what to do. I can write about whatever I want, whenever I want.

The personal finance field is fairly homogeneous. Despite not fitting in based on appearance or location, I realized long ago that search algorithms such as Google are fairly objective. All they want is the best content to show their users. Therefore, even though I am not a part of the majority, I am able to effectively compete based on the quality of my content. Today *Financial Samurai* continues to receive about one million organic visitors a month who don't care what I look like. All they care about is whether I can help them solve a financial problem.

When the system is stacked against you, not feeling like your future will be determined by someone else is huge. All any of us want is an opportunity to compete in a system that is not too rigged. If you feel the system is unfair, you must find different ways to overcome it.

Do not rely on society to help you. Do not depend on the government to save you. Focus on what you can control. If you adopt this mentality, I'm confident you will build more wealth than the average person.

We all have a desire to feel secure. By owning real estate and/or a small business, you can achieve some of that security for yourself and your children.

YOU GET A HOUSE, YOU GET A HOUSE, AND YOU GET A HOUSE!

One goal to consider is owning one property for every member in the family. This way, none of your family members will ever lack affordable housing. If you buy a property when your child is born, by the time they are an adult you might own the property free and clear. Saving and investing for something specific is a powerful motivator.

If you want to increase your chances of being involved in your adult children's lives, you can take this goal a step further by buying multiple properties near you. Providing affordable housing in a growing city is a wonderful incentive. However, you will ultimately have to let your children choose their own adventure. Even if they don't take you up on your housing offer, at least you will have assets that generate rental income.

Invest in Physical Real Estate or Online Real Estate?

Whatever your background and reason for wanting to invest in real estate, there have never been more options available than there are today.

I mentioned in chapter 3 that physical real estate and online real estate (private eREITs, public REITs, real estate ETFs, and real estate crowdfunding) are among my favorite passive-income investments. Jump back to that chapter for a quick recap on why.

The great thing is that you don't have to choose to invest in one or the other. You can do both as you have the funds, and your asset allocation in either investment can evolve with you.

For example, one path to consider as your wealth grows is to own physical properties while you have the time and energy to hold them for as long as you practically can. If you do sell, reinvest your newly liquid cash into online real estate if you no longer have an interest in managing rentals. This is what I did after selling my San Francisco rental house in 2017.

I reinvested $550,000 of the house sale proceeds into a real estate crowdfunding fund consisting of eighteen properties, a real estate ETF called VNQ, and a couple of public REITs. Most of the properties in the real estate crowdfunding fund have done well, but some have been zeros, hence the importance of diversification. Meanwhile, VNQ has been a steady gainer with a 2%+ dividend yield. Not only have my reinvested proceeds provided 100% passive income since 2017, but they have also outperformed San Francisco real estate since then. It's nice to have real estate exposure without having to worry about broken refrigerators, late rent, leaky windows, or a revolving door of tenants.

While both investment options have their pros and cons, let's take a closer look at how they compare.

The Case for Investing in Physical Property over Online Real Estate

With price appreciation, rental income, and tax breaks, physical property should be a core part of your investment portfolio. However, I want to focus on a key intangible reason rental properties may be an optimal choice over online real estate—and that's family security.

All parents should be worried about their children's futures. The ROI on a college education continues to go down. Globalization is making everything hypercompetitive. And black swan events like a global pandemic are preventing adult children from launching.

There is no joy in inheriting a dividend-paying investment portfolio. However, with rental properties, the adult child can market the property, screen tenants, run background checks, negotiate the lease, coordinate move-ins and move-outs, make sure all insurance policies are in place, collect the rent, and maintain or improve the properties. There is a tremendous amount of satisfaction in finding great tenants at a market rate. And even if your adult children find satisfying careers, if you've taught them about the benefits of real estate investing since they were children, they might be more inclined to take care of the properties when they are older. After all, they will likely inherit these properties after you are gone.

When my son turned three, we decided to plant two magnolia trees in front of one rental property close by. I explained to him that the trees needed to be watered every week for the first two years in order to successfully root. He nodded. Every week thereafter, we'd walk over to the rental property and water Herbie and Huggie, whose names he chose. Over time he will learn all there is to know about real estate investing. And as the trees grow with him, I hope, so will his knowledge about taking care of the rental for his own good and his desire to do so.

For those of you who are not parents, rental properties provide the passive income needed to help you lead the life you want. Rental properties tend to provide a higher yield than online real estate or most other asset classes. Further, given the potentially higher dollar value of your rental property purchases, the absolute income and appreciation amounts will likely be much higher as well.

The Case for Investing in Online Real Estate

Real estate crowdfunding (REC), also known as real estate syndication, has emerged as one of my favorite ways to diversify into real estate without the work involved in managing rental properties. Your investment is 100% passive, freeing you up to live your life while still getting exposure to the real estate market. It also gives you the flexibility to invest in properties anywhere in the country, particularly in the heartland or the South, where valuations are lower and net rental yields are higher.

If you happen to own real estate in an expensive coastal city, real estate crowdfunding enables you to more surgically invest in different areas of the country using the BURL methodology. Further, you can invest in different real estate asset classes such as office, industrial, hospitality, and multifamily.

For example, when the pandemic hit, office and hospitality commercial real estate suffered. However, storage facilities and multifamily properties boomed. You could have strategically invested in these real estate asset classes on a platform like CrowdStreet.

And as I mentioned in chapter 3, you don't have to take on a mortgage and go all in on one property if you invest in online real estate. Fundrise, with billions under management, for example, has a minimum investment amount of only $10. In other words, with online real estate investing, you can start small and work your way up, just as with stocks.

The 70/30 move is to build your physical rental property portfolio in your twenties and thirties. As you're building up your down payment, you should also invest in online real estate to keep up with the real estate market. Once you're in your forties, start transitioning more of your portfolio to passive online real estate investments. You can always hire a property manager to manage your physical rental property portfolio.

Ideally, you will find the maximum number of rental properties you feel comfortable managing. Once you hit that limit, invest all your remaining funds and cash flow earmarked for real estate in online real estate investments.

Buy This: Real Estate in the American Heartland

If you want to get rich, you should focus on trends. Once you get the trend right, the rest tends to take care of itself. In my opinion, the next moneymaking trend is investing in the heartland of America through real estate crowdfunding or private real estate syndication deals. (For reference, the heartland comprises Alabama, Arkansas, Illinois, Indiana, Iowa,

Kansas, Kentucky, Louisiana, Michigan, Minnesota, Mississippi, Missouri, Nebraska, North Dakota, Ohio, Oklahoma, South Dakota, Tennessee, and Wisconsin.)

If you can't buy physical real estate in the heartland, you can still find opportunities through real estate syndication deals. In 2022 and beyond, forces like taxes, politics, and flexible work environments will all help boost the value of heartland real estate over the next decade. These are the movements leading the trend:

1. There may be a net migration out of blue states into red states due to lower prices.
2. As our country gets older, more retirees may move out of blue states to stretch their retirement dollars.
3. The remote-work trend will continue and accelerate due to technology and flexible work-from-home options.
4. Income growth may be higher in red states due to demographic shifts.
5. The state and local tax (SALT) deduction cap hurts higher-priced properties in higher-taxed states. If the SALT deduction cap were lifted, then owners of higher-priced properties in higher-taxed states would benefit more.
6. Now that investing in real estate around the country is more efficient, capital will naturally flow toward states with higher cap rates and away from states with lower cap rates.
7. The expansion of who can invest via real estate crowdfunding will lead to an increase in demand and prices.
8. The rise of more real estate crowdfunding platforms will increase the supply of capital, thereby increasing the demand and prices of previously hard-to-tap investments.
9. The heartland's share of the foreign-born population has risen from 23.5% in 2010 to 31.1% in 2019. It is likely going to continue going up, providing more positive demographic tailwinds that will boost real estate demand.
10. Growing diversity in the heartland will likely attract more diverse people who feel more comfortable living among their own. In thirty years, the heartland will look more like coastal states. For a fascinating look at the evolution of diversity in the heartland, please see research from the Brookings Institute called *The Changing Face of the Heartland*.
11. Foreign real estate investors, who may have been shut out during the pandemic, may start flooding the U.S.

When you can earn rental yields 3X to 5X greater without having to maintain the property, you should be all over it.

Ideally, I want to aim for a roughly fifty-fifty split between owning physical rental properties in places such as San Francisco and Honolulu, where I plan to live, and investing in properties in the heartland, where valuations are lower and rental yields are higher.

Invest in Physical Property Locally or from Afar?

Folks who live in areas with high property prices are especially tempted to buy where prices are cheaper and rental yields are higher. But flying somewhere to buy physical property and managing it from afar can be very difficult.

My advice is to buy physical investment property from afar only if you have someone you trust to manage the property. The cost of hiring that person must also leave you with enough of a margin to make the investment worth it. A property manager usually charges about one month's rent. Therefore, if eleven months of rent still provides enough income to generate positive cash flow, then you are probably okay, especially if property prices continue to increase. Without a trusted property manager, all the headaches of running a rental property—from burst pipes to rowdy tenants—are amplified when you're too far away to deal with them. The stress you will feel, even with a property manager, will eat into any joy that comes from making a profit.

Further, when buying nonlocal property, you need to invest a high enough amount to make your time and hassle worthwhile. For example, let's say you have a $1 million net worth and earn $150,000 a year. Buying a $200,000 single-family home out of state that generates a net rental income of $600 per month probably isn't worth the headache. Instead, it's smarter to surgically invest in real estate from afar through a diversified REIT, a private eREIT, a real estate ETF, or crowdfunding. The REIT managers and crowdfunding platforms vet the deals for you, and the sponsors manage the deals so you don't have to. And the best part: it's not on you to chase anyone for rent, plow snow, or call a plumber when the dishwasher turns the kitchen floor into a wading pool.

Invest in a Vacation Property or Stay Free to Vacation Where You Want?

For the majority of people, buying a vacation property is a waste of money. You simply won't use the property enough to justify the costs. The financially optimal move is to remain untethered and travel where you want. Part of a great vacation is exploring a new place. Always having to go back to your vacation home may eventually start to get boring.

Before you buy, be honest about how often you will actually utilize the property. A vacation property is a total luxury expenditure for lifestyle purposes, not for investment growth purposes.

As a baseline rule, never buy a vacation property if you depend on rental income to afford the property. That income is constantly at risk due to a variety of factors—from economic downturns to weather. Even if you follow my 30/30/3 rule and have 10% of the home's purchase price in savings, a vacation dry spell can hurt your finances if you depend on that income to pay your mortgage.

Further, the hassle of maintaining a vacation property often causes more stress than it's worth. Ideally your investments will be as passive as possible. Owning and renting out a property with year-round tenants is hard enough. Factor in a revolving door of weekly renters and it's like taking on a part-time job. Sure, you can hire a management company to handle the logistics, but that cuts into your margins, and you're still vulnerable to rental dry spells plus the usual headaches that come with homeownership.

I appreciate that there is a whole subculture of folks making good money with short-term rentals via platforms like Airbnb and VRBO. The reality is that those properties require either time and effort or a lot of extra cash flow so you can hire someone else to do that work for you. It's a young person's game. From a purely passive-income perspective, a vacation property is a double sucker punch of being high-maintenance with inefficient economic returns.

With this in mind, I have a strict vacation property buying rule: **Lifestyle First, Income Second.**

I came up with this rule after gleaning wisdom from an investor who has decades of experience on me. Back in February 2017, during a hot-tub party at the Resort at Squaw Creek (I own a vacation home there—not the best financial decision, but more on that soon), I got to know a fellow owner who had retired five years earlier as a partner at a major law firm. He told me something surprising after I asked him what his future plans were for his property. He said, "Just continue to enjoy it. I'd never sell because the property is worth an insignificant amount as a percentage of my net worth today. I'll just leave the property to my kids to enjoy."

Given that this was a hot-tub party, not a personal finance one-on-one consulting session, I didn't dig deeper into his finances. But since the retired lawyer was twenty years my senior with adult children, I realized I had just seen the future that I want for my family.

Since first coming up to Squaw (now called Palisades Tahoe) in 2001, I've always imagined it to be a place where I could take my kids during their school holidays. During summer vacation, we can go hiking, mountain biking, river rafting, kayaking, and waterskiing.

During winter break, we can go sledding after seeing who makes the best snow angels. Lake Tahoe is magical.

If I'm able to fulfill my vision of hanging out with my little ones at the Resort during their entire childhood, the intrinsic value of my vacation property will dramatically increase. Even though I've suffered a financial loss, that's secondary because the property is now paid off and is a small percentage of my net worth.

Dreams don't always align with the reality of our finances. That's why I've created this rule—to protect us from making an irrational and overly emotional decision before we can truly afford it. In order to never have your vacation property feel like a burden, my rule is to **spend no more than 10% of your net worth on a vacation property purchase price (not down payment).**

For example, if your net worth is $3 million, spend no more than $300,000 on a vacation property. If your net worth is $500,000, then probably no vacation property for you. This handy chart serves as a vacation-property-buying-101 guide:

VACATION PROPERTY BUYING GUIDE

Spend no more than 10% of your net worth on the purchase price with at least 20% down.

Net Worth	Max Vacation Property Purchase	Thoughts
$500,000	$50,000	Avoid time-shares like the plague
$1,000,000	$100,000	You can own a cabin in the woods
$2,000,000	$200,000	Deluxe cabin with indoor plumbing and electricity
$4,000,000	$400,000	About the median price of a home in the U.S.
$5,000,000	$500,000	The range of options starts opening up
$10,000,000	$1,000,000	You can finally start really living it up

Source: FinancialSamurai.com

The guide basically says that you shouldn't even consider owning a vacation property until you have at least a $1 million net worth. Even then, you won't be able to get much until you have a net worth of over $5 million.

If I had followed this vacation property buying guide, I would have saved myself a lot of money and heartache by not buying my vacation property in 2007. In 2007, my net worth was about $2.2 million, but I spent $715,000 on a vacation property (32.5% of net worth). Over the next couple of years, my net worth dropped to about $1.5 million due to the global financial crisis, which meant my vacation property purchase price grew to an aggressive 48% of my net worth.

Any asset that's worth less than 10% of your total net worth starts feeling like a relatively insignificant amount of money. And when the property comprises such a small portion of your wealth, your reasons for buying it become more about lifestyle.

Even if you can afford the property, think of the purchase from every angle. Challenge yourself to answer these questions honestly:

1. Will you use it often enough?
2. Would you prefer to see new places?
3. Will buying this vacation property make your life better?
4. Do you plan to own your vacation home forever?

During downturns, vacation properties are often the first type of properties to get hit, since nobody needs a vacation property. A multiproperty owner would first consider selling a vacation property before selling their primary residence. Further, fewer people will be willing to splurge on vacations during difficult times. Therefore, vacation property rental income will likely decline as well.

Eight Steps to Correctly Value a Potential Investment Property

I can't encourage you to invest in physical real estate without teaching you how to value and analyze properties. I've learned a lot since buying my first property in 2003, and I want to help you avoid my mistakes and benefit from the wisdom I've learned.

So as I close out my discussion of real estate, I'll leave you with my step-by-step process for figuring out whether an investment property is worth your precious time and effort. Come back to this for a quick guide to running the numbers any time you're considering buying a property. Remember: for the time and energy that owning physical real estate requires, the profits *have* to be worth it.

Before you crunch any numbers, know that your investment strategy should mainly be about income. Your core task is to figure out the income a property can realistically generate year after year. While there may be a lot of data available to you, the property's current and historical income figures are what matter most. At the end of the day, an investment's value is mainly based on its current and future cash flow.

1. **Calculate your annual gross rental yield.** Figure out the realistic monthly market rent based on rents for similar nearby properties that you find online. Multiply that

number by twelve to get your annual rent. Now take the gross annual rent and divide it by the market price of the property. For example:

$2,000 per month × 12 = $24,000 per year

$24,000 ÷ $500,000 = 4.8% gross rental yield

This calculation gives you a quick snapshot of the yield you could make if you paid 100% cash and have no ongoing expenses.

2. **Compare your gross rental yield with the risk-free rate.** The risk-free rate is the ten-year bond yield, which has largely declined over the past forty years. All investments need a risk premium over the risk-free rate; otherwise, there is no point in risking your money investing. If the annual gross rental yield of the property is less than the risk-free rate, either bargain harder or move on.

   Ideally, you want your gross rental yield to be at least 3X the risk-free rate of return. After all, you will have insurance, property taxes, maintenance expenses, turnover, and potentially a mortgage to pay for.

3. **Calculate your net operating income (NOI), cap rate, and net profit.**
   - NOI: NOI equals all rental income from the property, minus all reasonably necessary operating expenses. The NOI calculation *excludes* mortgage payments, taxes, and capital expenditures. Investors use NOI mainly to judge a building's ability to generate revenue and profit and to cover the payments on a mortgage if one is needed. NOI is beneficial for making as close to an apples-to-apples comparison as possible when evaluating investment properties.
   - Cap rate: The property's cap rate is calculated by dividing the NOI by the property's asset value. For example, a $1 million property that has an NOI of $40,000 has a cap rate of 4%. You will then use the cap rate to compare the property against other potential real estate investment opportunities. The higher the cap rate, the more attractive the property is to investors, and vice versa.
   - Net profit: Net profit equals all rental income from the property, minus all expenses to operate and own the property. Everything—mortgage interest, insurance, HOA dues, marketing expenses, and property taxes—is included. Your net profit is your bottom line.

   When it comes to investing, everything is relative. For example, cap rates in San Francisco for one- to three-floor buildings have historically averaged 4%. Therefore, if you find a building for sale with a 5% cap rate, you might have found yourself a great deal. However, a building with a 5% cap rate is not attractive if it is located in Jefferson County, Texas, where the historical cap rate is 9.2%.

4. **Calculate the price-to-earnings ratio of your property.** The P/E ratio is simply the market value of your property divided by the current net profit.

   For example, let's say an investment property is selling for $500,000 and has an annual net profit of $5,000. The P/E ratio of the building is $500,000 ÷ $5,000, or 100. Whoa! It will take a new owner one hundred years of net profits to make back their investment.

   You would want to buy this property at a P/E ratio of 100 only if you believe you can materially boost rental income over the years or if you believe the property will significantly increase in price.

   If you believe you have the ability to boost the annual net profit from $5,000 to, say, $20,000, then you might really only be buying the property at a P/E ratio of 25 ($500,000 ÷ $20,000). If you can turn around and sell the property at a P/E ratio of 50, then you would receive $1 million gross ($20,000 × 50), for a $500,000 gross profit.

5. **Forecast the property price and rental expectations.** The P/E ratio, cap rates, and gross rental yields are only snapshots in time. The real opportunity is in properly forecasting the future.

   The best way to do this is to see what has happened in the past via online charts provided by DataQuick, Redfin, and Zillow and have realistic expectations about local employment growth. Are employers moving into the city or leaving? Is the city allowing lots more building permits in the pipeline? If more supply is created compared with demand, expect prices to soften, and vice versa. Is the city in financial trouble and looking to gouge owners with more property taxes? If so, your NOI calculation may be too optimistic.

   Understanding housing supply is key. Real estate tends to go through boom-and-bust cycles because real estate developers cannot perfectly time the acquisition and development of properties. For example, in Austin, where real estate price increases have topped the nation in recent years, real estate developers might be more incentivized to acquire land now due to potentially higher profit margins. But by the time a developer is finished with construction in two years, there might be a glut of supply.

   As a savvy real estate investor, you always want to be aware of both demand and supply of housing. Ideally, you want to invest in cities that have risen the least and also have the smallest amount of supply upcoming. Conversely, you may want to avoid cities that have seen the biggest increase in prices while also having the largest increase in upcoming supply.

6. **Run various pricing scenarios.** Take your realistic property price and rental forecasts and run three scenarios: realistic, blue sky, and bear market. If rents decrease for five years at a pace of 5% a year, will your finances be okay?

What about if mortgage rates for thirty-year fixed loans increase from 3% to 5% in five years? How will higher mortgage rates dampen demand if there is not a commensurate boom in job growth? Your property's value will likely depreciate or at least stop appreciating. Thankfully, interest rates usually rise due to an increase in economic activity and higher inflation expectations.

If the principal value declines by 20%, will you be mentally okay with a 100% decline in equity, assuming you put down 20%? If you put down less than 20%, will you be mentally okay with paying a mortgage for a property with negative equity?

Always run a bearish case, a realistic case, and a bullish case as your bare minimum. This way, you can make more realistic financial plans.

7. **Be mindful of taxes and depreciation.** Almost all expenses related to owning a rental property are tax deductible, including mortgage interest, insurance, maintenance, advertising, and property taxes. Think about owning a rental property like owning a business.

Depreciation is the process used to deduct the costs of buying and improving a rental property. Rather than taking one large deduction in the year of purchase or improvement, depreciation distributes the cost over time (27.5 years, to be exact, based on the modified accelerated cost recovery system). Depreciation is a noncash expense that reduces your net operating income. Given that your NOI is lower, your tax bill will be, too.

Let's say you buy an investment property for $1 million. The building is valued at $600,000 and the land is valued at $400,000. You can depreciate only the value of the building, not the value of the land. Therefore, to calculate your annual depreciation, take the building value of $600,000 and divide it by 27.5 to equal $21,818.

Each year when you do your taxes (Schedule E), you get to deduct $21,818 in depreciation expense. Owning a rental property is one of the best ways to earn tax-efficient income.

8. **Always check comparable sales.** The easiest way to check comparable sales over the past six to twelve months is to punch in the property address on Redfin, which I believe has better price-estimation algorithms than Zillow. But you might as well check both because it's free and easy to do.

THE 1% RULE

The 1% Rule is another handy rule for figuring out how much to pay for an investment property. The rule's equation is: 100 × monthly rent = maximum purchase price of a home. In other words, if a property rents for $5,000 a month, the maximum price you should pay is $500,000.

Unfortunately, the 1% Rule is almost impossible to follow in more expensive markets, where cap rates are often below 5%. In such low-cap-rate cities, investors are often banking on capital appreciation.

The 1% Rule works better in lower-cost areas of the country, where cap rates are higher and price appreciation is slower. However, even in places like the heartland, it's hard to find properties trading at only 100X monthly rent anymore.

Online you will see the tax records and sales histories of comparable properties. You need to compare your target property's asking price with previous sales and consider what has changed in the interim to make sure you are getting a good deal.

THE FINANCIAL SAMURAI WAY

- Real estate acts like career insurance for you and your children in a competitive world of unequal opportunity. Its real value may be more than just its income or potential selling price—it may be the emotional security of knowing you control your own destiny.

- Invest in trends. Specifically, invest in the heartland and the South. Postpandemic, there's no going back to the way things were.

- If you insist on buying a vacation property for lifestyle purposes, spend no more than 10% of your net worth on the purchase price. A vacation property is generally not a wise financial decision. It is a lifestyle decision.

- Build your physical rental property portfolio while you're in your twenties and thirties, or while you still are relatively energetic and unencumbered. Once you find the optimal number of rental properties you can manage, invest the rest of your capital allocated to real estate in online real estate opportunities that are completely passive.

- Always crunch the numbers and estimate various scenarios before making an offer.

PART THREE

Work While Maximizing Your Wealth

Your career will likely be your number one moneymaker for the first part of your financial journey. I'll show you where to look for high-paying jobs and how to get promoted faster than your average officemate. You'll also learn how to strategize a lucrative exit from your job that will keep the money rolling in long after you've left your post.

Finally, you'll see how a side hustle can be your secret weapon for achieving financial freedom sooner rather than later. In an increasingly permissionless society, you'll learn about the importance of establishing a brand outside your day job to increase your chances of success.

Chapter 10

Think Strategically About Your Career

Your career is your number one wealth generator—at least in your younger years. It will be your main source of cash that you'll leverage into investments, which will bring you more cash and eventually financial freedom. Please don't mess it up.

You can't reach financial independence if you don't earn enough money today to aggressively save and invest. I hear from so many folks who struggle with this. The truth is, you probably have the power to earn a higher salary than you realize. Your first step is to land a job with great pay—and I'll show you how to do that in this chapter. Then work strategically so that you get promoted often—you'll learn how to do that in the next chapter.

Ideally, you want to choose a profession you love that also pays you a lot of money. But if you can't do what you love, at least do something that pays well. If you want to achieve financial independence sooner, be practical with your career choice. You can always do what you love outside of work or when you no longer need to work.

Sure, you may have to endure more stress and longer hours than the average person. But in return, you should get paid more than the average person as well. France's thirty-five-hour workweek sounds nice. So does America's forty-hour workweek. However, if your goal is to reach financial freedom sooner, be prepared to work more hours than the average person.

Spend the first twenty years of your career building as strong a financial foundation as possible. If you do, by the time you're in your forties, you will have plenty more options with your career and, ultimately, your life.

Life is both long and short. Focus on maximizing your earnings when you have the most energy and are the least encumbered. When you are older, you will be glad you did.

Be Strategic in Your Job Search

I understand that many people reading this are already deep into their career and industry. If you're in a low-paying industry and have the time and desire to switch, *do it*. If leaving is not an option for whatever reason, it's time to think side hustle, and you can jump to chapter 12.

The advice in this chapter is for anyone early- or midcareer, and for folks looking to offer support and guidance to their kids or mentees.

If you're in college or just starting your career, you're in the best position of all. Target jobs in a lucrative industry and work your ass off to get really good at something. While working, build a vast network of supporters who want to bring you up with them. If you're still in school or willing and able to go to graduate school, choose courses that will make you qualified to work in high-paying industries. Then work your ass off some more.

Focus on the industries that often pay six figures straight out of school. Those include venture capital, investment banking, management/strategic consulting, high tech, and internet. Apply to the top companies in each field.

Here is a list of some of the top-paying companies by industry as of this writing. Most of these firms will pay you a healthy six-figure salary within five years of joining, if not immediately.

Venture capital: Sequoia, Benchmark, Accel, Draper Fisher Jurvetson, Kleiner Perkins.

Investment banking: Goldman Sachs, Morgan Stanley, J.P. Morgan, Barclays, Bank of America and BofA Securities.

Private equity: The Blackstone Group, KKR, Warburg Pincus, The Carlyle Group, TPG Capital, Neuberger Berman Group, Thoma Bravo, GI Partners, Silver Lake Partners.

Strategic consulting: Bain, BCG, McKinsey, Monitor, Arthur D. Little, Booz Allen Hamilton, Oliver Wyman, Kearney.

Software: Microsoft, Adobe, ServiceNow, Dropbox, IFS, Guidewire, Cornerstone, Secureworks, Vertafore, Procore, Asana, Autodesk, Intuit, Salesforce, Qualtrics, Twilio, Atlassian, VMware, Shopify.

Tech hardware: Apple, Samsung Electronics, Hon Hai Precision, Dell Technologies, Cisco Systems.

Internet: Google, Facebook, Netflix, eBay, PayPal, Airbnb, Quora, Uber, Pinterest.

IT consulting/accounting: KPMG, Deloitte, Ernst & Young, PricewaterhouseCoopers (PwC).

Oil, mining, commodities trading: Vitol, BHP, Glencore, Cargill, Koch Industries, Trafigura, Archer-Daniels-Midland, Gunvor Group, Noble Group, Bunge, Phibro.

Computer and movie animation: Pixar (*Toy Story*), Weta Digital (*The Lord of the Rings*), Blizzard Entertainment (*World of Warcraft*).

Real estate investment trusts: Vornado Realty Trust, Equinix, Simon Property Group, American Tower Corporation, Brookfield Asset Management.

Real estate tech: Fundrise, Opendoor, Cadre, Zillow, Redfin.

Financial tech: Stripe, Personal Capital, Affirm, Klarna, Chime.

Here is a look at high-income opportunities by industry and occupation.

Engineering: Mechanical engineers, electrical engineers, software engineers, structural engineers.

Health care: Doctors, hospital administrators, specialists, nurse practitioners, physician assistants.

Big government: Reach any top tier position in the federal or state government, and you will make six figures a year along with a nice pension. There are more than 400,000 federal employees making over $100,000 a year.

Government contracting: *MarketWatch* reported that the average total compensation for a navy, army, and air force contractor is about $180,000, according to a 2016 report by the Defense Business Board. Today the average total compensation is even higher.

Education: Principals, head coaches, professors. The average salary for an elementary school principal in the U.S. is $110,000.

And if higher education is not for you, there are many careers that pay very well and do not require a college degree to get started. You just need to have the desire, motivation, work ethic, and perseverance to get there. They include:

Law enforcement and firefighting: Police officers and firefighters with a couple of decades' worth of experience regularly earn over six figures a year. Add on their well-deserved lifelong pensions, and you've got a recipe for financial success.

Real estate: There are plenty of real estate agents who make six figures a year. With commissions staying stubbornly high at 5%, sell $3+ million worth of real estate a year to earn six figures (part of your commissions go to the brokerage firm).

Public-sector jobs with pensions: As interest rates have declined, the value of a lifetime pension has gone way up. For example, to generate a guaranteed income of $50,000 a year might have required $1 million back in 2000. Today you'd likely need close to $2 million to reliably generate $50,000 a year.

On the next page is a chart that illustrates the immense value that pensions can bring.

A common practice for pension owners is to find another career after retirement. If you do this, you'll get double the income, since a pension pays out regardless of what you do postretirement.

My friend who is a union electrician makes $170,000 a year. He will also get a pension of $5,000 a month when he retires at fifty-five in five years. What's more, he isn't allowed to work more than thirty-five hours a week. Let's not forget the $35,000 a year he makes doing side jobs with all that free time. Not too shabby.

High-paying jobs can be more attainable than they sometimes seem. If you're just starting out, or guiding a young adult as they navigate career choices, think beyond the stereotypical high-paying industries. The same goes for if you're looking to optimize a career you've already started. Six-figure incomes can be found across a huge range of industries. You just need to know where to look. And then work like crazy to gain the skills, network, or do whatever else you may need to do to land those jobs.

THE VALUE OF YOUR PENSION UNTIL YOU DIE

Annual Pension	Reasonable Rate of Return	Probability of Payout	Value of Pension
$35,000	1.0%	75%	$2,625,000
$35,000	1.5%	75%	$1,750,000
$35,000	2.0%	75%	$1,312,500
$35,000	2.5%	75%	$1,050,000
$35,000	3.0%	75%	$875,000
$35,000	3.5%	75%	$750,000
$35,000	4.0%	75%	$656,250
$35,000	4.5%	75%	$583,333
$35,000	5.0%	75%	$525,000
$35,000	5.5%	70%	$445,455
$35,000	6.0%	70%	$408,333
$50,000	1.0%	70%	$3,500,000
$50,000	1.5%	70%	$2,333,333
$50,000	2.0%	70%	$1,750,000
$50,000	2.5%	70%	$1,400,000
$50,000	3.0%	70%	$1,166,667
$50,000	3.5%	70%	$1,000,000
$50,000	4.0%	70%	$875,000
$50,000	4.5%	70%	$777,778
$50,000	5.0%	70%	$700,000
$50,000	5.5%	70%	$636,364
$50,000	6.0%	70%	$583,333

Value of pension = (annual pension amount ÷ reasonable rate of return) × probability of payout

Once you die, the value of your pension goes to zero because it is usually not transferrable.

Source: FinancialSamurai.com

IF YOU CAN'T WORK FOR THEM, MAKE THEM WORK FOR YOU

Higher-paying jobs tend to attract the most candidates. Therefore, landing one of these jobs will be extremely competitive. You've just got to keep on networking and applying, because landing a job is often a numbers game. If you have a 1% chance of getting an interview, then you need to apply to about a hundred jobs to get that interview. And if you have only a 25% chance of getting the job after interviewing, then you need to land at least four interviews.

But let's say you get rejected by everyone, as I did in 2011 and 2012 when I was considering a new career in tech. Then what do you do?

If no publicly traded company gives you a chance, then simply buy shares in the company. Turn the tables, make them work for you, and earn a nice return.

The shares I purchased in 2011 and 2012 in Apple, Google, Netflix, Tesla, and Facebook have all done well. The positions have now grown large enough that I no longer feel bad ordering fries with my $1 double cheeseburger at McDonald's. Thanks for working so hard, folks!

As a Financial Samurai, always try to see the positive potential in a suboptimal situation.

Follow Your Passion or Follow the Money?

When I was a kid, I wanted to be a professional tennis player. But my topspin backhand and serve were not good enough to compete. Therefore, I decided to focus on maximizing my earnings in the finance industry and play USTA League tennis outside of work.

At least once a month, I'd play a competitive match and pretend I was on the circuit. Off the court, I would work on my shots, eat healthier, and stretch more. Win or lose, I usually had a fantastic time pursuing my passion for tennis. I went from a 4.0-level player to a 5.0-level player in six years. Suddenly, I was playing against the D-I college tennis players I would watch while in school. The progress was thrilling.

But I realized that if I had to make a living from tennis, I would come to hate the sport. There are four Grand Slam championships a year, the pinnacle tournaments of tennis. They are located in Melbourne, Paris, London, and New York City. In order to be invited to qualify for the main draw, you need to be ranked in the top 250 in the world, unless you get a wild card. From the flight expenses to the lodging costs to the lifestyle changes required to have even a 0.1% chance of making the pros, I knew that the time, money, and happiness costs weren't worth it.

If you are good enough at your passion to compete at the highest level, give it a go so that at least you can say that you tried. The same goes for starting a business with your brilliant idea. Give your passion a good three years to see if you can make a sustainable living out of it. After three years of grinding away, if you're not gaining traction, it's time to move on and find a job that pays.

Join a Sexy Start-up or Work for an Established Organization?

There's a chance you'll run into an opportunity to work for a start-up on your hunt for that great-paying job. Should you go for it? Probably not, if you want to make the most money. Probably so, if you want to gain the most responsibility and learn.

One of the main misconceptions in Silicon Valley is that joining a start-up will guarantee you riches beyond your wildest dreams.

The truth? Joining a start-up will more likely make you poorer than richer. Those sexy start-up stories are just not reality for the vast majority of entrepreneurs and early joiners. The disproportionate amount of media attention is focused on the winners, with the losers swept under the rug, never to be heard from again.

The way start-up culture works is that, in exchange for lots of hard work, you are paid *below* market salary and stock options that you hope will become winning lottery tickets when the company is acquired or goes public (the salary discount is often in the 30% to 50% range in return for options). There is a long road to walk before you find your gold. And even if you stick around for the long run, you may end up finding only a leprechaun.

Most venture capitalists say they count on one out of ten of their investments being a home run to make up for their five to seven busts. The other three or four companies in their portfolio just tread water, neither making nor losing money. They call these "dead-pools" or "zombie companies."

Therefore, even with all of the due diligence you put into evaluating a potential employer, your chance of striking gold through your stock options may be about 10%. Meanwhile, your chance of getting paid a salary below market rate is almost 100%.

Let's say it takes on average five years for you to realize your liquidity-event riches. Here is an example to demonstrate the difference between working at a start-up and working for an established company:

Work for Start-up X

Title: head of sales

Salary: $120,000

Age: 31

Options: $200,000

Benefits: health, dental, no 401(k) match because the start-up is losing money

Work for Procter & Gamble

Title: head of marketing for some body wash

Salary: $250,000

Stock grants: $50,000 a year

Age: 31

Benefits: 401(k), 401(k) matching, dental, health

In five years, joining the start-up will have made you poorer. The start-up employee will have earned $600,000 in salary and $200,000 in options for a total value of $800,000. Over the same time period, the Procter & Gamble employee will have earned $1.25 million in salary and $250,000 in stock grants for a total value of $1.5 million. The monetary difference is $700,000, assuming that the start-up is still alive in five years but treading water and not really growing. Probability: 50%.

Let's say the start-up goes bust after five years. In this case, the start-up person has earned $600,000 in total compensation because his $200,000 in options are now worthless. The person at P&G now has made $900,000 ($1,500,000 to $600,000) more in five years, assuming P&G stock hasn't grown. Probability: 40%.

Finally, let's say the start-up is a raging success and grows by 5X in five years. You managed to be one of the top fifteen employees and saw your options grow by 5X as well. Your options are now worth about $1 million, ignoring dilution. Therefore, the total value of your compensation is $1.6 million ($1,000,000 + $600,000). In this scenario, you are finally ahead by $100,000, assuming no dilution and no growth of P&G stock. Probability: 10%.

Now let's calculate the outcome for the start-up employee in terms of expected value:

$800,000 × 50% = $400,000 (zombie company)

$600,000 × 40% = $240,000 (goes bust)

$1,600,000 × 10% = $160,000 (win the lottery)

Your expected value is $800,000 (calculated by adding up the above) versus $1.5 million going the P&G route. The difference is $700,000 in just five years. Of course, if your start-up grows by more than 5X in five years, you will have made the right choice going the start-up route. However, the chances of winning the lottery like that are slim.

So as a start-up seeker, you have to ask yourself:

1. Is the pay cut over five years worth it?
2. How will I feel after dedicating twelve-hour days at below market rate, only to see my company fail?
3. Will my résumé be tainted if I work for a failed start-up, or will it be enhanced?
4. Will I regret not having taken the risk if the start-up becomes a huge success?
5. Do I love the culture of the firm?
6. Can I gut it out for long enough to see the financial reward?

There are many possible scenarios that could play out. You are free to play around with the probabilities. Just be realistic with your expectations. If the top venture capitalists can't consistently pick winners more than 10% of the time, you probably can't either.

Now, you may be thinking, "Sam, what about an acquisition (as opposed to an IPO)? Couldn't that produce some returns?" Here's my response to that scenario. When a start-up does get acquired, it is the founder or founders who usually walk away with something meaningful. Sizable payouts typically aren't going to the employees beyond the first 10% who joined. It's simply the way the economics work.

But if, even after reading this, you can't resist the chance of finding a start-up pot of gold, you must do the following:

- **Ask what percentage of the company you will own after receiving your equity offer.** Don't just accept a random share count and be happy. Specifically, ask about your ownership percentage. Do the math on what your percentage ownership is worth and what you think you can do to grow the company's overall value. A 0.1% ownership in Facebook is massive. However, a 0.1% ownership of a $1 billion company is still only $1 million before tax and equity dilution. And not many companies ever get to a $1 billion valuation.
- **Pretend you are an investor and do the math regarding how much the start-up could realistically sell for and to whom.** The best measure is comparable companies that sold. Now take your equity stake and multiply it by the potential sales price. This is your maximum take because you may be diluted over time due to new investors.

- **Ask for much more than you are being offered.** Remember, most start-ups fail or go nowhere. Therefore, it's best you fight for a higher salary in addition to more equity.
- **Join as a cofounder for more aligned risk and reward.** Or join at the **series C or later stage**, when you can command a higher salary and have a much higher chance of a successful liquidity event.

The 70/30 move is to join an established company right after graduation that will pay you the greatest amount of money possible over the next ten or so years. Once you have a solid foundation and plenty of experience, then you can consider joining a start-up in a more senior role if you still want to. If the start-up is successful, your increased equity will be that much more meaningful.

Further, once you're in your thirties, more people will naturally take you more seriously. With more confidence, more knowledge, more work experience, and a bigger bank account, chances are higher you will make a more informed decision.

If you so happen to join the wrong start-up, then make sure you learn as much as possible to prepare yourself for the next opportunity. Remember: **if you're not earning, you had better be learning**.

The most important thing we can do is assess our situation honestly and enjoy the journey. If we work our hardest, then we'll be more content with whatever the outcome. But boy, the allure of potentially winning the lottery sure is hard to deny!

Take Cash (Salary) or Take Equity?

I just touched on the challenges inherent in an equity offer, but let's take a closer look in case you're ever faced with this decision when joining a company. Your optimal choice will depend a lot on the company itself. In most cases a cash/equity split will tilt more toward the cash side. But some companies may give you the option of more equity over cash. What to do?

To decide between more equity and more cash, if you have the option, here are some things you need to consider.

1. **Make an honest assessment of your cash-flow needs.** Calculate an income level that covers all your basic needs at the very least. Living paycheck to paycheck is stressful and will hurt your quality of life. But you might also be inspired to work harder if you don't have anything to spare.

2. **How strongly do you believe in management?** Does the C-level team have relevant industry experience with a long track record of successful execution? Or are they recent college graduates who have a great idea but no experience executing a vision? Management can be young and inexperienced, but they better have someone who's experienced to guide them through the land mines.

3. **How big is the market opportunity?** Every start-up sees a huge market opportunity; otherwise it wouldn't launch its business in the first place. The better question is, what is the *real* market opportunity? Overestimating the potential customer base is an egregious error that will severely affect the business model.

4. **How much income and net worth are enough to make you feel satisfied?** I understand it's hard to know until you get there, but you've got to make some assumptions.

5. **Do the venture capitalists have some preferential clause?** In case of a liquidity event, some VCs stipulate a 2X or greater minimum return before shareholders get paid. That can result in a much lower return (60% rather than 100%, in some cases) for employees. Ask your potential employer for any details.

6. **What is the cliff and vesting schedule?** A one-year cliff means that you must work at the company for one year before getting your first year's options. If you get fired or leave a day before the one-year cliff, you get nothing. With a four-year vesting schedule, your 40,000 options are granted over four years at 10,000 a year. Most companies vest every month after the initial one-year cliff.

7. **How many shares are there outstanding?** 40,000 shares sounds nice, but if there are 1 billion shares outstanding, 40,000 is just 0.004%. How much equity you receive depends upon when you start at the company and your negotiation skills.

8. **What is the current value of each option?** There are a couple of values to consider: the value as reported to the IRS for regulatory purposes and the value management believes the company is worth to outside investors. Choose the conservative route because valuations aren't real until a company gets acquired or goes public.

9. **What happens to your options if the company gets acquired?** Let's say you're one year in and the company gets acquired. Do your options immediately vest, or do you lose the remaining three years of a four-year vest? Everything is negotiable. If the acquiring company wants you to stay, they'll do whatever it takes to make you whole or perhaps give you more incentive to stay.

10. **What is the ultimate monetary goal of the company?** Is senior management planning on selling to a bigger fish while private, or going the IPO route? Figure out the

grand vision by speaking to management and asking about the time frame to get there.

At the end of the day, if you've decided to join a start-up, your primary goal should be to make as much money as possible while also learning as much as possible. Ideally you've done your due diligence and you're aware of the track records of the various venture capitalists and investors. Therefore, the 70/30 decision is to try to get as much equity as possible versus cash. Getting more equity is consistent with your belief that the company has tremendous upside and that you want to own more of it.

The extra below-market-rate cash compensation likely won't change your life if there is a liquidity event. However, the extra stock compensation may. If the start-up fails, at least you learned a lot and gained a bunch of experience for your next opportunity.

Job Hop or Remain a Loyal Soldier?

Company loyalty is overrated in this day and age. Long gone are the days of pensions and opportunities to work at one company for life. Being loyal is, sadly, now a 30/70 move. Instead, for maximum financial gain, **you should job hop every two to five years during your twenties and thirties.**

When I left Goldman Sachs after two years to join Credit Suisse, it wasn't by choice. I knew my third-year-analyst position was not getting renewed, so I had to find another opportunity. However, because I ended up staying at Credit Suisse for eleven years, I likely gave up well over $1 million in lost income. I know this because two years before I ultimately left, I received a two-year guaranteed offer from a competing bank in New York City for much more.

The reality was that I was damn tired of the industry. More money wasn't going to make me happy. Nor was leaving my friends behind in San Francisco to return to New York City. So I turned it down. I don't regret my decision to stay, but the fact remains that I made a lot less money by being a loyal soldier.

It's sad that loyalty is often rewarded with below-market pay. I call this the loyalty discount. Companies are not incentivized to keep up with market pay. Instead, they are incentivized to pay you as little money as possible, hoping you won't notice or until you threaten to quit. As a result, it is up to you to sell yourself internally if you think you are underpaid.

The late, great John Wooden of UCLA basketball fame never made more than $36,000 a year during his time coaching the UCLA Bruins from 1948 to 1975. When Wooden started coaching the Bruins in 1948, he made $6,000, equivalent to about $60,000 when adjusted for inflation. In Wooden's final year, the 1975 season when he won his tenth NCAA title, he made $40,500, or roughly $185,000 adjusted for inflation. Not bad, but Wooden could have made so much more had he entertained offers from other teams.

Nick Saban, on the other hand, coached football at Toledo and Michigan State before joining LSU in 2000. After great success at LSU, he bolted for the Miami Dolphins in 2005. Miami offered him five years and $22.5 million. After two years of a mediocre record with the Dolphins, Saban entertained an offer from the University of Alabama that paid him $32 million over eight years. Then in 2021, after winning six national championships, Saban negotiated another eight-year contract worth at least $84.8 million.

In other words, if you are any good, it pays to job hop for more money.* Job-hopping also resets an employer's vision of you, which may be helpful if you started at the bottom. To some employers, you'll always be the inexperienced newbie, no matter how well you perform. It's similar to your parents still treating you as a child even though you're a middle-aged adult.

And if you are really good and comfortable with where you are, it pays to negotiate as much money as possible from your existing employer, as Nick Saban did. Once you've proved that you can consistently deliver the goods, your employer would be foolish not to pay you top dollar. When an employer loses a valuable employee, there is often three to six months' worth of lost productivity.

If you're good, don't bother sticking around if your employer doesn't offer a pension and isn't willing to pay you market rate. Get paid what you are worth.

Further, firms have proved in this volatile and hypercompetitive business environment that they will fire and lay off employees to cut costs and appease shareholders. Being a fifteen-year veteran used to mean something. Now it just means you may be too expensive and not as hungry as you once were.

We have a responsibility to be loyal to the firm that provides for us. But we have a bigger responsibility to be loyal to ourselves and to our family. If a firm is underpaying or mistreating you, speak up. It is literally taking away opportunities from you and the people you love the most.

If you plan to stay at your firm long-term, you should speak up about your compensation at least every two years. In your year-end review, it's up to you to remind your manager of all the great things you've done for the company. Make sure to highlight your first-half wins as well. It's very easy for people to forget.

---

* In 2021, Coach Lincoln Riley left Oklahoma after only five years, getting a massive ~$110 million package to join USC. And Coach Brian Kelly left Notre Dame for LSU for a ten-year deal worth $95 million plus incentives.

It really is great to be happy with what you have. Just don't leave too much money on the table. Ultimately, by underpaying you, your employer is robbing you of your time.

It's Good to Be Career Selfish

As I mentioned earlier, and this is worth repeating, the 70/30 move is to job hop every two to five years in your twenties and thirties. Make sure that each job hop resets your pay and title at least one notch higher. By the time you hit your forties, you will have consistently made the most money the market could bear.

For those of you who are super ambitious, it's worth working hard to see how far you can go in your career. Be willing to relocate wherever the best job opportunity is while you're still young and unencumbered.

If you get to a multiple-six-figure income level, shoot to last for at least ten years while saving 50% or more of your after-tax income. Eventually you'll accumulate a large enough financial nest egg that you can do whatever your heart desires.

Not a day goes by that I'm not thankful for having worked brutal hours in my twenties and early thirties.

Being free is absolutely priceless. Do not get distracted by the YOLO crowd who are desperately trying to show off their fabulous lives in order to justify why they aren't willing to work as hard.

THE FINANCIAL SAMURAI WAY

- Be strategic in your field of study and in your job search. If you want to make more money, focus on industries that pay the most.

- Do not underestimate public-sector jobs or any job that offers a pension. In a low-interest-rate environment, the value of a pension increases. After twenty years, employees with pensions often retire early and find a new job. This way, they get to earn double income.

- In your twenties, you can join a start-up to learn, but you likely won't earn much. Once you're in your thirties, you can really start making a healthy income at a start-up with all the knowledge and skills you've acquired.

- If you do join a start-up, try to get as much equity as possible. More equity is consistent with your bet that the start-up is going to be a winner. Getting more cash won't make as much of a difference.

- If your company refuses to pay you market rate after you perform well, you should leave. Your goal is to maximize your income during your career and save the world after hours or once your career is over. You and your family come first, not your employer.

Chapter 11

Make Your Money and Then Make Your Exit

As a financial freedom seeker, there's a high chance you don't want to stay at your job forever.

Even if that's not the case, even if you love your job and want to stay for decades, it's smart to have a career strategy that will keep you earning a top salary in your industry.

Here's the thing: being a great worker simply isn't enough. Too many people make the mistake of thinking that if they do a good job, they'll eventually get promoted and paid what they're worth. Unfortunately, that's just not how it works in most companies. Meritocracy is a lost art.

Your strategy should focus on two goals: to do your job extremely well and to become well-liked. And to achieve both, you first need to understand your place in the company.

In your twenties, you're an expendable cost center to your employer. You don't know anything and you're spending most of your time learning. Just having you around may cost the company more than you're bringing in. Therefore, focus on minimizing your company's costs as much as possible. That entails getting in every day before your boss and leaving after them, asking what more you can do, and adding value in whatever way you possibly can.

There is no excuse for *not* working extra hours in your twenties. Forget about work-life balance when you're that young. This is your time to work long hours, learn as much as possible, and become indispensable. Figure out how to differentiate yourself. Hustle to become so good at what you do that losing you will bring your manager a great deal of pain. It may take six months to hire your replacement and three months to get that person to the level at which you were operating. Become so good that the company can't afford to lose you.

Don't let someone outwork you. If someone else is consistently working ten hours a week more than you, over the course of a year, that's an extra 520 hours. Now, if someone is also smart and is well-liked while also working longer hours than you, then your chances of getting ahead are slim to none.

The payoff of doing incredible work and building relationships is twofold. Not only will it help you get paid and promoted during your career, but it will also help you end your career with a dollop of whipped cream and a cherry on top when you leverage your value into a hefty severance package.

The Art of Getting Paid and Promoted Faster

Most companies are consensus driven in terms of who gets paid and promoted. Becoming invaluable and well-liked is essential to getting ahead. You cannot be passive in your job.

Many people I know (myself included) hate self-promotion. We'd like to believe our good work alone will rightfully get us to the promised land, but it's just not true when many people are involved. Excellent work is essential, but you also need a balanced strategy of *actively selling yourself.*

Balanced means selling yourself 50% externally and 50% internally. The more valuable you become to your customers (selling yourself externally), the more valuable you become to your firm.

If you don't have a revenue-generating role, then it's even more important not only to do your work well but to spend at least 50% of your time becoming the most well-known, helpful, and likable person in your department (selling yourself internally). Most of what follows pertains to this internal salesmanship.

Tooting your own horn is a very delicate process that can easily backfire. You know that person who always sends out blast emails to tell everyone what they've done? Don't do that. Instead, work on building relationships throughout your company. Here's how.

1. **Treat your bosses and your colleagues as clients.** This will lead to organic self-promotion. Think about it: Your clients are your moneymakers. They give you business and promote you to others if they love working with you. You treat your clients with respect. You figure out ways to make your clients like you and keep coming back to you for more help because they see you as a valuable asset in their business.

    If you approach your bosses and colleagues with this mindset, you'll have a similar outcome as you would with a client: they'll keep bringing you business; they'll want to keep working with you; and they'll promote you to others at every opportunity. But if you treat your boss and colleagues like competitors, the exact opposite will occur.

    When you treat your coworkers like clients, you're creating a symbiotic relationship instead of an adversarial one. And that can be rare—especially in cutthroat industries. I understand it's hard to be an ally when everyone is competing for one promotion, but you've got to be the better person. You can't stab people in the back. Hold yourself to a higher standard and treat every single colleague—even your competitors—like a client.

    Once you've built your support network, getting paid and promoted is an inevitability because everybody in the company will be cheering for your success.

    Even if someone doesn't like you, they won't be able to speak out against you for fear of retribution from all those who do like you. The naysayer will look like the jealous colleague, and nobody wants that. Never underestimate peer pressure and politics when it comes to promotion!

2. **Promote your boss first.** Folks rarely think about how they can support their boss. They see their boss as someone who is there to support and mentor them and forget that the need goes both ways. After all, your boss is likely under more stress and also wants to get paid and promoted.

    A hugely effective strategy for building an internal support system is to promote your boss to other people—especially to their bosses. Give them credit. Eventually they'll appreciate it and bring you along with them. Every boss is also trying to succeed. They have their own insecurities and are trying to climb the ladder. The more you can promote your boss, the better your chance will be of getting ahead.

3. **Why talk to the ass when you can talk to the head?** Whether your goal is simply ensuring your survival or boosting your career to light speed, you must develop relationships at the very top of your organization. When you've got the ear of your boss's boss, you are golden.

For the first two years at my previous job, I studied my department's organization chart and made a point of developing relationships with all senior leaders (head of equities, head of prime brokerage, head of derivatives, head of sales, head of research, etc.).

I shot every single one of them an email to invite them for a drink or lunch (on me) to hear about their roles and responsibilities. I wanted to see how I could help them do their jobs better. Nobody turned me down because nobody turns down a free lunch from someone who just wants to listen and help out where he can. If buying lunch for someone is not practical for you, invite them to coffee.

During my first year at Goldman Sachs, the other analysts and I asked Michael Mortara, one of the founders of the mortgage-backed securities market and president of GS Ventures, to breakfast. It was an amazing experience that taught me an important lesson: no wall existed between the peons of the organization and the elites who took helicopters in to work from their homes in Connecticut.

The people at the top are just like us. And they are just like you. Do not be afraid. Develop direct senior relationships.

4. **If your boss speaks Korean, you too shall speak Korean.** This is where brownnosing comes into play. You should try to like what your boss likes, without making it seem forced. If you know that your boss grew up in Korea, has a Korean wife, loves soccer, and went to Ohio State University, you better learn all you can about Korean culture, the World Cup, and Buckeyes football.

If you are caught making fun of Korean culture, calling soccer a boring sport, or rooting for the Michigan Wolverines, your career just imploded.

Brownnosing is perhaps the hardest thing to do well in the workplace. If you are a poor brownnoser, it becomes blatantly obvious what you are doing. My recommendation is to work on defense first, i.e., learn everything *not* to do.

Be careful not to say or do things that are insulting to your boss's sensibilities. If you know he's a hard-core Republican, then telling him you're going to a Democratic fundraiser is unwise. If you cannot assimilate, at the very least don't overtly run counter to all your boss's views.

Once you've mastered defense, you can slowly roll out offensive brownnosing one element at a time. He loves the San Francisco Giants? Well, so do you, as you memorize the entire lineup and come up with pitching rotations.

His favorite charity is Save the Whales? What a coincidence! You are a regular Marine Animal Rescue donor! Her favorite TV show is *Breaking Bad*? Funny, because you've memorized all of the classic Walter White lines ("I am not in danger, Skyler. I am the danger!"). In short, your goal is to build commonality.

5. **Treat your junior colleagues with respect.** Finally, the greatest test of character is how you treat people who have no leverage or influence over you. If you've been lucky enough to ascend, become a mentor to any and all junior employees who seek your help. Remember, one day your junior employees might become senior employees, and they will never forget the people who helped them along the way.

Ultimately, getting ahead at work takes building a network of supporters. Managers simply want to promote people they trust and like.

Go Back to Work or Become a Stay-at-Home Parent?

Big salaries and fancy promotions require so much time and effort. If only we were doing it all in a vacuum. The reality is that life happens at the same time, and when big life and work choices collide, the 70/30 move can feel impossible to identify.

One of the most stressful choices for parents is whether or not to go back to work after having a baby. Once you have a child, should you continue to be all in on your career, or—if you have the option—should you or your partner stay home to care for your child full time? It's a legitimate dilemma, because the reality is that it's extremely difficult to be a great parent *and* a great employee or entrepreneur at the same time. Something often has to give.

Remember, we're talking about *optimal* choices here, and there's a lot to consider when it comes to career and family. Ultimately, the decisions you make will be about creating a life where you, your partner (if you have one), your kid(s), and your career can thrive within the best possible scenario for your circumstances.

So let's consider you and your partner first. Before I became a father, I suspected I couldn't become a great dad if I continued to work sixty-plus hours a week in investment banking. I spoke to plenty of colleagues who worked these hours, and they all lamented never having enough time to spend with their children and the toll that it had taken on them personally.

Many parents, especially working mothers, told me they felt a tremendous amount of guilt being at the office all day. When I asked why not take a break from work, they usually said *they couldn't afford to quit the money*. They also feared if they walked away, they'd miss out on critical promotions.

Guilt is mentally draining and can really weigh you down if left unchecked. It's important not to overlook your mental health if you're feeling overwhelmed. So step one is to keep your happiness and well-being at the forefront of your decision. If you and/or your partner design a life around making the highest possible salary, then you must be okay with not spending as much time with your family as you'd like. It's very difficult to have it both ways. You might reason that by making more money up front, you can spend more time with your children later on.

Now let's consider the potentially optimal scenario for your kid(s): being able to spend as much time as possible with their parents before going to preschool or kindergarten. This is not my attempt to tell you how to be a great parent. Because unlike work, parenting is *very subjective*. There are no title or pay increases, only endless care you must provide in hopes that your child enjoys their youth, learns new things, and grows up to be a good person.

But we should be able to agree that the more time we spend with our children, the higher the likelihood that we may *become* better parents, all else being equal.

And the more we spend time with our children, the higher the chances that they will love us and turn out to be good citizens.

OVERCOMING GUILT BY SPENDING MORE TIME THAN AVERAGE

How much time is enough to feel like a good parent? To answer this question, we must look at the average amount of time parents spend with their children a day. In America, the average amount of time university-educated moms spend with their children is 120 minutes a day. The number falls to just 85 minutes a day for university-educated dads. For parents without a university education, the time spent drops by roughly 20% each.

If you want to at least feel like you're doing a better parenting job than average, spend more than these average amounts of time a day with your children.

But What About the Money?

Despite the desire to spend more time with your children, there's still your career—and your goals for financial freedom—to consider. Again, something often has to give. If we want more quality time with our kids but we also want to make great money so we can have financial freedom sooner rather than later, how can we achieve both—or either one, frankly—without forfeiting our well-being along the way?

For years, I thought the best solution was to forsake my career and go all in on being a father. This is one of the reasons my wife and I waited so long before deciding to have kids. We felt we needed to save way more money than we had been because I was never going back to work. I now regret having waited so long. What I now realize is that if you want to prioritize your family when you become a parent and still make a good income, it doesn't have to be an all-or-nothing proposition. This is especially the case today, when many employers are offering more flexibility.

So as a first line of action, if you feel stuck choosing between work and family, especially as a parent to young children, you must capitalize on society's postpandemic movement toward more flexible employment. If you feel you absolutely can't leave your job for a few years after having a child, challenge your employer to offer some compromises. Even if you're working all day and need childcare, working from home at least part of the week will cut your commuting time. That's time you can put into family and into your personal well-being.

But even the most flexible job won't solve the career-or-family dilemma. You cannot work well, even if you're working from home, and raise your kids yourself. We must learn to let go of trying to be great at everything, at least temporarily.

The 70/30 Parenting/Work Combination

If you are willing and able to take time away from your career to care for your kid(s) full time, the optimal scenario is to have one working partner to ensure financial security and one full-time parent to ensure maximum childcare.

If the full-time parent can be a full-time parent for two to three years, until the child attends preschool, this combination may be ideal for the child and the full-time parent's career. In such a scenario, the child gets the maximum amount of care from that parent during the most important years of development. Parental guilt is minimized as a result.

Meanwhile, two to three years away from work is not long enough to derail a career you will ultimately return to.

Ages two to three are when most full-time preschool programs start. Once your kids are in school, you no longer have to spend all day with them. Now that you only have to drop them off and pick them up, it's easier to go back to work, especially in a more flexible work environment. And if your work schedule doesn't allow you to pick them up, perhaps a family member, friend, or sitter could. And if not, extended care until you can pick your child up is often available.

Of course, your child won't receive as much love and attention at preschool as when you were taking care of them at home. However, your child will learn important social skills and participate in new activities that would otherwise not be available at home. A great preschool is usually a place of joy and learning for a child.

Being out of the workforce for two to three years won't greatly impact your career in this more empathetic and flexible world. You should have little problem getting a similar type of job with similar pay should you wish to reenter the workforce. In fact, your future employer might look positively on your commitment to family in this age of constant job-hopping. Bosses who are also parents are keenly aware of your struggles. They tend to be more understanding when childcare issues come up. Therefore, strategically, you may want to work for someone who also has children.

Another potentially optimal scenario, if you and your partner have flexible jobs that you don't want to fully leave, is to work reduced hours or opposite schedules so you can trade off childcare responsibilities. This way, both of you are still plugged into the work environment while also being able to spend more time with your young children.

I wish someone had clearly explained to me this two- to three-year time frame during my most gung-ho career days. I would have been much more serious about trying to start a family when I was thirty-two, instead of trying at age thirty-six and thirty-seven, after I left work.

Given that you will love your children more than anything else in the world, you want them to be in your life for as long as possible as well. And if you can get your employer to provide subsidized health care and paid parental leave, as more employers are doing today, then you might actually feel like you are able to have it all, at least for a moment.

Take Advantage of Freelancing for More Flexibility

Finally, another powerful combination is for one partner to have a full-time job and one partner to freelance part time. Depending on your abilities, the opportunities to make equal (if not more) money freelancing are tremendous today.

For example, back in 2015, there was one point when I was freelancing as a marketing consultant for three fintech start-ups at the same time. I made $10,000 a month from each for a total of $30,000 a month. It was then that I realized how much more flexible and lucrative working as a freelancer could be. Unfortunately, I couldn't keep up the pace after three months and dropped two of the three clients.

If you have more than five years of work experience, you likely have the knowledge and skills to freelance for companies. Companies appreciate freelance work because they don't have to pay benefits or make long-term commitments. If you believe in your skills, you can make good money freelancing while also spending more time with your children.

At the end of the day, you must ask yourself, what will you regret missing out on more—career and money opportunities or your child's first years? There isn't one right answer here. But if it would make you happier to be home with your baby, I think it is worth it to at least try for some level of work flexibility during the first two or three years of your child's life. There will always be another dollar to make. Just be aware that being a full-time parent for the first two years may be the hardest job you'll ever do!

Quit Your Job or Strategize Your Layoff?

Please don't get fired or quit your job. Instead, get laid off. If you quit or get fired, you get no benefits. But if you get laid off, you may receive a severance, unemployment benefits, and more. A baby panda dies in the woods every time you quit your job or get fired. Negotiate a severance and leave on your own terms with money in your pocket.

One winter day in 2011, I got to talking with a friend who had been laid off right before getting his year-end bonus. He was pissed because our bonuses in banking usually accounted for 20% to 70% of our annual total compensation.

Despite missing out on what would have been at least a $100,000 bonus, he told me he got twenty-four weeks' worth of severance for the eight years he was at his firm. Given that he had a base salary of $160,000, his severance amounted to about $74,000.

I had heard of fellow employees and competitors getting severance packages multiple times before, especially during the depths of the global financial crisis. But this was the first time it clicked for me that negotiating a severance was my ticket out of banking.

In February 2012, I asked my boss if I could be let go with a severance and all my deferred compensation. In exchange, I would introduce my junior colleague, whom I had hired, to all my clients and ensure a smooth transition over a two-month period.

Surprised by my proposal, my boss told me he'd get back to me. After two weeks, he agreed because he had realized my heart was no longer in my job. Saving the department a six-figure salary plus benefits was attractive, since times were still uncertain. Further, an eleven-year employee successfully providing a smooth transition over several months was appealing. Usually employees provide two weeks' notice and head to a competitor. Instead, I told them I was leaving the industry altogether.

When all was said and done, my old firm put together a severance package that paid for between five and six years of my normal living expenses. Not only did I receive a nice lump-sum severance check, but I also got to keep all of my deferred stock and cash compensation, paid out on its normal schedule. Finally, I got to keep all the "toxic assets" employees were forced to buy in 2010. Those investments turned out to be home runs when they finally paid out five years after I had left my job in 2012.

With at least five years' worth of living expenses covered, I decided to travel extensively with my wife until she also negotiated a severance in 2015 at age thirty-four. During this time, I also got to work writing on *Financial Samurai* in the way that I wanted to, not because I needed to generate online income.

The Difference Between Getting Fired and Being Laid Off

There's a big difference between getting fired and getting laid off (also known as reduction in force, or RIF). Getting fired is almost always due to *cause*. Perhaps you sucker punched your boss or harassed a colleague. You don't want to get fired because it may leave a mark on your employment record. Nor should you quit your job if you don't have to.

There's also a significant difference between a person who gets laid off by surprise and someone who is able to negotiate a severance. If you can plan your layoff ahead of time, you can better dictate when you want to leave, how much severance you get, when to use your paid time off (which typically must be paid out as part of your severance, if unused), and what to do next. The key is to help your employer during the transition process and to be flexible.

The vast majority of workers quit their jobs when they want to start a new job, go back to school, or go all in on a side hustle. Most people don't think there's any other way. Perhaps people are simply too afraid of confrontation because they don't know how to approach the situation.

If you want to leave your job, try to get laid off with a severance package. Don't just quit and walk away with nothing. The longer a runway you can provide your bosses, the better. Finding a replacement employee could take months. And even after the replacement employee is on board, it will probably take them months more to hit their stride. During this time, energy is wasted on searching and training.

Therefore, if you want to negotiate a severance, you must have the emotional intelligence to consider how your departure negatively impacts your colleagues, your boss, and your firm.

One CEO of a public company told me he was irate at one of his executives for giving only two weeks' notice. If this executive had come to him about a succession plan, the CEO would have gladly approved a multimillion-dollar severance package.

In addition to getting severance, here are some of the main reasons why it's beneficial to exit the company via layoff.

1. **Getting laid off typically makes you eligible for government unemployment benefits.** Quitting your job or getting fired makes it much more difficult to collect unemployment benefits. The rationale is that if you quit your job, you don't need the money, so why should you get to collect unemployment benefits? Usually, a phone call with your state's unemployment department will be conducted about two weeks after you file your claim, to see whether unemployment benefits are justified (e.g., if you left because of unsafe working conditions).

2. **If you have deferred compensation in the form of stock or cash, you are eligible to receive these assets during the scheduled time table.** Let's say your firm pays a portion of your annual compensation in stock. Deferred stock compensation generally vests over a three- to four-year period. If you've been at your firm for at least three to four years, the deferred compensation starts really adding up and could equal a full year's salary or more. If you decide to quit your job, then you will likely receive none of the deferred compensation. However, if you get laid off, you have a much greater chance of receiving all your deferred compensation on its normal payout schedule.

3. **You can get all your unused vacation days paid.** The company should pay you for your unused vacation days if you quit, but there is no guarantee. One of my biggest mistakes during my severance negotiation process was taking five vacation days to go

to Hawaii a couple of months before I left. If I was smart, I would have used my sick days instead to take time off for a mental health break. Each unused vacation day, up to a limit, is worth one day's salary. Therefore, I missed out on receiving an extra five days of compensation.

4. **You will not receive a negative mark on your employment record.** Quitting your job shouldn't leave a negative mark on your employment record, only getting fired for cause. However, you just never know if you leave your employer on bad terms. It is much better to negotiate an amicable departure so that if a potential future employer calls up your old employer for a reference, chances are higher that your old employer will be supportive.

5. **You may get continued health-care coverage for the duration of your severance.** Legally, most companies must provide the option of COBRA coverage for eighteen months after separation. But this means the former employee has to pay the full premium at the employer-negotiated group rate. As part of your severance negotiation, ask your company to continue covering the cost of your health-care premium. My severance package included full 100% subsidized health care for six months.

   This is real money that shouldn't be taken lightly, since there's no guarantee that you'll succeed in whatever new thing you want to do. If you negotiate really well, your old employer might pay 100% of your health-care insurance for months.

Always Try to Negotiate a Severance If You Plan to Leave

Negotiating a severance requires courage, understanding of how the process works, and empathy for your boss's and colleagues' needs. The more you can understand your company's needs and the more flexible you can be to help achieve those needs, the more likely your employer will be willing to offer you a severance.

Even if you are a high-performing employee, as my wife was when she negotiated a severance in 2015, you can negotiate a type of severance that works for both sides.

My wife's manager came up with an agreement for her to work just three days a week, versus five, while continuing to receive her full-time salary until they found her two replacements. In essence, for six months my wife got a 67% raise while feeling much less stressed.

Once her two replacements joined her office, she spent a couple of months training them to the point of satisfaction and then left with a severance package valued at over $100,000 in total.

If you want to really get into the nitty-gritty of severance negotiation strategies, I wrote an e-book called *How to Engineer Your Layoff: Make a Small Fortune by Saying Goodbye*. You will learn how to set up the framework to successfully negotiate a severance. Even better, you won't need to hire an expensive employment lawyer once you're done reading.

THE FINANCIAL SAMURAI WAY

- It's not good enough to be good at your job. You must sell internally as much as you do externally.

- If you want to conquer guilt as a working parent, beat the average time spent with your child (120 minutes per day for college-educated moms, 85 minutes for college-educated dads).

- If you decide to become a full-time parent, it doesn't have to be forever. Going back to work after two to three years is soon enough that you can likely get a similar job with similar pay.

- Never quit your job; get laid off and try to negotiate a severance. If you planned to leave anyway, there is no downside.

Chapter 12

Get Your Side Hustle On

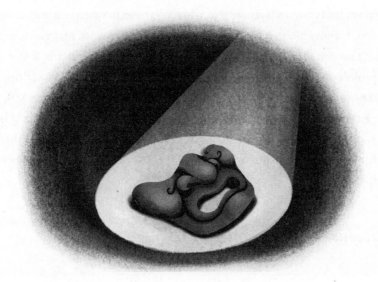

Work while others are sleeping so you can eventually play while others are working. This is a mantra I'd like all of you to embrace as you strive for financial independence. You have to do something hard to appreciate what is easy.

If you want to achieve financial freedom sooner, then you must find ways to make more money. Yes, your job is likely going to be your main source of income. However, job security is no longer what it once was. Find a way to maximize your day-job income with raises and promotions while also earning income on the side. This is where your X factor comes in.

Your X factor in your plan for financial freedom is your side hustle.

Every once in a while, I go jogging along the mansions in Pacific Heights on Broadway Street in San Francisco. I specifically choose this area because it's inspirational to see the beautiful houses. All of the homes are valued between $10 million and $80 million. And guess what? The majority of the owners are entrepreneurs.

This jog, and the megamansions, are what inspired me to invest and start *Financial Samurai*. I realized there was no way I could ever afford such a home by simply working a day job.

And while I still can't afford one of those mansions, I'm grateful they inspired me to start my side hustle. It is truly a fantastic feeling to build something out of nothing and create an asset that is potentially worth something significant.

Your side hustle can be as big or small as you want to make it. The goal is to create a new revenue stream that you can leverage if or when you need to when you're no longer working a day job—and, above all, to have an outlet for meaningful work that you love to do.

You can't do extraordinary things if you do what everybody else is doing. And taking on a side project doesn't have to be permanent. Think of it as a temporary opportunity; if you adopt the side-hustle culture for too long, it can lead to burnout, especially for parents with kids. However, the average hours worked a week in the U.S. has actually been declining for decades. As a result, the hurdle to get ahead is relatively low. Put in the work today because things could get a lot harder down the road as the world becomes increasingly more competitive.

U.S. Average Hours Worked per Week

Source: Census Bureau (Data: Nov-21, Pub: Dec-21)

The Glorious Morning

Just as saving before spending money is an important practice in personal finance, so is conquering the morning. If you can conquer the morning by doing the important things first, the rest of the day will feel like gravy.

Don't wait until you're completely exhausted from your day job to focus on your own ideas and side projects. Instead, work on them before your job begins.

If the average person starts hitting the snooze button at 7:00 a.m., try waking up at 5:00 a.m. for a year to work on something you're passionate about. Then try it for another year. Two hours a day of extra hustling, for two and a half years, enabled me to grow *Financial Samurai* into a website with momentum and income-generating potential.

Turns out, anyone can be productive given the gift of *over seven hundred extra hours* in a single year. You don't have to be smarter than anybody else. You just have to do things other people aren't willing to do.

If you aren't a morning person, work on your side gig in the evening. Few financially successful people I know work only forty hours a week or less. Forty hours a week is an artificial construct. These entrepreneurs, multimillionaires, even billionaires, are often working sixty hours or more out of a 168-hour week. Only after at least ten years of extra hustle might they finally take things down a notch to enjoy the fruits of their labor.

Thanks to the internet, it is easier than ever before to start side projects and create more money engines. Sticking with it, though, is still the hard part for most people. But not for Financial Samurais. The secret to your success is unwavering commitment.

This chapter focuses on not just why to have a side hustle but also *how.* It covers the opportunities of the gig economy, online businesses, our permissionless society, and the abundance of a side-hustle mindset. You'll learn what needs to happen before you can retire from your primary career to focus on your side job—or how to have multiple hustles instead.

There are people out there who are not as talented as you, not as educated as you, and less experienced than you, who maybe even don't work as hard as you, but they are more successful than you simply because they had the courage to put themselves out there and you didn't.

Everybody has something to give. Don't doubt your talents! You never know what might happen until you try.

The Samurai Side Hustle

Here are some real-life examples of people who had success side hustling.

Let me tell you about my friend Harry Campbell of *The Rideshare Guy*. Harry was an aerospace engineer for Boeing in his twenties, making roughly $90,000 a year at his peak.

In 2014 Harry recognized that the Uber and Lyft ridesharing phenomenon was going to be big. First, he side-hustled after work by giving rides that generated anywhere between $20 and $40 an hour.

Then, as more and more drivers joined the platform and his hourly earnings declined, Harry pivoted to making money online. Instead of driving for eight hours to make $160, he got paid $100 to $1,000 every time someone signed up to drive through the link on his website. The secret was writing well-crafted articles about driving for Uber and Lyft that organically showed up in online search engines.

At age twenty-eight in 2015, just ten months after starting *The Rideshare Guy*, Harry took a leap of faith and quit his engineering job. He had been side hustling for twenty to thirty hours a week on his site on top of his forty hours a week at his day job.

Today, *The Rideshare Guy* is one of the largest websites for information about the sharing economy, including grocery delivery and micromobility (scooters). The site generates over $1 million in revenue annually and has several freelance employees.

NOW MEET TWENTY-SIX-YEAR-OLD SHERRY from San Francisco. During the day, Sherry worked in accounting making roughly $85,000 a year. After work and on the weekends, Sherry would get her exercise by walking other people's dogs.

She first started walking dogs using the Rover app. In the beginning, Sherry charged $15 per hour, with Rover taking a 20% cut. Sherry was immediately taking home $300 to $350 a month working an extra twenty-three to twenty-seven hours a week.

After about three months of accumulating positive reviews, Sherry began charging $20 an hour. She would also occasionally sidestep Rover altogether to save on commission. Her income soon grew to over $500 a month.

Six months in, some of her clients started asking her to house-sit, which brought in $240 to $350 a night for an eight- to ten-hour shift.

After a year of side hustling, Sherry grew her client list to over thirty clients who regularly pay her $2,000 to $3,000 per month on top of her ~$7,000-per-month salary.

With the help of her side-hustle money, Sherry bought a two-bedroom condo in Hono-lulu in 2018 for $500,000 that has since appreciated in value by at least 20%. She generates about $500 a month after expenses renting it to long-term tenants.

By the time Sherry is forty, she plans to pay off her condo and earn over $2,200 a month in passive rental income. When the time comes, she will likely take things down a notch.

HOW MUCH MONEY DO YOU THINK one guy can make selling hot tub and pool chemicals? $10,000? $25,000? $50,000?

Meet Matt Giovanisci. Matt has worked in the pool industry since he was thirteen years old. His first summer job was stocking shelves at a local pool supply store in South Jersey. He worked his way up the ladder until he became the marketing director of the company when he was twenty-five.

In 2008 he was making $40,000 a year without a college degree. That's also when he started his side project: *Swim University*, a blog and YouTube channel teaching home-owners pool and hot tub maintenance. In 2011, Matt got laid off from his day job. He took the opportunity to work on *Swim University* full time until he could replace his original salary. In 2021 *Swim University* earned over $500,000 in revenue and over $450,000 in operating profits, thanks to the site receiving over five million visitors.

FINALLY, LET ME SHARE MY STORY. It was in July 2009 that I finally decided to start my side hustle, *Financial Samurai*. At the time, I had no delusions that the site would make any money. All I wanted to do was connect with like-minded people who were trying to make sense out of the financial chaos. Instead of taking up drinking or smoking to cope with my fear, uncertainty, and doubt, I took up writing personal finance advice.

In October 2011, I found myself hiking up Santorini with my wife on a sunny, seventy-eight-degree day. After several hours of walking around, I found myself at a bar on top of the cliff. Somehow, my wife still had the energy to explore, so I was left alone with my thoughts. I ordered an overpriced Mythos beer for 8 euros and took in the scenery. The bar had wi-fi, so I checked my email and saw that an old advertiser in London wanted to place an advertisement on *Financial Samurai* for $1,000.

Still in disbelief, I wrote back, "Sounds good!" Within thirty minutes, I had published the ad and received the funds via PayPal. That was the moment when I knew everything would be all right if I left my job. I ordered another overpriced Mythos beer and soaked in the sun.

By 2017, *Financial Samurai*'s operating profit surpassed my old day-job salary. But the best thing is, running the site is way more fun and much less work than being in finance. Plus, I can run the site from wherever there is internet access.

Today I'm still side hustling by writing this book. When an editor at Portfolio, a Penguin Random House imprint, contacted me with this book idea, I was flattered and once again responded, "Sounds good!"

When you start a side gig, if you stick with it long enough, you will encounter unexpected opportunities. Take advantage of them! The key is to just keep going.

The Side-Hustle Mindset

Whether they know it or not, Harry, Sherry, and Matt are prime examples of the Financial Samurai side-hustle mindset. This mindset includes a blend of grit, creativity, and endurance that you'll need to rise above the nonstarters and quitters. To help get you started and keep you going, keep these tenets in mind:

1. **Participate in the new permissionless society.** There are people making big money every day without the traditional prerequisite credentials. For example, you no longer need a fancy degree to get a job in tech. You just need to know your tech.

   In the personal finance world, there are some very successful bloggers who are doctors, journalists, engineers, cooks, and schoolteachers. Most do not have a finance background. All they did was start a site and get creative.

   You don't need radio experience to start a podcast.

   You don't need acting experience or a Hollywood agent to start a YouTube or TikTok channel.

   You don't need a college degree to be successful.

   There are no gatekeepers. There's not actually anyone "in charge" on the internet—something that's especially wonderful for historically marginalized groups, as we discussed.

   You don't need to wait on anyone else to start publishing what you know. Start now. In many situations, there's literally no cost to do so.

2. **Show up and stick with it.** What I just said was partially untrue. Because *of course* there's a cost: your time and your effort. Producing consistently good work is not easy.

But that's precisely why it works! Because others don't have the fortitude to stick with it.

Show up when others don't. Over time, you'll get better at your craft.

3. **Work while others sleep or play.** You'll race ahead of them while they're not looking. Waking up at 5:00 a.m. and working on your side hustle for two hours each morning for a year will lead to 730 hours of output. Instead of spending three hours watching football on Sunday, be a producer instead of a consumer.

4. **Fake it until you make it.** A lot of people give their work or products away for free in the beginning because they don't have the confidence that anyone will pay for them. And that is totally okay. In fact, it's a proven strategy among creators. Folks regularly build up their expertise by writing, recording, and vlogging about a topic on their website for years. Then, once they've established themselves as an authority, they sell products.

5. **Do something you'd do anyway.** A side hustle is best when it's something you'd be doing for free anyway because you love the work. The more you enjoy the work, the longer you will stick with it.

6. **Be willing to make sacrifices.** The side-hustle mindset is waking up an hour earlier or staying up an hour later in the evenings to work on your personal side project. It's skipping the Netflix special you wanted to watch. It's taking weekends to sprint on an idea instead of hanging out with friends. Often it means asking your partner or parents for favors: "Can you watch the kids for two extra hours every Sunday so I can work on this project?" You don't have to adopt the side-hustle culture forever. Make the most of your time and energy while you have it in order to work less when you're older and less motivated to grind.

7. **Take risks and adapt.** The side-hustle mindset is about being willing to go outside your comfort zone and risk feeling dumb if your idea doesn't work out. It's about being curious about the cause and effect, the action and reaction, of your own efforts. It's about creating learning habits that help you get better as you go.

Being a Financial Samurai with a side hustle comes with incredible power—the power of working on something of your own choosing, and the power of potential. When you work to create a product, to put something into the world that wasn't there before, you are literally inventing a new channel for your own income.

Start a Side Hustle at Any Age

The best time to start a side gig is when you have a stable job with benefits, not when you have no source of income. Consider the first two years of growing your endeavor an incubation period with little downside risk. See if you enjoy the process.

Passive income is a core part of financial independence, but the early years of your side hustle will likely be very "active." In other words, it is a hands-on thing that requires your direct attention and effort, even if only for an hour a day, or for thirty minutes on lunch breaks, or during long weekend sprints. There's a reason it's called "hustle."

A big part of your thinking needs to be about how much time you have to give and when.

That is why it's ideal to start your first side hustle when you are as young as possible, but the truth is, it's never too late to start. No matter where you are in life, your current stage and experience have something to offer. The 30/70 move is to never launch because you're afraid you've missed the boat. Let's look at the benefits of starting a side job during different life seasons.

Early twenties (earlier if possible): This is when you should invest at least 50%+ of your free time in your side project. You are time wealthy and likely full of energy. During the weekends, build the life that you truly want! Of course, you want to excel at your day job and have a life, too. I know this sounds like a lot—and frankly, it is. But if you're very focused on financial independence, building your side hustle early can pay huge dividends later on. Most people look back and kick themselves over how much time and opportunity they wasted when they were younger. Work as hard as you can, as early as possible. It will be exhausting. You may be overwhelmed at times. Take breaks when you need them. Also remember that the grind is only temporary, and it will be worth the big payoff when you achieve your goals.

If you're not ready to work on your side gig yet, then get in the side-hustle mindset. Treat your day job as a side hustle by finding ways to do extra work to get paid and promoted faster. Moonlight by taking communication classes so that you can become a more eloquent speaker and writer. It doesn't matter how brilliant you are if you can't get your point across in an effective manner. In addition, you can side hustle by actively learning new skills to job hop.

Late twenties, thirties: The average American has children by their late twenties or early thirties. As much as we love 'em, little kids are a *ton* of work and a significant expense.

Kids are the ideal motivation for working to achieve financial freedom but can also be the single biggest obstacle to it. Once kids arrive, generally speaking, your available time for a side job is dramatically reduced.

Even if you don't have children, by your thirties you are likely busting your butt at work, climbing in your career, possibly taking on more responsibility, managing people, on the hook for hitting numbers, etc. There's no cruise control setting at work. This makes a side hustle harder.

I'm not saying don't do it. I started *Financial Samurai* right after my thirty-second birthday, while I was working sixty hours a week as an executive director. It wasn't easy, and I didn't even have kids until I was thirty-nine! But the fear of losing my job during the global financial crisis finally catalyzed me to start. My hope is that you can start before you feel like your back is against the wall.

Forties: You're firing on all cylinders. You're more confident, more efficient, and maybe you have people to delegate to.

But if you're like me, it's possible that you're well on your way to burnout. At age forty-five, I can barely keep my eyes open after 10:30 p.m., whereas when I was in my twenties and thirties I could stay up until 1:00 a.m. and wake up by 6:00 a.m. five days a week no problem. And if you've had any financial strain along the way, that stress has probably prematurely aged and exhausted you.

There is a bright side to your exhaustion, though. Experience. With more experience and less tolerance for taking crap from bad bosses and colleagues, your chances of creating a successful side hustle go way up.

Fifties, sixties: The same argument goes for your fifties. Or even your sixties. Why not?! The kids, if you have them, are out living their lives. And just like that, you have free time and a quiet house again. And your expenses are down!

Sure, it's also possible that your energy is waning, but there's no reason you couldn't start working on a side project as a new income stream. What can you commit to working on for the next ten years that gives you purpose?

If you've already reached financial freedom, your side hustle will keep you engaged and give you purpose. If you haven't (yet!) reached financial freedom, a side hustle is going to be an important part of your income-stream portfolio.

Seventies and beyond! By now, hopefully, you have no need to earn extra money. Your main goal should be to stay active and do only things that give you meaning.

To stay mentally active, my seventy-five-year-old father has edited most of my posts and newsletters since 2015. In exchange, I pay him a modest salary. I want to pay him more, but he refuses. My father's side hustle has brought us closer together because we are constantly interacting every week about new topics.

It's never too late to try new things.

Hustle Offline or Hustle Online?

There are two main types of side hustles.

First, there's the "gig economy" side hustle. This is the practice of getting a second job, or a freelance or contract gig, that you can do outside of and in addition to your usual working hours.

Some of these gigs are physical, offline, brick-and-mortar work where you are somewhat limited in the amount you can do because there's a finite number of stores or clients in your location.

A physical side gig might mean getting a night job at McDonald's, a morning job at Starbucks, driving for Uber or Lyft, or delivering packages for Amazon. Other examples are babysitting, house-sitting, dog walking, caregiving, tutoring, and teaching tennis (like yours truly).

There are also a ton of online side gigs you could spend your time on. Examples include designing logos for start-ups, freelance writing for websites, doing voice work, teaching piano, or editing podcasts. You'll still have a boss or a client to make happy, but you'll have a lot of flexibility in your schedule, which is what makes online side gigs so popular for people who also have day jobs. No one cares if you're designing websites at 3:00 a.m., as long as the work gets done.

If your side hustle comes in the form of a side gig like this, great! You have two revenue streams—your main job and your second job or gig work. You're also making connections, meeting people, seeing new perspectives—you're out in the world getting your steps in, so to speak. All of which is energizing and keeps you and your finances healthy. Who knows? Your side gig may lead to a better-paying full-time job opportunity.

That said, you are always working for someone else, at *both* jobs, and possibly not creating your own unique brand, content, and product that you get to reap benefits from down the road.

That's why your best kind of long-term side hustle, if your goal is financial freedom, is *not* the side gig. Gigs are great when you have energy, but they are less great as you get older and your energy fades.

Instead, the second and best type of side hustle is building something from scratch and creating your own unique product. Your brand is what will set you apart from your competitors. Your own product is what will make you unique. When you're thinking of side hustling, think about something that is scalable.

For example, instead of teaching piano one-on-one or to a group online, create a unique piano lessons course under your brand. Once you create your product, you can then sell it to many people without having to do correspondingly more work.

Before the 1990s, you couldn't create a side hustle online and scale it so easily. Today you can by leveraging the internet. To me, creating something of your own is the best way to do work you love, whenever you want, with people you like.

As with everything good, you've got to put in the work. Let me provide you with some potential operating profit for talented content creators (bloggers, YouTubers, TikTokers, podcasters, etc.) who are willing to produce unique content three times a week or more. Here's what I think is possible for 70% of those who try.

Year 1: $1,000–$10,000
Year 2: $10,000–$30,000
Year 3: $30,000–$50,000
Year 4: $50,000–$100,000
Year 5: $100,000–$250,000
Year 6: $150,000–$350,000
Year 7: $200,000–$500,000
Year 8: $300,000–$600,000
Year 9: $400,000–$800,000
Year 10: $500,000–$1,000,000+

As you can tell from the progression, there is a high correlation between time, effort, and money. Too many content creators quit in the first year, negating all their effort in the process. By year five, a content creator could earn more than the top college graduates who land the most lucrative jobs. The secret to your success is unwavering commitment. Stay consistent and keep going for as long as possible.

The *Financial Samurai* website can theoretically reach more than 4.7 billion people online through search engines, word of mouth, organic promotion, and advertising. Of course, not every human in the world with an internet connection is going to visit my website. My point is just that they *could*, whereas not everyone in the world could walk into your retail store or restaurant or hotel.

Having your own website is now more valuable than ever because it can't be shut down. Nor can you get laid off, as so many employees were during the pandemic. Think about your website as a dynamic résumé where you can tell your story to the world.

Your goal is to be unshutdownable, no matter what happens in the economy.

If you can't shut down a business, its earnings are more defensive. If earnings are more certain, then the overall business is even more valuable.

In fact, an online business is one of the strongest asset classes today. It's no wonder many private equity companies, public companies, and larger media assets are trying to buy the most promising cash-flowing websites.

If you don't want to create your own website, you can always buy existing ones and go from there. The key is to build a recognizable brand that helps differentiate you from the crowd.

Further, please don't wait until you are an expert to start. In 2006 I came up with the idea to start *Financial Samurai*, but I waited until 2009 to launch the site because I thought I should first have ten years of financial experience under my belt.

Had I started in 2006, the site would be even larger now, and I could have left my day job at least one year sooner. There are plenty of people with little to no relevant experience making money on YouTube, TikTok, Instagram, and their own platforms. The key is to just start. Once you start, you will figure out your own brand.

When to Make Your Side Hustle Your Main Hustle

As we've discussed, the side hustle usually starts small, unpaid, and unglamorous. It requires a mountain of willpower and discipline because you usually don't see progress or returns for a year or longer. But once you gain momentum, you may reach a point where you wonder if you can promote your side hustle from part time to full time.

Your framework for making this decision is simple. With your side hustle, you have to:

1. Cover your base needs
2. Truly enjoy it

There are a lot of extra benefits to a traditional career, like company-provided health insurance, a 401(k), a network of colleagues, maybe equity and stock options. You want to take a panoramic look at what you're leaving behind, and make sure your side project still replaces it enough to cover your base needs and happiness.

I've calculated that your side job/business needs to generate about 30% to 60% more than your day-job salary to fully replace that income plus the job's benefits. Here's a chart that explains why. As an employee making $100,000, you get so much more and often have to pay less to keep yourself afloat.

It's worth noting that if you forsake your job for your side hustle, you are reverting to

HOW MUCH YOU NEED TO MAKE AS AN ENTREPRENEUR OR FREELANCER TO REPLACE YOUR DAY-JOB INCOME

What You Get as an Employee	Value	Comments
Income	$100,000	Base salary, does not include bonus
Retirement benefits	$10,000	401(k) matching + profit sharing if any
Subsidized health care	$6,000	Single or family
Paid time off	$5,770	Three weeks of paid vacation
Life insurance	$500	Term life insurance = 5X salary
Short-term and long-term disability	$7,000	Paid parental leave and disability beyond six months
Ongoing employee training	$1,000	Continuing education classes
Automatic minimum raise	$2,000	At a minimum to keep up with inflation
Subtotal	**$132,270**	

What You Don't Have to Pay as an Employee	Value	Comments
Employer FICA tax	$7,650	Employer pays 7.65% for both employee and employer
State franchise tax	$800	Minimum annual tax in California for businesses
Business accountant	$1,500	Got to get your finances right
Bookkeeper	$1,500	Someone to keep all your records in order
Capital expenditure	$5,000	Computer, phone for your asset-light business
Travel	$4,000	Business trips to see clients and go to conferences
Meals	$3,000	Your own and prospective clients'
Office	$7,200	Your home office or coworking space
Marketing expenses	$3,000	Got to help get your name out there
Subtotal	**$33,650**	

An entrepreneur needs to make between 30%–60% more to replace a day-job income.

Source: FinancialSamurai.com

one income stream. Let's say all this time you've been making $100,000 a year at your "real job," and you have also been pulling in gravy from your side hustle—so much that your side gig almost matches your primary career income, and you're tempted to hire yourself out of your job.

This could look like: $100,000 (career) + $90,000 (side project) = $190,000 income combined. This is when you want to make sure you haven't already adjusted your lifestyle to that combined income—because if you have, then dropping the day job and going back to a $90,000 income is going to hurt.

Side-Hustle Income as a Percentage of Gross Annual Day-Job Income

To further think through how and when a side project can graduate to center stage, let's take a look at your side-hustle revenue in phases. The benchmarks below show side-hustle income as a percentage of your gross annual income.

10% of gross annual income: If your side hustle makes less than 10% of your gross annual income, please don't leave your day job just yet.

25% of gross annual income: You're building momentum. This might be an early indicator that you should figure out how to spend more time on your side gig while still having a job.

50% of gross annual income: You really have something here. Things are getting exciting. Give yourself a six-month goal of reaching 75% of gross annual income.

As I mentioned at the outset of this book, my general savings recommendation is to save at least 20% of your after-tax annual income and eventually try to get to a 50% after-tax income saving rate or higher. Therefore, if your side hustle is generating 40% to 50% of your gross annual income, you have just about enough side-hustle income to live a normal life. You just need to be okay with not saving for a period if you decide to leave your day job. If you are very bullish on your side hustle's growth, then you'll be back to saving money in no time.

75% of gross annual income: If we have a clear plan for how to reach 100%, and it's working, then the more risk-tolerant among us will make the leap here. Risk is mitigated if you have been in your day job for a while and you're in a position to negotiate a severance.

If you're not ready to jump, this is where you give yourself *another* six-month plan and circle that date on your calendar. That's when you will leave your day job if all still looks good.

100% of gross annual income: Even the more conservative among us will probably make the leap into full-time side hustle when it is bringing in 100% of our day job's gross annual income. All you're probably thinking about at work is your side gig. Therefore, you probably owe it to your colleagues to negotiate a severance and move on. With a strong correlation between effort and reward, your day job is likely holding you back from earning much more.

Now that we've covered the financial expectations for quitting your day job, let's discuss the second part of committing to your side hustle full time—the question of love.

A quick test for whether you love your side hustle:

1. Are you having fun?
2. Are you doing something you would do for free?
3. Can you see a sustainable growth path?

Yes? Then you've scored yourself a lifestyle business, which means you have struck Financial Samurai gold: a fulfilling, well-paying lifestyle business where you call the shots—and where your effort directly correlates to your reward.

No? That's okay. Plenty of side hustles are born of necessity or ambition, and you are willing to accept the grind because you know you are in total control of the direction and revenue. If your side project is like that, consider putting a timeline on it.

I also want to throw in a healthy reminder here that for maximum wealth building, it might be best to keep your biggest income source, your career, for as long as possible and keep your side hustle, if you don't truly enjoy it, where it belongs—on the side as a source of extra income.

One of my greatest discoveries about work is that work is so much more fun when you don't need to work! It's a feeling similar to when you get into college at the beginning of your senior year of high school. With your future set, high school suddenly becomes a blast.

Therefore, if you can tolerate your boss and colleagues, feel free to keep your seat for as long as possible. You might find that your work and colleagues become more tolerable the more money you make from your side hustle. Further, you can build up your all-important taxable investment portfolios even more.

Pursue a Lifestyle Business or Hope for the Big Payout?

Over poker one night, some friends and I got to talking about what we always talk about: entrepreneurship. Out of ten people at the table, four worked at start-ups, three worked at Google, one was a high-tech lawyer, one worked as a medical correspondent for CNN, and then there was me.

Down about $185 for the evening, I started lamenting what the money would cost in side hustling. Several hours of work at least, I thought. That was sobering. No thanks to my opponent landing a king on the river against my pocket queens!

With side hustle on the brain, I asked this of the poker sharks sitting with me:

Would you rather make $15,000 to $30,000 a month and work only two to four hours a day?

Or would you rather make minimum wage working twelve to eighteen hours a day for two years, with a 25% chance of selling your business for $100 million and netting yourself a cool $25 million—and a 75% chance of being left with nothing but your experiences? (That 25% chance, by the way, was a *generous* hypothetical.)

I purposely left the question open-ended to see what the various responses would be. Immediately they started doing the math to figure out what the capitalized value of $15,000 to $30,000 a month would be, based on life expectancy, compared with the expected value of the big payout. After all, we calculate expected value all the time in poker. (The realistic value of choosing the lifestyle-business route, by the way, is anywhere between $4 million and $20 million.)

But instead of calculating their way to a decision, I encouraged my fellow players to go with their gut. Because even when true numbers are staring us in the face, we messy humans tend to go with gut decisions informed by hope, chance, luck, ambition, and maybe outright delusion.

Surprisingly, or perhaps not, given that they were sitting at a poker table, every single one of them chose option two: the big potential payout. A couple of the entrepreneurs in the game already had a $100 million buyout goal in mind for their own businesses.

As the night wore on, I finally heard someone take the other side after losing over $800 in a $2,600, three-way pot when his straight got flushed out.

"Well, $30,000 a month for working only a couple of hours a day isn't so bad. I think I'll go with that."

I chuckled to myself. I knew he'd come around. They usually do.

At the end of the day, your side hustle's main purpose is to provide you a better lifestyle. Going for the big payout is a long shot. You will likely fail. But if you understand the odds, hopefully, even if you fail, you will feel good that at least you tried. Besides, even if you start feeling like you made the wrong move, you still have up to a 30% chance things could eventually turn around using my 70/30 philosophy. Hope is a powerful motivator for change.

Just know there are plenty of extremely successful moon-shot entrepreneurs who are no happier than the average person. With tremendous money comes tremendous responsibility. If you have thousands of employees and everybody counting on your every move to survive, are you really free?

Make sure your side hustle fits into the lifestyle you want to live. For the majority of people, I believe choosing the lifestyle business over a potentially massive fortune is the correct 70/30 decision.

THE FINANCIAL SAMURAI WAY

- Starting a side hustle can help you build extra income to save and invest. It might one day supplant your day-job income. You won't know until you try.

- Don't wait until you're an expert or everything is perfect to start. You can figure things out as you go.

- Once your side-hustle income can cover your basic living expenses, you have the potential to leave your day job behind. However, a job is a security blanket that enables you to take more risks outside of work.

- Start-ups that get acquired for big bucks or go IPO get all the fanfare. However, most start-up employees don't end up making a fortune. Instead, consider going the lifestyle business route and see if it brings you the ideal combination of money, autonomy, and freedom. If that's not enough, you can always level up.

- View your weekend as a time to recharge but also as a time to build the life you ultimately want. The hard work you put in won't last forever. But the results may.

PART FOUR

Focus on the Most Important Things in Life

Getting your career and investments right is just one part of your wealth-building strategy. The reality is money is only a means to an end: to live your best life possible.

Choices like the schools you attend, your life partner, whether to have kids, caring for family members, and even how you eat influence your wealth potential and overall satisfaction.

Once you are on the right path to financial independence, your goal is to optimize everything else that matters most.

Let's explore how life outside the spreadsheet will impact your dreams of financial freedom.

Chapter 13

Invest in Education

I can't stress this enough: education will set you free.

It's true from a financial freedom perspective, and it permeates every other part of your life. Education will empower you to make better choices. It will help you figure out a career path, where to invest your money, how to pick a life partner, how to build a business, and how to be a happier person because you understand and empathize with different cultures and different ways of thinking. The more education you have, the more confident you will be.

And to be clear, I am not talking only about formal education. You don't need a fancy degree, or any degree at all, to become financially free. Having a college-level degree will give you access to more employment opportunities. It is the 70/30 choice that improves your odds of achieving financial independence, but it is not required. That's a big reason I'm so excited that education is now largely free online. There is a low barrier to entry. Most top universities post their syllabi online, and there are endless other options for free and low-cost learning, from blogs and podcasts to courses at your local library.

Some of the angriest people I encounter are the least educated—and again, I am not talking about prestigious degrees. I am talking about any kind of education that allows you to see and understand different perspectives or gives you the confidence and self-esteem to feel good about your life choices. That education can be exposure to different cultures through reading or traveling, or even just pausing long enough to listen to others' opinions that are different from your own.

A strong mind is an open mind. Learn from those who disagree with you so you can continually improve.

One of the greatest gifts a parent can give to a child is an education—that is, sending them to school and, equally important, spending as much time with them as possible and explaining to them why things are the way they are.

Education is also the best thing we can gift to ourselves. But the choices around *how to spend* on education can get confusing fast, especially through the lens of trying to achieve financial independence. From private preschools to elite universities, there is no ceiling to how much we can spend on learning. And then there are the free options that can arm us with the same level of knowledge. When is education worth the expense? This chapter answers that question.

I understand that folks will be reading this book at various life stages. My hope is that my advice will help parents who are trying to make optimal decisions about their kids' education, and help them guide their teens as they make their own choices about school. I also wrote this for anyone who feels stuck in their career. Education is among the best tools to help you break out of a bad work situation.

As you read ahead, and as you figure out your own optimal choices, please remember that your 70/30 move is to **always be learning, regardless of the educational format**. Believe that there is always something more to learn. The knowledge and skills you accumulate play a crucial part in the amount of income and opportunities you can command.

Don't Chase Prestige at All Costs

I want to stress an important point: after your first couple of years of work, nobody cares about whether you went to a prestigious university, or *any* university.

Well, I take that back. Two groups of people care: parents, so they can brag to their friends at the next social event, and graduates who have little to no work experience.

Hiring managers pay attention to where you got your degree when you've just graduated because your education is usually the main piece of information they have to go on. Remember, entry-level employees are a cost center for companies. Your goal is to show them that taking a chance on hiring you is a low-risk move. Excellent grades from a top-ranked school are a strong signal to employers that you're a reliable hire. But after you get your first job, your hiring potential is all about what you can do and how well you can work with others.

This means a degree from a top school will give you a better chance of landing a job interview out of school. And if all other things between competing candidates are equal, the person with a top GPA from a higher-ranking school is likely to have a better shot at getting the job.

Your school's ranking also tends to carry more weight in certain industries. Companies in banking, technology, management consulting, and big law mainly recruit from the top twenty-five schools. If you or your child have your heart set on working in one of those industries, then be strategic about what school you choose. Contact the career office to learn which companies recruit at the school.

But there are exceptions to attending an elite university, of course. We all know people who went to state schools or schools not ranked in the top twenty-five and got great jobs out of college, even jobs in the industries I just mentioned. I'm one of those people.

I graduated from the College of William & Mary, a public university in Virginia that isn't a target school for the investment banking industry. And my first job out of school was as a financial analyst at Goldman Sachs—where the acceptance rate for a front-office job was and still is only around 5%.

I didn't know anyone at Goldman who referred me for the job. I didn't have any special advantage. All I did was work relentlessly on getting good grades, study the markets every day, and then get on a bus at 6:00 a.m. to attend a job fair in Washington, DC, while my peers slept in.

Once there, I got grilled by the recruiter, who asked me how many times the Federal Reserve had changed interest rates in the past couple of years, where I thought the market was headed, and what I thought about the prospects of various companies. It was a harrowing process that I thought I had failed. However, a month later, I was invited back for more interviews. I navigated fifty-five interviews over seven sessions before I finally got a job offer.

I'll get into more detail in a minute about whether it's worth paying to attend an expensive, high-ranking school. For now, I want to emphasize that getting a prestigious degree is not the be-all and end-all of your success.

If you don't go to a top school, you can do other things to improve your chances of getting hired upon graduation. Things like getting on the damn bus, submitting more résumés, going to more career fairs, building more relationships, getting straight As, or starting a side hustle/business in a field you want to work in. You're not stuck if you go to an average school. You just need to be motivated to work on other parts of your résumé to show employers that hiring you is not a big risk.

After your first two or so years of work, your hiring potential becomes all about what you can do and the network you create. Instead of thinking about college as a guarantee of riches, think about college more as employment insurance that doesn't always pay out.

So what to do? **Go for the best education you can afford**, because ultimately, the school you choose is all about getting those first opportunities. Once you have the best opportunity, it's up to you to show what you can do. And once you show you can get the job done, more opportunities begin to snowball.

The best *you can afford* is an important qualifier. Don't chase prestige at all costs. It's not worth sinking yourself into six-figure student loan debt just to improve your chances of getting a hot job out of school. If you're determined to work in an industry that values prestigious degrees and you can't get scholarships, consider going to a cheaper school for a year or two, getting phenomenal grades, and then transferring to a higher-ranking school. Or go to a midrange school that you can afford and blow recruiters away with your high GPA and impressive extracurricular activities. There's no reason college students can't gain significant relevant work experience during the summers and winters.

If you're midcareer and feel stuck in your job, use education to level up. You can always start over in a new industry by either going to graduate school or getting a certification from a top-ranked school in a specific area. Online certificates are a great alternative to pricey four-year degrees and graduate programs if you know exactly what you want to do and can get certified in that.

Above all, make sure you're getting educated for a purpose—the pursuit of prestige should be a very secondary purpose.

Pay Up for Private School or Go to a Lower-Cost Public School?

If it doesn't work out for you to attend an elite private university, you're not alone. According to the Education Data Initiative, 13.8 million or 78.9% of undergraduates attend public institutions; 21.1% attend private institutions. I'm part of the 78.9%. I applied to only one private institution, Babson College, because I was interested in entrepreneurship. However, I was neither smart enough to get a large scholarship nor wealthy enough to afford to pay full tuition.

However, I did attend international private schools when I lived in Asia (paid for by the U.S. government since my parents worked in the foreign service) and attended public high school and college in the States. I found very little difference in the quality of education between my private middle school and my public high school.

Upon graduating from William & Mary after thirteen years of diligently working, saving, and investing, I reached a modest level of financial independence at thirty-four. Life has been good post–public school. The ROI was tremendous, given that William & Mary tuition was only $2,800 a year versus $22,000 a year at comparable private schools at the time.

Change is in the air when it comes to school rankings. Public schools are starting to climb the charts as institutions are adjusting how they evaluate a school's status. *Forbes* is among those leading the charge. It changed its 2021–22 college-ranking criteria so that it considers whether a school makes itself accessible to lower-income students who can't afford high tuition. *Forbes* now also factors extensive data on student outcomes into its rankings.

Under *Forbes*'s new methodology, several public universities surged up the rankings between 2019 and 2021 (the rankings took 2020 off). UC Berkeley jumped from #13 to #1; UCLA from #38 to #8; UC San Diego from #79 to #15; and the University of Florida from #70 to #25. Harvard, meanwhile, dropped from #1 to #7.

Wherever a school may land on the ranking charts, we all know there's no guarantee that you'll do anything special (indeed, that you'll *be* anything special) just because you went to a private school, or to college in general.

If you send your child to private school and pay full tuition, there is only one guarantee: you will spend a small fortune.

So let's try to remove my bias in favor of public schools so we can objectively analyze the decision to attend public or private school by simply doing some math.

I understand that many parents send their kids to private school for religious reasons, for smaller class sizes and more attention, or for a more customized program if their child has special needs. These reasons all make sense, and if your family's needs require you to go the private school route despite the costs, go for it. You know what's best for your family.

And of course, some folks attend private school for free or reduced tuition through scholarships or other support programs. That's fantastic! By all means, take full advantage. The possible scenarios and reasons for attending any particular school are endless and beyond the scope of this conversation.

My goal here is to help people who are struggling with the decision between public and private school if the choice to go to private school requires a huge financial commitment on their part and if their needs, or their child's needs, would be equally—or nearly equally—met in either school system. My calculations are relevant for all school levels, from pre-school to college.

This exercise is also valuable for other groups:

- Students who want to understand the true cost of their education and the sacrifices their parents make in order to make better choices with their careers
- Parents who make too much to get financial aid but not enough to feel like they can comfortably afford private school
- Students and parents who feel bad for attending or sending their kids to public school or have a tinge of envy for those kids who do go to private school

So if you're considering private school for yourself or for your kids, you can start with this simple equation for determining whether you can afford it at all: **your household income should be at least 7X the net tuition per kid before you can consider paying for private school.**

In other words, if annual tuition is $20,000 a year, and you only have one child, your household income should be at least $140,000. If your child gets an $8,000-a-year scholarship, then your minimum household income should be at least $84,000. Private school tuition tends to get more expensive the higher up your child goes. However, hopefully, your household income will continue to grow as well. That, or your child continues to receive scholarships to bring down the net tuition cost. Remember, you are still on a mission to aggressively save and invest to build passive investment income for financial freedom.

If you *can* comfortably afford private school based on my 7X tuition guide, you can feel good about going for it—all else being equal. If you decide the private school is not for your child, you can always transfer to a public school and save on tuition. As I said earlier, go for the best education you can afford because the school you choose is all about getting those first opportunities. And better first opportunities snowball into greater opportunities down the line.

If you're considering private preschool, the key opportunity it provides is more direct access to private grade schools. If you're considering a private high school, the key opportunity is if it is a "feeder school" for certain well-ranked universities.

The private-versus-public debate is especially relevant to parents who do not have access to public preschools. Preschools in many cities are private, and not cheap. If your only option is expensive private preschool, then you should absolutely try for the highest-rated school, all else being equal, because the application fee and tuition are similar.

Whatever grade level you're considering, let's focus on the actual cost of going to private school over public school. Because even if you *can* afford the private school tuition, there's still the question of whether it's worth spending the money. It can be hard to figure out the answer without a framework for your decision-making.

Let's start by calculating how much it will cost to send your child to private school for K–12 and four years of college. On the next page is a chart outlining the costs of real private school tuition for the Chinese American International School in San Francisco for K–8, San Francisco University High School for 9–12, and Princeton University for four years. Further, families generally have to pay an additional $500 to $5,000 a year in donations, books, excursions, and so forth at private grade schools. These tuition rates are very similar in other big cities such as New York City, Boston, Los Angeles, Seattle, and Washington, DC. Expect tuition to continue to go up by 3% to 6% each year forever.

All told, if you plan to send your little one to private school in San Francisco starting with kindergarten in 2022, you will eventually spend at least $745,660 in tuition through college graduation. But if you invested the money instead and earned a conservative 5% compound annual return, you would end up with about $1,131,000 after seventeen years.

Therefore, it is highly reasonable to assume a total cost of over $1 million for a private school education (especially since my chart on the next page doesn't include the rising cost of tuition, or donations).

Now let's look at the potential financial benefits of going to college. According to researchers from the Georgetown University Center on Education and the Workforce, as summarized in a report entitled "A First Try at ROI: Ranking 4,500 Colleges," the economic gains for attending a private nonprofit college are $838,000 and $765,000 for a public college.

In other words, their data shows that the value of attending a private nonprofit college

THE TOTAL COST OF PRIVATE SCHOOL TUITION

Grade	Tuition*	Academic Institution
Kindergarten	$33,900	Chinese American Int'l School
First grade	$33,900	Chinese American Int'l School
Second grade	$33,900	Chinese American Int'l School
Third grade	$33,900	Chinese American Int'l School
Fourth grade	$33,900	Chinese American Int'l School
Fifth grade	$33,900	Chinese American Int'l School
Sixth grade	$33,900	Chinese American Int'l School
Seventh grade	$33,900	Chinese American Int'l School
Eighth grade	$33,900	Chinese American Int'l School
Ninth grade	$54,130	SF University High School
Tenth grade	$54,130	SF University High School
Eleventh grade	$54,130	SF University High School
Twelfth grade	$54,130	SF University High School
College freshman	$56,010	Princeton University
College sophomore	$56,010	Princeton University
College junior	$56,010	Princeton University
College senior	$56,010	Princeton University
Total Cost	$745,660	
If invested with a 4% compound annual return	$1,038,000	
If invested with a 5% compound annual return	$1,131,000	
If invested with a 6% compound annual return	$1,235,000	
If invested with a 7% compound annual return	$1,350,000	
If invested with a 10% compound annual return	$1,776,000	

* Tuition figures are as of 2021–2022. Tuition will likely increase by 3% to 6% a year forever.

Source: FinancialSamurai.com

is about $73,000, or 9.5%, greater than the value of attending a public one over the course of the average person's working career. Is that a significant difference or even statistically significant? It's hard to say, since there are so many variables that can determine a person's financial outcome postcollege. However, at the very least, we can compare the ROI difference of $73,000 with the actual cost difference to help make a more informed decision.

Interestingly, adjusting for cost of living, private grade school tuition is relatively cheaper in expensive cities such as New York, San Francisco, Honolulu, Seattle, and Washington, DC. If you're on the fence about sending your child to a private grade school, make sure to inquire about financial assistance.

Imagine What You Could Do with $1 Million

I'd like all parents and students who are considering private school to run this exercise. Instead of graduating with student debt, imagine if your parents said at the after-party, "Congratulations on graduating from college! You're free to pursue your dreams, live wherever you want, buy a house, and even start a family because here's a check for a million dollars." You'd be set!

If you graduated at twenty-two years old, invested the entire $1 million, saved and invested another $20,000 a year, and earned a 5.4% annual compounded return, you would end up with $3,192,000 by age forty. Being financially independent by forty with minimal effort would be pretty nice. But the really wonderful part would be having the freedom to do whatever you wanted *at the beginning of adulthood.*

Yes, there's also a possibility that having $1 million so young would make you a deadbeat. On the other hand, having a financial safety net could make you the biggest success ever because you could take huge risks. Look at Bill Gates and Mark Zuckerberg, who could afford to drop out of college because they came from wealth.

The key to making sure your kid has their head on straight with regard to money is having regular conversations about all aspects of wealth creation. The more you talk about various financial topics as your child grows up, the less of a shock it will be if you hand over a $1 million check. You could always spread the money out into multiple tranches based on various conditions for distribution if you felt that your child still needed time to mature.

At the age of twenty-two, I would have used $200,000 for a 20% down payment on a $1 million property in New York City. Then I would probably have stupidly blown $100,000 on a nice car and motorbike, because that's the sort of thing I did after my first full year of working. With the remainder, I would have invested $600,000 in stocks and $100,000 in bonds or a CD. The $1 million would probably be worth $4 million today. The New York City property alone would be worth ~$2.5 million and be fully paid off. Or maybe I'm just fooling myself with the benefit of hindsight.

If you decide not to give your child $1 million upon graduation, think what an extra $1 million could do for your retirement timeline. You could literally retire at least ten years earlier, based on a $100,000 annual spend. And for folks who live in expensive coastal cities and average closer to $200,000 a year in expenses, eliminating five years of work hell could be a godsend.

Saving time is truly the best thing you can do when you have a financial windfall. Each year you live reduces the percentage of time you have left. Think about how much money you'd be willing to give up to rewind time or live a life of leisure.

Here is a scenario to consider for parents desiring to send their kids to private school. What if you end up spending a fortune on private school tuition, only to have your children end up working in the same jobs as people who went to public school? Further, how will your adult children feel when they realize they delayed your journey to financial freedom by several years to help pay for private school? As your children mature, they should eventually appreciate the sacrifices you made for them.

If you send your children to private school, your expectations for your children will be higher. Further, your self-aware children will have higher expectations for themselves as well. One of the reasons why I chose William & Mary was because it was inexpensive. I could have paid off the $2,800 a year in tuition by returning to my old job at McDonald's for $4 an hour. The pressure to succeed was off, which enabled me to enjoy college more.

Remember, **happiness = results – expectations.** The more you pay for something, the more you want out of it.

If your household income is above 20X the annual net tuition per child, your expectations for your children may be more tempered. For example, even if your child goes to Cornell University for $61,000 a year in tuition alone and ends up with a minimum-wage job at the mall, you may not be too disappointed. After all, your household makes at least $1,220,000 a year. You might even start rationalizing that a minimum-wage service job might do your boy some good, since he's been so privileged all his life!

The bottom line: If your household income is 7X the annual net tuition per child or more, then you can send your kids to private school if you wish, especially if your local public school system is mismanaged. However, if your local public school system is well rated and your child can get into a great public university, then by all means go to public school and invest the difference.

BULLYING IN SCHOOLS

When I attended McLean High School, a public high school in Fairfax County, Virginia, I ran into a lot of trouble due to plenty of negative influences. Even though the district had top-ranked schools, I found myself occasionally defending myself from bullies.

One day, a big kid pushed me over while I was tying my shoe at my desk. He had been harassing me for a while, so I ended up punching him in the side of his face and smashing his glasses in the process. We both got suspended for a couple of days. Thankfully, he stopped bothering me after that.

In another incident, a bully came to school with a butterfly knife and threatened to cut me and anyone else who stood in his way. He had muscles on top of his muscles to boot. Everybody was afraid of him, so we said only good things to his face.

Then there was this other troubled kid who pushed smaller kids into their lockers and took their lunch money. He ended up going on *The Jerry Springer Show* to reveal all the problems he and his family had.

The one common denominator these bullies had was troubled households. Either their fathers were absent or abusive, or the families lived near poverty. Life was hard for them at home, so the bullies would take out their troubles on kids at school.

In retrospect, the most violence I ever experienced was during my time in school. Although I developed street smarts, it's important to find a safe and nurturing place to send your children to school so they can learn without fear. Find a school with a strong history of not tolerating violence. Further, identify schools that build strong partnerships with parents. The greater the parental involvement, the more likely the school will be a safe, nurturing learning environment. And most of all, ask your child if they feel safe.

Save for College in a 529 Account or Skip It?

Saving in a 529 plan explicitly for college and private grade school is a no-brainer. It's always a good idea to take advantage of tax-saving investment vehicles and compartmentalize what your money is used for. A 529 plan is similar to a "tax-exempt" retirement plan like a Roth IRA. The money you contribute to a 529 plan is posttax. However, the money gets to compound tax free and be used on qualified education expenses tax free.

Because of the passage of the SECURE (Setting Every Community Up for Retirement)

Act in 2019, the 529 plan received a functionality boost in 2020 and beyond. A 529 plan can now be used for

- all college tuition and qualified expenses;
- K–12 tuition and qualified expenses, up to $10,000 a year;
- apprenticeship programs and qualified expenses; and
- paying down a qualified education loan repayment for each of a 529 plan beneficiary's siblings, up to $10,000.

Given these benefits, if you have kids, contributing to a 529 plan makes even more sense. Always maximize the utility of your money by taking advantage of any benefits the government throws your way. Goodness knows they tax us hardworking citizens plenty!

However, if you contribute too much to a 529 plan, you may not be efficiently allocating your limited resources. Every dollar you contribute to a 529 plan is one less dollar you can contribute to your own retirement savings, your house down payment fund, or your around-the-world adventure with friends. (Still, in the worst case, if you contribute too much, you can always pass on the remaining funds to future generations.)

Deciding how much to contribute to a 529 plan is not easy. Here are some things you should consider to figure out the optimal amount.

1. **Identify the current and historical costs of attending select institutions.** Let's say you want your daughter to attend the College of William & Mary or UC Berkeley, two public universities with excellent reputations at a reasonable price. Go to the respective schools' websites and familiarize yourself with the current and historical costs of attendance.

   Once you've calculated the historical compound growth rate, use that growth rate to formulate your assumption about how much the college will cost by the time your daughter is eligible to attend. Then calculate how much you will need to earn and contribute to get there.

   Many parents who read *Financial Samurai* recommend accumulating enough to cover the costs of your in-state flagship school. I like this approach because it covers the bases and provides an important money topic of conversation when it comes time for your child to choose where to attend.

2. **Make a realistic assessment of the number of kids you will have.** Even if you do beat the odds and are blessed with more children at an advanced age, you still have

plenty of time to save and invest for their future. It's not like your expenses go from zero to thousands of dollars as soon as they are born. There's still enough runway to save.

3. **Carefully observe the cognitive abilities and interests of your kids.** Objectively observing your child's attributes is almost impossible. Of course you will think your baby is the cutest, smartest, best-looking, and kindest kid ever. But try hard to be objective by comparing the progress of your child with various milestones and other children the same age.

   When it comes to your kids, you don't want to suffer from the Dunning-Kruger effect—that is, be delusional and overestimate their competence. If you do, you will give your kids a false sense of security that will be smashed to smithereens in the real world. Praise effort, not results.

   Not everybody needs to or should go to college, let alone private grade school or private college. If your child dislikes learning about quadratic equations and would rather fix cars for a living, going to trade school is probably a much better move. Trade schools don't take as long or cost as much as college. Therefore, you won't have to save as much in your 529 plan.

   Match your child's education to their interests. Don't assume your children will go to college or get scholarships.

4. **Pay attention to 529 plan laws and politics.** Even though the SECURE Act passed, none of us are exactly sure how we'll be able to go about extracting our 529 funds to pay for things until we actually do. I fully expect to one day try to withdraw $100,000 and not be able to because I forgot to account for some random law.

   There is also an increasing chance that within the next twenty years, many more Americans will be able to attend reputable colleges for free. There is also constant discussion about student debt being canceled. When deciding how much to save for your child's education, pay attention to the tenor of the political conversation and how things are trending.

5. **Make sure you are saving enough for your retirement.** Regardless of who comes into power, it's always a good idea to make sure you're financially on the right track.

   Achieving financial freedom is much harder for parents because we must not only save for our own retirement but also fund our children's education. As a result, it is much harder to retire early or achieve financial freedom.

   But remember, your financial well-being should come first. After all, if you can't take care of yourself, how can you possibly take care of a child? You must be able to max out your tax-advantaged retirement plans and concurrently build your taxable investment accounts.

Just imagine how much better society would be if every kid grew up in a financially stable household where parents were less stressed out about finances and had more time to spend with their kids.

6. **Use realistic return assumptions.** None of us knows how our 529 plan investments will perform over the coming years. But we do know that stocks tend to return roughly 10% on average, while bonds tend to return roughly 5% on average since 1926. However, we all know that stocks and bonds do go down as well. Based on what we know about historical returns, a 60/40 portfolio may return an 8% compound annual return.

Changing 529 Plan Beneficiaries

If you save too much in your 529 plan, you can always change its beneficiary. Surely there is a relative with a child who could use some help. Worst case, if you remove funds for nonqualified expenses, you'll pay a 10% penalty on your gains. You'll also be subject to income taxes on the gains and may have to pay back any state income tax deductions you previously claimed.

However, for those of you who have estate values that may surpass the estate tax threshold, I strongly consider viewing a 529 plan as a generational wealth transfer vehicle. In other words, not only should you change beneficiaries for any money left over, you should also consider funding multiple 529 plans for as many loved ones and relatives as possible.

It's a more tax-efficient move to contribute $16,000 a year for five years to a grandchild's 529 plan than to have your estate pay a 40% death tax on the $80,000. Creating a family education endowment in a tax-efficient manner is a great way to ensure the survival of your lineage.

Get Your MBA or Go Without?

As an MBA holder from UC Berkeley, I should be very pro–business school. Unfortunately, it has become harder to justify the cost of an MBA due to skyrocketing tuition. In 2022, tuition at any of the top ten MBA programs in the U.S. ranged from $64,000 to $80,000 per year, with most being in the mid-$70,000 range. Once you add food and shelter, we're easily talking $100,000+ a year. Students are not only giving up two years of experience, but they're also giving up another $150,000 to $300,000 in median lost income.

Only if you are already rich, screwed up massively in college, want to take a long vacation (and are rich), love learning, got a nice grant, or despise your job and want a career change should you consider *paying to attend* an MBA program full time. MBA programs are not like graduate programs in the sciences or humanities, where scholarships are readily available. They are businesses and seldom give out free money to students.

If you are considering getting an MBA, please first check with your employer to see if it has a tuition-reimbursement program. It's a business expense for the company as well as a recruiting and retaining tool for its top employees. If you plan to pay the entire bill yourself, then do research on how you can deduct the tuition on your taxes. For example, if you earn under $80,000 the year you go to school (or $160,000 if you are married), you may be able to deduct all tuition and school-related fees. See more tuition deduction info at irs .gov/publications/p970, and check with an accountant.

All this said, getting an employer-funded MBA is the 70/30 decision, even if the school is not highly ranked. This combination minimizes your expenses, boosts your future earning power, and lets you keep working if you go part time, so you don't have to give up two years' worth of income while you're in school.

When I went to the Haas School of Business at UC Berkeley between 2003 and 2006, tuition was around $28,000 a year. I felt that was a steep price to pay, so I applied to the part-time program because my employer was willing to pay 80% of the tuition if I stayed on for at least two years after graduating.

It was a hard three years working and going to school part time. I was at the office all week, was in class Saturdays nine to five, and studied half a day on Sundays. But it was worth it. I learned practical skills that I use in every facet of life, from how to be a better negotiator and communicator to how to properly analyze cash-flow statements and real estate transactions.

But the main thing I learned in business school was confidence. I went from being a young man in my twenties who was intimidated by the senior portfolio managers to someone who could carry on a conversation with people managing billions of dollars. I finally understood everything they were saying in those meetings. With an added diploma and three more years of work experience, I started to finally feel like I belonged in the finance world.

Despite the ridiculously high cost of getting an MBA, you will likely not regret your experience. You'll meet interesting people, go on amazing school trips, and be forever part of a community. It's the journey that is most rewarding.

Just make sure you either work for at least ten years after graduating or make at least 10X the total cost of getting an MBA before you stop working, whichever comes first. After all, getting an MBA is all about maximizing your return on investment.

A top MBA essentially gives you more options and more connections. The people you meet in business school will mostly land good jobs. Some might even start successful companies. Ten years from now, your network will only be more powerful. Therefore, make sure you build good relationships and regularly keep in touch.

Remember, whatever you choose, getting an MBA is all about maximizing your returns. Don't let an MBA be an expensive two-year vacation. Instead, treat it as one of your most important lifetime investments.

THE FINANCIAL SAMURAI WAY

- Do not let the allure of prestige cloud your judgment. Elite private schools help graduates get their first opportunity at a job interview, but they are not the be-all and end-all of a person's success. Private school is typically not worth the expense if the cost of tuition will require you to sacrifice important financial goals.

- The goal of grade school is to provide a nurturing environment for learning where your kids feel protected and valued. If you can find this setting in a public school, then you've found the ideal situation. If not, then look to private school. The best schools have strong parental involvement.

- Once your household income is over 7X the annual net tuition per child, you can begin to seriously consider sending your child to private school, especially if your local public school system is poorly managed. However, the ideal situation is to send your child to a well-managed public school and invest the money you would have spent on private school tuition. You know your child's needs the best. If you can find a school that is more accommodating, it's probably worth the cost, even if you don't make 7X the annual net tuition. Education costs don't last forever.

- Just as contributing to a tax-advantaged retirement plan is a must, so is contributing to a 529 plan if you have children. Even if you contribute too much, you can change beneficiaries. If your estate is likely to surpass the estate tax threshold, fund multiple 529 plans to lower your estate's value.

- Getting an MBA is a growing gamble due to high tuition, increased supply of graduates, and time. Ideally, you'll have an employer subsidize your tuition while working full time.

- Keep an open mind. There is always something new to learn, regardless of the educational format. Reading a book like this one might be one of your best educational investments of them all.

Chapter 14

Nurture Your Love

Would you rather be rich and alone or poor with the love of your life?

Don't answer that—it's a trick question. The truth is, either scenario would be suboptimal.

Life isn't worth living if we're going to do it alone. What's the point of having money if you have nobody to share it with? The joy of spending money on your partner and your kids is often greater than the joy of spending it on yourself. So is the joy of spending money on those most in need.

But we do need money as much as we need one another. Anyone who says they'd rather live poor with the love of their life—and does it—will quickly see what a hard life it is. Nearly every part of your life would be limited by your financial constraints, from the basics, like what you eat, to the big-picture stuff, like which of your dreams you can pursue.

If you want to start a family, you'll stress over whether you can afford to have kids. If you do have them, you'll stress over the opportunities you can't afford to give them. The inability to provide your children everything will be a constant source of frustration. The data hurts: ~36% of divorces occur because of financial problems.

Thankfully, this isn't an either-or proposition. You can have love *and* money. That's the optimal scenario, which is why we should spend as much time focusing on our relationships as we do on optimizing our finances.

If you're single, that means prioritizing your search for a life partner. It's too easy to let work take over until you have nobody to share your success with. If you've already found someone, it means putting time each and every day into nurturing that relationship. It's easy to take someone you're constantly around for granted.

Love and money intersect constantly. This is especially true once kids enter our lives. Of course, kids cost a lot to raise, but that's only part of our responsibility. They soon become full-fledged adults who make financial decisions for themselves. It's our job to prepare them for that.

My core belief around love and money is this: **if we love someone, we should help them become financially independent.** This is true for our spouse and for our kids. Being financially *de*pendent is limiting at best—and debilitating at worst.

As you navigate what I hope is a life full of love and family, let's explore how you can make optimal 70/30 choices along the way. Our friends and family are what will provide us the most happiness and heartache in our lives. As a result, we must spend an equal amount of time, if not more, nurturing our relationships as we do striving for money.

Get Married or Cohabitate for Life?

Let's look at this strictly by the numbers. There are two key factors that come into play when determining whether marriage or cohabitation is the better financial move: taxes and Social Security.*

Married people who are high earners (typically $500,000 combined income and up) may be subject to an income tax penalty. Therefore, in order to save on taxes, you may want to just cohabitate.

Based on one calculation, using a marriage calculator by the Tax Policy Center, a $500,000 earner marrying an $80,000 earner would pay an additional $13,000 a year in

---

* I am referring specifically to the U.S. tax and Social Security systems.

taxes. After twenty years, that amounts to $260,000 in extra taxes paid! And if you had invested the $13,000 each year and earned an 8% compound annual return, you'd have about $642,000. Think about what you could do with all that money and decide whether getting legally married is worth it.

The exact rules change from time to time, and your tax bill will depend on several factors that are personal to you. Consult with your tax adviser and run the pro forma numbers using a free online marriage tax calculator to see what your additional cost of marriage would be. And most of all, discuss the implications with your partner.

The bigger—and often overlooked—factor is Social Security benefits. Being married offers more financial benefits when it comes time to collect Social Security, particularly if one spouse earns less than the other. The U.S. Social Security Administration allows a spousal benefit that can be as much as half of the higher-earning spouse's Social Security benefit. Each spouse can collect whatever benefit amount is higher: either the one that's calculated based on their own earnings, or the spousal benefit.

For example, let's say Susan's Social Security benefits based on her earnings are $3,000 a month. Meanwhile, her husband Mark's benefits based on his earnings are $1,000 a month. If Mark elects to collect Social Security at full retirement age (and not sooner) after Susan starts collecting her own benefits, he can collect a spousal benefit of $1,500 a month (50% of Susan's benefit) rather than collecting the $1,000 benefit based on his earnings.

The other huge benefit to getting married, when it comes to Social Security, is that the surviving spouse will continue to receive their deceased spouse's Social Security benefits. If you're not married, even if you've been living together for decades, the deceased partner's Social Security benefits disappear. Do the benefits the government promised you go to a relative or friend of your choice? No, if you die prematurely, the government gets to keep the money you paid in FICA taxes for all those years.

For the lower-income-earning individual with a lower net worth, the 70/30 move is to tie the knot. This way, you gain more financial security. And if your partner really loves you, they will try to make you financially independent during your marriage.

For the higher-income-earning individual with a higher net worth, the decision to get married is a little more difficult. You understand the often-cited statistic that roughly 50% of marriages end in divorce. Further, paying more taxes just to be officially married doesn't sound like a good trade. Therefore, even though it's not romantic, the 70/30 move is to get married with a prenuptial agreement or to cohabitate.

Getting married is easy. All it takes is paying a small fee and signing a few legal documents, and away you go. However, getting married is a massive legal commitment that requires careful planning when income and wealth levels differ greatly. Therefore, since so many marriages fail, entering into a prenuptial agreement is the rational thing to do, even if neither of you is very wealthy. If you come to a mutual agreement, it's easier to take the next step to marital bliss.

And to be clear, a prenuptial agreement doesn't necessarily mean the poorer partner gets the short end of the stick. Instead, you can look to a prenuptial agreement as a way to provide the poorer partner a way to achieve financial independence if the relationship turns sour. One friend of mine, who is worth about $20 million, married someone who was worth –$200,000. The prenuptial agreement stated that in case of a divorce after five years through no fault of either partner, the poorer partner would walk away with $2 million. Not a bad return for five years of marriage! Further, only a 10% hit to the wealthier partner's net worth if things sadly don't work out.

Ideally, you would both start from similar positions of wealth. In such a scenario, I wish you the best in building your wealth together. Starting a relationship with someone when you both have nothing and then growing your wealth to something significant is a tremendous feeling. Even if the marriage ends in divorce, splitting assets fifty-fifty is likely the right thing to do and won't feel as acrimonious.

Finally, if you want to keep things simple, just cohabitate. You can always hold a wedding ceremony and go forth like a married couple without making it legally binding. You don't need a marriage license to prove your love to your partner. Your actions are what matters most.

Marry for Love or Marry for Money?

Before you drop this book, aghast that I might suggest marrying for money, let's bring some logic to this question. The person you marry is going to be either your financial teammate or your antagonist, depending on whom you choose.

Do not marry for love at all costs. Yes, marry for love. But also marry someone who will make your life better, not worse. Marry someone who is going to be your best friend for life. But love isn't enough to keep your marriage together.

Consider a person's financial situation, intelligence, and general life philosophy before you decide to spend your life with them. If they're carrying heaps of credit card debt and haven't started saving for retirement ten years into their career, those are likely indicators that your financial future together will be fraught. Even if your finances are in tip-top shape, there's a good chance you won't want to carry all the burden of saving and earning for the family while your partner ties sandbags to your ankles.

Be aware of what you're getting into and have the hard conversations early. The chemicals of love during the first couple years of dating are strong. They make you easily see past your partner's shortcomings. Make sure you share similar money philosophies and set goals together. Whether or not you and your partner are a financial match will make your life together either much easier or much, much harder.

I know what I'm about to say will rub some people the wrong way, but I believe it to be true. All else being equal, if you have a choice, marrying someone you love who is well-off is an optimal decision, versus marrying someone you love who is struggling financially. By marrying someone who is financially secure, you get to leapfrog a generation of struggle. You yourself will have a greater chance of getting ahead because you'll be better connected and have more financial security to take more risks. Perhaps most important, your children will have greater opportunities.

In the end, love is a numbers game. Be bold. The more people you meet, the greater your chance of finding a great fit. For example, if you've got a 1% chance of finding your soul mate, you should probably try to meet at least a hundred people before giving up on love.

And if you can't find someone you love who is also well-off, then at least marry someone you love who is your equal. If you can find someone to marry who is of similar education, wealth, and ideals, you will have the optimal chance of building a successful life together. Planning for the people you meet is one of the main reasons why some people join organizations, both public and private.

One of the positives of not having a lot of money is that when it comes to making more money, you've got a lot more upside! When I'm down in the dumps, I always try to look at the upside scenario. Sprained my ankle? Thank goodness I didn't break it. Lost money on an investment? At least I didn't invest even more in the junker!

My wife and I met as poor college students. After she graduated, we decided to cohabitate from 2001 to 2008. By then, we had more money, but the global financial crisis was really putting a massive dent in our finances. It was then that I decided to propose, because I knew that even if I lost all my money, I didn't want to lose my wife, too.

Pay Up for a Fancy Wedding or Save the Money?

Keep it cheap, folks!

The average cost of a wedding in America in 2021 was $22,500, according a survey by

The Knot. If you live in Manhattan, the average spend is closer to $77,000, while San Francisco weddings average about $40,000.

With the median household income in America at around $69,000 according to the U.S. Census Bureau, spending $22,500 for a wedding is egregious. After paying taxes on a median $69,000 household income, the average couple is spending about 40% of their after-tax annual income on a wedding. It's pure insanity.

A typical wedding lasts only a day. The opportunity cost of not investing the money in your new future may result in over $100,000 in lost wealth. For example, if you invested $22,500 and it returned 8% a year over a twenty-year period, you would end up with $104,872.

Marriage is a leap of faith. Nobody goes into a marriage thinking they will break up. But divorces happen all the time. Therefore, let me provide you with some simple wedding spending rules that will give you a 70% or greater chance of making the optimal wedding spending decision.

If you follow *one* of these rules, I believe your marriage will last longer and you'll have more wealth than the average American who does not follow any of these rules. And if for some reason you divorce, or you end up having a lower household net worth for your age than the average, then you can simply blame each other for all your mistakes!

Please consider following one or a combination of two rules if you want to spend an appropriate amount on your wedding.

Wedding Spending Rule #1: Spend no more than 10% of your newly combined household income. This is the easiest and most practical wedding spending rule to follow. If one partner makes $60,000 and the other $80,000, then they should spend no more than $14,000 on a wedding. So in other words, to spend the average $22,500 on a wedding in America, a couple should earn at least $225,000. For the median household income of $69,000, consider spending up to $6,900 for a wedding instead. That $6,900 might not sound like a lot. But it forces you to think about a less expensive venue and invite only the people who matter the most to you.

Wedding Spending Rule #2: Spend no more than 3% of the value of your combined pretax retirement plans. Let's say at age thirty, one partner has a *Financial Samurai*–recommended $150,000 in their 401(k). At thirty-five, the other partner has a *Financial Samurai*–recommended $300,000 in their 401(k); this couple can spend up to $13,500 on a wedding.

When the couple's attention is drawn to their retirement savings plans, there will be a natural tendency to spend less, given that spending more means a later retirement. Remember, always be cognizant of how much time money can buy.

WEDDING SPENDING BASED ON TAX-ADVANTAGED RETIREMENT SAVINGS

Age	Years Worked	Retirement Savings	Wedding Spend (2% of Savings)	Wedding Spend (3% of Savings)
23	1	$10,000	$200	$300
24	2	$30,000	$600	$900
25	3	$50,000	$1,000	$1,500
26	4	$90,000	$1,800	$2,700
27	5	$100,000	$2,000	$3,000
28	6	$140,000	$2,800	$4,200
29	7	$150,000	$3,000	$4,500
30	8	$170,000	$3,400	$5,100
31	9	$220,000	$4,400	$6,600
32	10	$245,000	$4,900	$7,350
33	11	$280,000	$5,600	$8,400
34	12	$300,000	$6,000	$9,000
35	13	$310,000	$6,200	$9,300
40	18	$500,000	$10,000	$15,000
45	23	$750,000	$15,000	$22,500
50	28	$1,000,000	$20,000	$30,000
55	33	$1,500,000	$30,000	$45,000
60	38	$2,500,000	$50,000	$75,000

Median age for marriage is ~28 for women, ~30 for men, as of 2022.

Source: FinancialSamurai.com

Based on this rule, the average responsible American couple should spend between $4,000 and $10,000 on their wedding, not $22,500 or more.

Wedding Spending Rule #3: Spend no more than 50% of your combined side-hustle gross income. This may be my favorite modern-day wedding spending rule. Let's say the couple has a combined W-2 gross income of $120,000. In addition, they make

$24,000 a year selling T-shirts and trinkets from their online Etsy store. The couple can spend up to $12,000 on their wedding.

However, given that the couple spends 260 hours a year to make $24,000 in side-hustle money, they might be reluctant to spend $12,000 on their wedding; 130 hours of side hustling is a lot for just eight hours of fun!

As veteran side hustlers, they might even make a portion of their wedding a deductible business expense if they decide to set up a booth to sell their goods. As a side hustler, you tend to think more often about how to maximize income and minimize expenses. Just check with your accountant before making any tax decisions.

Wedding Spending Rule #4: Spend no more than 10% of your annual passive investment income. If the couple saves and invests aggressively for eight years to generate $30,000 in annual passive income, they're free to spend $3,000 on a wedding.

As a reality check, to spend $22,500 on the average American wedding, a couple would need to earn $225,000 in annual passive income. To earn $225,000 in annual passive income would require $5,625,000 in invested capital generating 4% returns or a 4% dividend. Therefore, this wedding spending rule is the most restrictive one of all.

However, the key to retiring early or achieving financial independence is generating enough passive investment income to cover your desired living expenses. Therefore, I love this wedding spending rule because it focuses a couple's attention on investing for their future. If following this rule is not feasible, then choose another one of my rules that is.

For older couples advanced in their capital accumulation, spending no more than 10% of your combined annual passive investment income might just be the perfect amount.

Wedding Spending Rule #5: Spend as much as your respective parents want to spend. If you and your partner are lucky enough to have wealthy parents who are willing to cover all the costs of your wedding, then go right ahead and accept their generosity. (But bear in mind, every time generosity is accepted, there might be a mental debt burden that will weigh on you. The next time your parents or in-laws want you to do something you don't want to do, you had better oblige. Otherwise, you will seem ungrateful.)

If your parents or in-laws are not wealthy, then please think about their financial future. They might be the most generous people, but it's up to you as their child to help them eventually achieve financial independence as well. Be gracious in accepting modest gifts, such as paying for the rehearsal dinner, the flowers, or a toaster oven. However, please don't accept money that will materially delay their retirement. I'm sure they will appreciate your thoughtfulness.

———————

BY FOLLOWING AT LEAST ONE of my wedding spending rules, you'll be able to get your marriage off to a more optimal financial start. And with stronger finances, you'll likely have less stress and fewer disagreements about finances.

If you're curious, my wife and I ultimately decided to have a sixteen-person wedding on a beach in Honolulu, where my parents and relatives live. Including two round-trip tickets from San Francisco and lunch at my favorite Korean barbecue restaurant, Yakiniku Camellia, the wedding event cost $3,100. I wore my favorite aloha shirt, pants, and slippers while my wife wore a $60 beach dress from Target. It was a blast!

WHAT ABOUT THE ENGAGEMENT RING?

There are some entertaining "rules" about how much someone should spend on an engagement ring. A couple of the common ones I've heard are the three-months'-gross-salary rule and the age rule (if your partner is thirty-two, buy them a 3.2-carat diamond).

The sparkle and excitement of proposing to your significant other tends to woo folks into spending more on an engagement ring than they likely should. Don't let marketing and societal pressure get to you! According to the 2021 WeddingWire Newlywed Report, the average cost of an engagement ring was $5,500. Although, 18% spent more than $10,000.

To keep things consistent, choose one of the first four wedding spending rules above to use as a guide for purchasing an engagement ring. But instead of using the combined gross income, pretax retirement balance, side-hustle income, or passive-income figures, use only the figures of the person buying the ring.

Sure, you may feel a little embarrassed if you show your friends a candy Ring Pop. Although nobody can tell if you get a cubic zirconia ring. Fight that feeling of not having something good enough and explain, if asked, that you guys are saving the money for your financial future.

There's no law that says you have to get a diamond engagement ring. Once you've built up a greater amount of wealth, you can always "upgrade" to a nicer engagement ring if you want to. You can use this opportunity to renew your vows as well.

Combine Your Finances or Keep Separate Bank Accounts?

There is perhaps no better gift than the gift of financial independence. I'm not talking about showering your spouse with riches once you get married. I'm talking about supporting your spouse in making their own fortune in addition to contributing to the family fortune. And the optimal move is to keep a joint account *and* separate bank accounts to minimize friction.

After all, financial independence by definition includes being financially independent from each other. Many of us remember the sheepish feeling of having to ask our parents for money growing up. The same feeling exists as an adult without your own bank account. In fact, the feeling of asking for permission to spend money may feel worse as an educated, working adult.

One reader, a stay-at-home mom who left her career as a chemical engineer after her first child was born, shared with me that she's always second-guessing whether she should spend on even the simplest of indulgences. Her husband earns a salary working at a tech company and he controls their finances.

"I miss the feeling of being able to make my own money and spend money without having to explain myself to my hubby," she shared. "For example, when my back and hands were starting to kill me from having to rock my youngest to sleep for an hour each evening, all I wanted was to get an hour-long massage. But instead of charging $120 on our joint credit card, where he checks each line item, I decided to just spend $20 in cash on a chair massage at the mall because I was afraid he'd complain that he could easily give me a massage for free! I love my husband's frugal ways, but his massages don't come close to what professional hands can do."

Over the years, I've had over a hundred people tell me they wish they had their own money to spend freely without fear of judgment from their spouses. Many who made less or were stay-at-home parents have told me financial dependence on their spouses made them feel resentful and trapped. If you're not convinced that separate bank accounts are necessary or worth it, consider these very useful reasons for having them.

Reasons Why Each Partner Should Have Their Own Accounts

Reason #1: The release valve. The common reason for each spouse wanting their own bank account is the desire for independence. There's no greater feeling than being free to do whatever you want with your own money. Because it is impossible to agree 100% on every single aspect of life—nor should you have to—having your own bank account provides a release valve when partners don't completely see eye to eye on a particular expense. Without a release valve, the chance of arguments (and ultimately divorce) increases.

Reason #2: The insurance policy. Having independence is just one reason why each spouse should have their own separate bank account. After all, before the partners met, each enjoyed independence for years. The other reason for having your own financial account is insurance.

Let's say something bad were to happen to your spouse and the legal system somehow tied up their assets in probate despite a clearly written will. Or perhaps your life insurance company decides not to pay out on the policy you spent fifteen years paying for. Who knows what snafus await after an unfortunate event. They happen all the time.

If you have your own finances, you can more comfortably wait out the storm while the legal system makes you whole. In other words, your bank account is your worst-case scenario. Knowing that my wife has her own healthy bank account will let me die more peacefully, assured that at the very least, she'll do just fine without me and our accumulated wealth and vice versa.

Reason #3: The financial trainer. Just as a workout buddy helps motivate you to do one more set or eat one less slice of pizza, your spouse can help motivate you to earn and save more. By having separate financial accounts, you can clearly see where each of your finances stand. You can challenge each other to see who gets to a certain savings amount first. Or if your starting amounts are vastly different, you can challenge each other based on a percentage increase amount. The number of different challenges and the ways to get there are endless, just like the many different types of side hustles and investments one can undertake to boost their income.

The ultimate goal is to push each other to achieve optimal finance performance while *concurrently* building a stronger financial life together. If you completely commingle your funds, it's hard to tell exactly how much you've contributed to the household. The murkier your contribution, the easier it is to feel demotivated or misinformed.

So far, I've addressed separate financial accounts for two working spouses. But how does a stay-at-home spouse expect to earn their own money if they don't have a job? Well, that's easy.

Being a stay-at-home parent is easily worth *at least* the median income of your city. In reality, being a stay-at-home spouse is often much harder than having a day job, since it can be 24-7 for the first several years of a child's life.

If you don't believe so, then take the number of hours your stay-at-home spouse works and multiply it by the average hourly cost for day care or a nanny. That is the amount of money they deserve to make, spend, save, or invest, as that is their effective contribution to the household income.

If you believe in happiness, then you believe in equitable financial independence for both spouses. And if you believe in financial independence, then you should not be opposed to each spouse having a separate bank account plus a joint account.

The ultimate goal is to create household wealth together while also ensuring that each spouse never loses their freedom.

Have Children When You're Young and Broke or Wait Until You're Older and More Financially Established?

Your children will be your most precious assets in the world. Any amount of money doesn't compare. Therefore, you'll logically want to be with them for a greater percentage of your life. And when you one day dare to dream of being a grandparent, you may wish you had had children even sooner.

Having children is one of the great equalizers because you don't need to be rich to have them. Of course, the cost of raising children is an entirely different matter. However, given that children are a great gift, it is only logical for some parents to want to have more of them, even if they lack great wealth. I didn't really understand this phenomenon until I had my own. But that's normal; it's impossible to understand what it's like to have children until you have them.

We waited so long mainly because I was overly focused on my career. I didn't think I was ready to be a dad without first feeling settled at work and having a large financial buffer. All the propaganda about the cost of raising children scared me into waiting. The last thing we want to do is have children and not properly care for them. Our children deserve better.

So we waited until we felt we had enough of a financial nest egg. And then we had to wait for almost three more years because our biology did not cooperate. They say the average couple without fertility issues has a ~15% chance of conceiving with each attempt.

Therefore, the average couple would need to try seven times with accurate ovulation tracking before succeeding. However, staying pregnant is another challenge.

LET'S CREATE A MORE SUPPORTIVE WORKPLACE

When it comes to starting a family, people need to be supported in the workplace and at home. Questions such as "When are you going to have your first baby?" or "When are you going to have another child?" may seem innocuous, but they can bring about emotional pain.

Between 10% and 25% of known pregnancies end in miscarriage. Chances are high the person you are speaking to may have experienced one, or they may be struggling with infertility. Perhaps they do not want to have a child (or more children) or are navigating the complex surrogate or adoption process. Nobody owes anyone else an explanation about their family plans. It is best to stay mum about another person's parental status unless they voluntarily bring it up. You never know what someone is going through—or whether they want to talk about it with you.

If you are a manager, please be more empathetic to a pregnant colleague who has to visit the doctor, leave a meeting to use the restroom, or take time out to pump when they're back from parental leave. Pregnancy can be very uncomfortable and can also negatively affect sleep. The postpartum period can also be extremely challenging due to the need to feed the baby every one to three hours. Hormonal crashes do happen, which may lead to periods of depression. Further, there may be bodily trauma inflicted during childbirth, especially during a C-section or particularly difficult natural birth. As our ob-gyn once said, "Nine months to give birth, nine months to heal." Yet here in America, we do not have a federal paid maternity leave law.

As you figure out your career, do your best to find a company that supports at least one month of paid parental leave for both partners (although one month is absolutely not enough, it is the bare minimum). The best companies are now providing both parents three to four months of paid parental leave to be used within the first twelve months of a newborn's life.

If there is ever a time to pay for childcare support, it's during the fourth trimester (the three months after giving birth). Hiring a night doula to help with pumping, feeding, cleaning, and sleep can be extremely helpful. But of course, overnight care is not cheap.

The optimal age to have a baby is based on two variables: biology and finances. From a biological standpoint, the younger you have a baby, the better. Being younger offers a higher probability for a couple to get pregnant, stay pregnant, and give birth to a healthy baby.

By age twenty-eight, roughly 23% of a woman's eggs have chromosomal abnormalities (are not genetically normal). By age thirty-eight, that percentage increases to 48%. By age forty-two, the percentage increases to a shocking 83%. Chromosomal abnormalities are one of the main reasons why older women may have a more difficult time getting pregnant and have a higher chance of experiencing miscarriages. The body tends to know when something is wrong.

Younger parents also tend to have more energy, which helps in the newborn months, when sleep is scarce. Then those babies become toddlers who will climb the kitchen counters or lick the power outlets the moment you look away.

As a forty-five-year-old dad of a kindergartener and a two-year-old, I'm reminded of my age every time I bend over to pick up my little ones. My lower back aches and my knees sometimes buckle if they bend too far. Oh, to be twenty-five again! But then I realize that because we are older parents, we don't have the same financial stresses as some younger parents have. There will always be trade-offs.

That said, I'm going to jump to the optimal answer here: **have a baby as soon as you're financially and emotionally stable enough to do so.** But let's get specific. Based on biology and economic wealth potential, the ideal age range to have a baby is between thirty to thirty-four. In this age range, you've likely accumulated a comfortable amount of wealth and know what you want to do with your life. Further, you're in an age range when your biology likely still cooperates. Forced to pick a number, I believe the best age to have a baby based on biology and economics is thirty-two.

Let's dig deeper into the economics of having a child. Kids are expensive. According to the U.S. Department of Agriculture, the cost of raising a child from birth through age seventeen was roughly $233,000 in 2015. When you factor in inflation, the cost rises to roughly $284,000. Then add college tuition, room, and board, and the figure easily jumps to roughly $500,000—or well over $1 million if you plan to send the child to private school (see chart in chapter 13).

It's important to have your financial house in order before having children because raising a child is truly one of the hardest things you'll ever do. You'll be constantly tired, worried, and stressed. Your day-to-day happiness will likely take a plunge during the initial years of your child's life as your free time disappears and your energy gets zapped. But things get better over time, and the joy you experience from having kids will fill your heart.

Working sixty-plus hours a week in banking was relatively easy compared with my first three years as a stay-at-home father. The stakes are much higher as a full-time parent. One missed second could result in a lifetime change. Adding money problems to the equation is guaranteed to put a strain on your relationship and happiness.

Before having kids, my wife and I would seldom argue. If we did, it would be about silly stuff like, "Why did you cook enough for fifteen people at a potluck? If the fifteen people coming all cooked for fifteen people, we'd have enough food for two hundred and twenty-five people!" But after we had children, these funny incidents that didn't matter became more agitating because we were both constantly tired. That's why figuring out your money *before* having kids is extremely important.

Career and Financial Guidelines to Consider Before Having Kids

There's an old saying, "Have children and the money will come." The reason is that once you become a parent, most people will do everything possible to provide for them. At the same time, children are expensive and take a tremendous amount of time and effort to raise.

Therefore, here are some financial guidelines you should consider before having a baby. Please note I'm assuming you've already found the right stable partner. If you are currently experiencing marital problems, having a baby to try to fix your issues will not likely work.

1. **A career milestone target.** Having a baby may or may not derail your career progression due to workplace discrimination and necessary time off. Given this potential reality, you might consider having a baby only after **achieving at least a third promotion**. The first promotion doesn't count for much, since you're going from junior bottom-feeder to less junior bottom-feeder. But by promotion number three, it's clear you're actually creating a lot of value for your organization. Three or more promotions is not a fluke. You should feel confident in your career and in your earning power by then. If you happen to lose your job, you can be assured that you've got good enough skills that other companies will want you too.

2. **An income target.** According to Princeton economist Angus Deaton and psychologist Daniel Kahneman, $75,000 is the income level where happiness no longer increases the more you make. They partnered with Gallup to survey 450,000 Americans

in 2008 and 2009. Thanks to inflation, that income level is closer to $100,000 a year in 2022.

I argue happiness no longer increases once a couple earns closer to $250,000 if you live in an expensive coastal city like San Francisco or New York. According to the U.S. Department of Housing and Urban Development in 2018, a San Francisco family of four with an income of $117,000 per year is considered "low income." In San Francisco, you can actually qualify for subsidized housing if you make $117,000 a year or less for a family of four. Therefore, having a household income of $85,000 to $100,000 in a noncoastal city or $200,000 to $300,000 in a coastal city before having kids is a reasonable target. With such income, you'll ideally be able to afford to buy a home, comfortably pay for children's expenses, and save at least 20% of your salary for retirement.

But of course, you can certainly have kids on a lower income. Statistically, most do. It's just that providing for them in a less stressful way may be harder. Divorce rates tend to trend slightly lower the higher a couple's household income gets.

Nathan Yau of FlowingData reports that, according to the 2019 American Community Survey, once you get to a $200,000 median household income, the divorce rate declines to a roughly steady 30%. It's only when you reach a $600,000 household income that divorce rates decline again to about 25%.

If you want to make optimal decisions with a 70% or greater chance at succeeding in marriage, generating a higher household income is a logical way of improving your odds, especially after having kids.

3. **A net worth target.** Coming up with a net worth target before having children can be fun and an extremely motivating way to build wealth. This way, the more you want children, the more determined you will be to grow your net worth.

Back when I was working, I set a goal of having a $1 million net worth before having kids. I remember setting this goal because a buddy at my first job told me that was his goal. Stayton had graduated from Yale, was on the more profitable U.S. equities desk, and is now a hedge fund manager. Our upbringings were quite different, yet we were colleagues. As an impressionable young man, I liked the sound of a $1 million goal, so I went with it. It was as if Stayton implanted an idea in me, as Cobb did in his wife, Mal, in the movie *Inception*. Once the idea took hold, there was no changing my mind.

I became fiercely focused on my career, saving, and investing for over a decade so I could reach that goal. There was no time for family in my twenties and early thirties.

It's clear now that a $1 million net worth goal before having children was completely unnecessary, especially since I would have continued to build wealth after having children. My parents raised my sister and me just fine without being millionaires. Why the hell did I ever think I needed $1 million to be a competent father?!

Answer: peer pressure and the high cost of trying to achieve a comfortable lifestyle in an expensive city. For my entire postcollege career, I've lived only in New York City or San Francisco, the undisputed two most expensive cities in America. Therefore, be very careful about letting other people's lifestyles influence your own, including mine!

Having a net worth that is equal to **2X to 3X your gross income** offers enough stability to start having kids if you've also hit your career milestone and income target. In other words, if you and your partner are making a combined $100,000 a year, a net worth of $200,000 to $300,000 is a reasonable level to bring new life to the world. The key is to be on the right financial track because chances are high that your wealth will continue to increase over time with proper financial habits.

Whatever age you feel is ideal to start having kids, consider starting a year *before* that ideal age because it takes on average seven months to conceive if you have no issues.

The last thing you want to do is wait until you are 100% financially ready to have a baby and then not be able to have one because your body won't cooperate. In such a scenario, you may be filled with regret for years. Remember, when it comes to having a baby, we are following the 70/30 framework to give ourselves the best chance of making the right decision without wasting too much time.

You might not want a family now if you are 100% focused on your career. However, you may feel differently as you get older. Starting a family requires tremendous planning. Understand the statistics with regard to biology and come up with financial targets. Have regular dialogues with your partner in advance. The battle against time is one none of us will win, and the earlier we can prepare, the better.

THE BEST TIME TO GET LIFE INSURANCE

Life insurance tends to be an afterthought for many in their twenties and thirties. However, if you plan to buy a home with a mortgage and start a family, getting life insurance is the responsible thing to do.

The best age to get life insurance is around age thirty. And the best type of life insurance to get is a thirty-year term policy. At this age and term, it's like locking in a thirty-year fixed mortgage at an all-time low. The longer you wait to get life insurance, the more expensive the premiums tend to be.

After age thirty, the average person's life tends to get a lot more complicated. You not only may have more debt and new little ones to support, but your spouse might leave their job to take care of the kids. Then you might need to support two sets of parents as well. Losing an income source during your highest-earning years can be devastating.

Ideally, your life insurance policy will cover all debt and provide enough money for your family to live on until your children become financially independent adults. If you are able to pay off debt sooner or build much more wealth after getting a life insurance policy, you can always cancel it.

One of my mistakes was getting only a $1 million, ten-year term policy at age thirty-five in 2013. Given that I didn't have children back then, I decided to match the duration to when I planned to pay off my primary mortgage. I naively assumed I could always renew for another ten to twenty years at a similar rate if I ever had children.

However, an overzealous sleep doctor in 2017 diagnosed me with intense sleep apnea. The sleep center had recently opened and was hungry for business. I decided to do all the treatments the doctor recommended because, why not? Insurance was paying for almost everything. Finally I could use my insurance on something after years of not seeing doctors and paying high premiums.

As it turns out, due to my sleep doctor visits, when I went to renew my policy in 2017, my insurance carrier decided to quote me 11X more! My reasonable $40 a month premium for a $1 million, ten-year term policy would skyrocket to $450 a month if I were to renew. Some of the premium increase was due to age. But the predominant reason was sleep apnea.

Lock in an affordable life insurance policy before going to the doctor for non-life-threatening health issues. And expect your life to turn out differently than expected. Get life insurance before you need it most. It will be a lot more affordable if you do. Further, you'll be able to rest easier knowing that your family will be taken care of just in case the worst happens.

Financially Support Your Adult Children or
Let Them Fend for Themselves?

When I bought my first single-family home in San Francisco in 2005, my seventy-year-old neighbor stopped by to say hello. He was the godfather of the block, having bought his building back in the early 1970s. He gave me the inside scoop on all the neighbors. One neighbor stood out in particular.

He said the house across the street was purchased a year before mine by a family who wanted a place for their son to live while attending UC Hastings College of the Law. The purchase price? $1.45 million for a 2,100-square-foot, three-bedroom, three-bathroom house.

The son would host at least one fraternity-style party every quarter, but other than that, the house was pretty tame. The son continued to live in the house after law school.

For ten years, the son not only lived for free but made rental income by charging his two roommates at least $1,000 a month each. His $120,000+ law school tuition was fully paid for by the Bank of Mom and Dad. He also drove a $60,000 Audi S4.

Eventually he decided he no longer wanted roommates, so he sold the house for over $2 million. He then used the proceeds to buy himself an even nicer house in Pacific Heights, one of the most expensive neighborhoods in the city. Given that he received so much help from his parents, he has now leapfrogged his friends, who are mostly still renting in expensive San Francisco. At the time, I was envious because I couldn't afford to move up to Pacific Heights on my salary alone.

Providing financial assistance for adult children is a tricky situation. On the one hand, you want your children to be safe and have as many opportunities as possible. On the other hand, you don't want to spoil them to the point where they lose the motivation to provide for themselves.

Taking away from your child the dignity of working can lead to negative life ramifications in the future, like lower self-esteem, feeling like a loser, or lacking purpose, to name a few. For example, after I bought a smaller home in 2014, my new neighbor's son came back to live with them after college. Not a bad choice to save money for the first year or two. However, because he had minimal living expenses, he decided to spend the little money he was making at odd jobs on cars and motorbikes.

He never got motivated to go back to school to get his master's degree either, as his father had mentioned he planned to do. Today the son is thirty-two and still living in his parents' house, trying to figure things out. As parents, we want our children to build a life

NURTURE YOUR LOVE   261

of their own. We should take care of our adult children if needed. However, there comes a point when we must cut them off and let them live on their own, no matter how much it pains us!

Going Through the Muck

I started out flipping burgers at McDonald's for $4 an hour, and the experience made me not take any opportunities for granted. The last thing I wanted to do was go back to McDonald's and get yelled at each day by a power-tripping manager because I didn't do my best at my new job. This fear of going in reverse propelled me to not only work hard but also invest aggressively and start side hustles.

Being able to start with very little and work your way up is a blessing. It gives you perspective, so you're less likely to take the opportunities you have for granted. Giving your adult children everything takes away that important perspective. If the first car you drive is a new BMW given to you by your parents, you may be hard-pressed to appreciate any other car. Over time, if you can't comfortably afford to buy a BMW on your own, then you may end up extremely frustrated when you want to buy a new car.

Despite all the downsides of financially assisting your adult children, there are also real benefits, if they have their heads on straight. But whether you are providing money for food, transportation, or even a down payment on a house, it's important to *never* let your adult children think you are offering free money. Instead, the money is a loan that will be paid back by a specific time. In addition, charge a reasonable interest rate that is at least higher than the risk-free rate of return (ten-year bond yield). When they finally pay you back, they will feel an incredible amount of self-satisfaction. It is *then* that you can decide whether to forgive their loan or not.

If your adult child is willing to accept financial assistance, use the opportunity as a chance to emphasize your sound financial philosophies. Further, make sure they understand never to brag about the things they have, especially if you bought them those things. Your adult child thinking they hit a triple when they were born on third base is a surefire way to lose friends.

If you are a parent who is fortunate enough to accumulate wealth above the estate tax threshold, that is all the more reason to help your adult children while you are living rather than after you are dead. To pay a ~40% death tax on money above the estate tax threshold is a waste. It is much more satisfying to actually see your money help someone.

The key is to raise financially savvy children who understand the value of money. If you've been constantly teaching them about money and making them work for their money since childhood, chances are high you will have raised financially competent children.

Optimal Scenarios:
- Help your adult children financially if you believe they appreciate the value of money. Just don't let anybody know.
- Help your adult children financially but put strict conditions on when the money will be paid back and at what interest rate. There should also be a strict time limit in place after which your financial support will be cut off. This way, you and your children can plan for that ultimate break.
- Unless it is a life-or-death situation, do not help your adult children if they have never shown an interest in money. You will end up encouraging their poor financial habits. Let them live a suboptimal life until they can better appreciate money.

Set a Good Example for Your Kids

My dad is a frugal guy. So many of the money habits and philosophies I live by today stem from the examples he set for me as a kid. And one of the biggest lessons he taught me came from something incredibly small.

We were never allowed to order a drink when my family went out to eat. My dad said it cost too much and that we should order water with lemon instead. Besides, lemon water was healthier than a sugary soda. It's such a tiny thing, but I still think about it today. Dad didn't let his frugality stop us from enjoying a meal out. He found solutions to make it work financially. And it turns out, water with lemon *is* pretty good.

I remember sitting at the breakfast table with him one morning when I was a junior in high school as he showed me how to read a stock ticker. That was my first introduction to investing, and it led to my having a huge interest in finance and economics. My dad's early lessons inspired me to start investing my money in college, to work in finance, and to eventually start *Financial Samurai*.

Seeing my dad live according to his own set of money principles helped me understand personal finance fundamentals. When he taught me about investing and compounding interest, I learned that if I wanted $100 in my pocket, I had to first earn $120 and then pay taxes on it.

In addition, as someone who was making only $4 an hour at McDonald's, I was forced to realize how much $120 Air Jordans would really cost: about thirty-six hours working away over a hot stove making Egg McMuffins and Quarter Pounder patties I occasionally dropped. (Well, maybe I only needed to work thirty hours, since I made below the standard deduction threshold at the time.)

And if I invested that money instead of spending it, there was a good chance that $100 would double about every seven years, based on a 10% compound annual return. I applied that thinking when I got my first full-time job in 1999 and invested 50% to 80% of my after-tax income for the next thirteen years. I would not have had the financial cushion I needed to negotiate a severance at thirty-four if it hadn't been for my parents' money lessons.

My mother was equally frugal. She wouldn't let me leave the dining table until every kernel of rice was eaten. Today she is a grandmother who generously gives her money away. "I'd rather see my money go to helping others while alive than after I'm gone," she explained to me one day.

It's crucial to talk about money with your kids—and then lead by example. As you apply the principles in this book, bring your kids along for the journey in age-appropriate ways. The key is to explain why things are the way they are and to translate how much things cost in terms of time. If you can teach your children the reality that money is time and time is money, chances are higher they will make the most of both.

Show your teen a mortgage amortization schedule when you celebrate locking in a low interest rate on your new home. Let them see why it matters. Teach them the real cost of those Bluetooth earbuds if they put them on a credit card that they can't pay off when the bill is due. And show them how compounding interest works in their favor if they invest their money.

My dad's example set a great foundation for building wealth. But it did have one downside. For two decades, I had a hard time spending and enjoying my money. And to this day I don't live it up as much as I probably can afford. There's always that pull to be frugal and to invest more money.

Despite my frugality sometimes getting the better of me, I'm so grateful to my dad for teaching me how to be financially responsible. I'm also grateful to my mother for showing me how to be happy with what I already have. As a result, I've made it my mission to pass that learning on to as many people as possible, and above all to my kids. Now when we go out to eat, we sometimes even order water with *two* free lemon slices. All the taste, none of the calories.

Get Divorced or Stay in a Loveless Marriage?

They say divorce is expensive because it's worth it. Nobody gets married thinking they'll one day get divorced. However, overall, about 50% of married couples in America eventually divorce, the sixth-highest divorce rate in the world. Therefore, if you're thinking about getting a divorce, know that you are not alone. Please try not to feel ashamed for wanting to move on with your life. Divorce is as normal as making a wrong stock pick.

Although divorce can feel like a failure and a letdown to your family and friends, change your mindset. After trying your best to make your marriage work—through marriage counseling, third or fourth chances, interventions, and so forth—staying in a loveless marriage is a sunk-cost fallacy.

A sunk cost is a cost that has already been incurred and cannot be recovered. In other words, given that your marriage is no longer fixable, it is best to take your losses and move on. The sooner you gain the courage to move on, the less you will let a broken relationship keep you down.

Do not let a bad marriage prevent you from seeking happiness on your own or with someone else. If you do, you let your antagonizing partner win. Staying in a bad marriage keeps your partner from seeking happiness elsewhere as well. There are millions of people out there looking for love. Surely you could be compatible with at least a handful of them.

Too many people let the judgment of others keep them from doing what they want. A female reader revealed to me that she doesn't love her husband but stays with him because she doesn't want to feel the shame of being a divorcée. What would her parents and friends think about her breakup? What about her $200,000 wedding at the fancy resort with over four hundred guests? She wants to "get their money's worth" by staying together for at least ten years. This is a sunk-cost fallacy.

Instead, her solution to an unhappy marriage is to see other people in secret to fulfill her emotional needs. After all, she lives in a nice home, eats at fine restaurants, and frequently goes on nice vacations. But she's not fulfilled, and neither is her husband.

The harder you try to save your marriage, the less guilty you will feel once you finally divorce. Therefore, do everything you can to try to make the relationship work. Set a one-year time limit to make amends. If after one year things don't get better, make a change.

The one large complication to divorce is when kids are involved. Ideally, two parents stay happily together until their kids leave the nest, and then the parents divorce. Of course, it's hard to hide growing discontent from your kids. But this is a strategy that seems to have worked well for my friend Pete, who decided to get a divorce and remarry after his son's first year at university. By then, Pete and his ex-wife felt they had done their best for their now twenty-year-old, mature son. Now it was time for them to find happiness with new partners.

If there were ever a clear sign that parenting is hard, just observe how common it is for parents to divorce after having children. Even though a loving, two-parent household is ideal, parents still get divorced because their relationships have become unbearable. Children are a joy, but they can also put tremendous strain on a marriage.

You have the right to happiness, just as you have the right to financial freedom. Don't let anybody tell you otherwise!

SUNK-COST FALLACY OR RATIONAL DECISION?

Justy, Keiah, Rebekah, and Wes crash-land on a tiny island in the Pacific. For one week, they subsist on coconuts and mangoes. Then one day the fog suddenly clears. With her laser vision, Keiah tells the group she sees land about thirty miles away.

After much debate, Justy, the most determined of them all, successfully convinces the group to try to swim ashore. The mangoes and coconuts are almost all gone. It is time for them to do something about their suboptimal situation. The water is calm and over eighty degrees. So they go for it.

Thirteen hours of swimming and several shark encounters later, the group can finally make out the details of the shore. Rebekah encourages the group by shouting, "Just thirty more minutes and we will all finally be dry, safe, and free!"

But just minutes away from shore, Wes inexplicably tells his fellow swimmers, "You guys go on ahead without me. I'm too tired to continue." Wes then turns around and swims thirteen hours back to the deserted island.

When it comes to making optimal decisions, always be aware of how much time and money you've spent getting to where you are, what is the incremental cost of continuing, and whether you will enjoy the ultimate outcome. You may have spent a fortune on your goal, but if achieving it will make you worse off, then it may be best to give up and start anew.

In Wes's case, it seems obvious he should have kept swimming to shore. However, what we may not know is that Wes is a wanted fugitive who decided he'd rather not get captured and tortured in jail for the rest of his life. He'd rather take his chances with the sharks in the name of freedom!

THE FINANCIAL SAMURAI WAY

- Friends and family provide the most happiness and heartache in our lives. Thus, it's worthwhile to spend more time and effort nurturing your relationships.

- Look for a life partner who is financially secure. Not only will you live a more comfortable life, but so, potentially, will your children. But if it comes to choosing between the love of your life who is poor and someone you like who is rich, go for the love of your life as long as you have a similar money mindset. You can always find ways to make more money, but you might never have a chance with that special someone again.

- If you believe in financial independence for yourself, you should also believe in financial independence for your spouse. Therefore, it makes sense to have both separate and joint financial accounts. This way, each partner always has the freedom to spend money the way they see fit, while jointly working to build greater financial security together.

- The best age to have a baby is determined by biology and economics. After about ten years of working after high school or college, you should be able to build some sort of financial momentum and understanding of what you want. Therefore, if you want to start a family, shoot to have your first baby by around age thirty-two. The difficulties of getting pregnant and staying pregnant start increasing after thirty-five.

- Help your adult children financially if you feel they appreciate the value of money and hard work. However, charge interest and set a target date for when you will get paid back. When they are able to pay you back, that is when you can decide whether to forgive their loan. Don't take away their pride of making it on their own.

- You deserve to be happy. Don't let the sunk-cost fallacy cause you to stay in an unhappy marriage for longer than you want. Try your best to make your marriage work. Go to therapy, and seek counsel from friends and family. But if there is no improvement after a year, it's time to move on. Divorce is no longer taboo.

Chapter 15

Live Like a Financial Samurai

I t's easy to get so lost in the numbers when striving for financial independence that we forget the point of it all. Remember: we don't chase financial freedom for the money itself. It's the *freedom* piece that we're after. When we're financially free, our time—our most finite and precious resource—becomes entirely our own.

I have friends who are worth hundreds of millions of dollars and are no happier than the average person because they don't have the freedom to do what they want—shareholder concerns, employee issues, and an overwhelming amount of responsibility always get in the way. Our *why* can get buried in the noise.

And too often we confuse our *why* with the allure of prestige and social status. We spend money on things we don't care about to get validation from people who don't matter.

As you pursue your goal of achieving financial independence, remember your core values. Do a gut check to make sure you're focusing on the things that really matter to you, at whatever life stage you're in. Don't get fooled into playing the status game.

Strive to Be Rich and Famous or Aim to Be a Rich Nobody?

Fame can be a curse if you are not careful. Once you get a taste of it, you might get addicted to the endless dopamine hits, which eventually make you numb inside. Instead of seeking fame and fortune, focus on just the fortune part so you can live your life on your terms.

Once you become famous, your most precious asset, time, rapidly shrinks away, as someone always tends to want something from you. On the other hand, if you are a rich nobody, you can more adeptly weave in and out of society without anybody noticing. And given that your ultimate goal is financial freedom, it is only consistent that you have time freedom as well.

Unfortunately, the more money and fame you have, the more you may be judged. "Nobody is self-made" and "You didn't build that" are two favorite retorts from critics. Although it is true that building a great fortune often requires a tremendous amount of luck, you also want to feel good about the work you've put in to get to where you are. Further, you want to conserve your precious life energy by not having to constantly defend yourself for the sacrifices you made to get to where you are. When in doubt, nod and move on.

Therefore, your optimal solution is to practice Stealth Wealth. With Stealth Wealth, you'll be able to expertly deflect any unwanted attention you might receive by blending into any type of environment. Ultimately, you must stay humble, especially as your wealth grows.

Here are ten guidelines for the Stealth Wealth practitioner.

Stealth Wealth Rule #1: Never drive a nice car to work or to any public setting. Nothing inspires judgment quite like seeing what kind of car a person drives. Drive an economical, safe car so that when you run into your coworkers, they won't suspect you're wealthy. Or take public transportation. You don't want to roll into the office in a Benz and have your boss see you. Their immediate thought will be to cut your bonus since you are doing so well.

Driving up to your salary-negotiation meeting in a Bentley isn't going to work in your favor either. Neither is owning a nicer car than your landlord's, which he'll see every time he comes over to address an issue. Instead, drive the safest and most economical car you can.

When cops huddle for breakfast thinking about which car they want to ticket, do you think they are going for the guy in a ten-year-old Toyota Corolla or the guy in a new Lamborghini Huracán?

Having a modest car is the number one easiest way to practice Stealth Wealth.

Stealth Wealth Rule #2: Be careful whom you give your home address to. People love to snoop online to see what you paid for your house. Not only will they see what you paid for your house, but they'll also be able to tell whether you're underwater or have huge equity. Instead of giving an exact address, you can give them cross streets and a description of the house, e.g., *I'm at the corner of Jackson and Teller. Brown wood-shingle house. You can't miss it.*

Inevitably, they will find out your exact address if they pay attention, but delay access to that information for as long as possible. Your house is your sacred abode. Protect its privacy. I recommend claiming your house online by logging into Zillow, Redfin, and other platforms. Then remove all photos of your home or upload different photos to throw lookie-loos and robbers off the scent. You can even decrease your number of bedrooms and bathrooms from what the online platforms have on file.

You most certainly don't want your property tax assessor to think you live in a mega-mansion. I clearly remember that during the global financial crisis, the property assessor would continue to value properties higher in order to charge more in property taxes. This was despite obvious indicators that property prices were weakening. I had to battle the property assessor's office for three years in a row to stop them from continually increasing my property tax bill. And you know what? I won each appeal. But wouldn't it be nice if each city did the right thing and valued your property fairly every year? Don't count on it. During downturns, cities are incentivized to raise property tax revenue even further.

Your home is the easiest way to blow your Stealth Wealth cover. Be careful.

Let me share an innocuous story about how giving out your home address can make you a target. After one reader's child got accepted to a new preschool, the administrator blasted out an email to all new parents saying the school would be dropping off a welcome bag to their homes. My reader and his wife thought it was a nice gesture.

However, in addition to being nice, it turns out the school was canvassing new parents' homes to compare the homes' apparent values with those listed on Zillow and Redfin. In other words, the delivery person was acting like a drive-by home appraiser, so that when it was time to send out fundraising letters, the school could better segment its donation asks to improve yield.

My reader, who lives in a $3 million house, was asked for a donation of $2,500, while another parent, who lived in an apartment worth much less, was asked for a donation of $500. They found out because they were friends and showed each other their donation request letters.

From a fundraising standpoint, it was smart of the school to differentiate their donation requests. However, as the person being scouted, you might not appreciate such a targeted solicitation. By giving out a P.O. box instead, you have more control over other people's perceptions of you.

Stealth Wealth Rule #3: Don't flash your bling. Whether it's your Panerai watch, Birkin bag, Armani suit, or Louboutin shoes, keep them at home if you don't want people to know you can afford the real thing. People who practice Stealth Wealth do not flash their bling.

Resist the urge to brag about your material things. After all, the quality things that you buy are for your own pleasure. Pretend you don't know luxury brands or how much things cost. You can just say you like how they look.

Stealth Wealth Rule #4: Never reveal your full income or wealth. Without question, never reveal the full extent of how much you make. Only those who are insecure, seek adoration, or want to make money by teaching you how to make money enjoy flaunting their wealth. There's an inverse correlation between how much wealth you have and how much you show. You're an invisible tycoon, remember?

If you have a particularly high income level and you're hanging around with people who make a fraction of what you make, be cognizant of that. Be aware that the median national household income was $67,521 in 2020, according to the U.S. Census Bureau. Earning anything more than 2X your state's median household income will slowly bring you under fire.

The people bragging about their income are people with some of the lowest self-esteem. They are clearly seeking attention to make up for the lack of attention they receive at home.

Stealth Wealth Rule #5: Spread your assets around. Do not become one of the biggest landowners in your community. Do not become one of the biggest shareholders in a private equity deal unless you really, really believe in it.

Spread your investable assets around so people can't really tell how much you have. Diversification also ensures that your wealth doesn't take a beating in case of violent downturns.

Chopping up their assets and putting them into different LLCs is one of the best ways the rich practice Stealth Wealth. They usually use a lawyer to be each LLC's representative.

Stealth Wealth Rule #6: Learn to be humble. Not everybody had nurturing parents, attended great schools, is fully able, was born in a developed country, or got lucky breaks. If you had any of these things, know that you are privileged. And because you recognize your privilege, it is important to stay humble.

When you start visiting other communities, you may realize that despite all your hard work, you may still be luckier than most. The better understanding you have of others, the less chance you'll come across as an arrogant snob. Take every chance you get to travel internationally, learn another language, and live abroad.

When someone eventually confronts you about your wealth or success, attribute most of your success to luck. There are plenty of people who work just as hard as, if not harder than, you but haven't been as lucky. If you attribute much of your success to luck, people will naturally back down. You can take things a step further by buying them a drink and asking about their situation to show that you care. So many people just want to be heard.

Stealth Wealth Rule #7: Praise others for their success and highlight your failures. Always be encouraging and positive about other people's milestones. People who are insecure tend to be the ones who want to toot their own horn the most. Instead, be proactive in highlighting the success of others. Not only will other people appreciate your love, but you will also be seen as a confident and thoughtful person. So bite your tongue and try not to one-up someone else despite the successes you have. Give glory to others. Be happy for them and never belittle their achievements. Instead, always highlight the team who helped make things happen.

Instead of talking about your wins, point out your failures. Your failures are what will endear you to others because everybody has failed at multiple things in their lives. To only talk about your achievements is a low emotional-intelligence (EQ) move.

Stealth Wealth Rule #8: Volunteer your time. Donating money is one thing. It's easier to do when you have a lot of money. However, even if people find out that you donate a lot of money, they will still judge you for not donating enough or not donating to a worthy enough cause. Therefore, in addition to donating your money, donate your time. If you're out there being a Big Brother or Big Sister for a child who needs a mentor, how is someone going to look down on you? You don't need to be there, but you are. Because you care.

Stealth Wealth Rule #9: Get your estate plan in order. Getting your final affairs sorted out well before your time ends is undebatable. One great way to protect your wealth is by setting up revocable living trusts. You don't want your heirs to go through a public and potentially messy probate court fight for what they think they should get. Further, probate often costs more and takes longer. Trusts are all about leaving a legacy without other people getting up in your business. I also recommend putting businesses you own under someone else's name (a proxy, usually a lawyer) or under the shelter of a trust. Keep inquisitive people guessing. A trust within a trust, just like a dream within a dream.

If you're unwilling to hire an estate planning lawyer to set up a revocable living trust to protect your assets and your family's privacy, then at least write a will. This way, your heirs will know your intentions. Supplement your will with a letter of instruction, which has more specific details about your online passwords, secret files, handymen to contact, and more. Please go to the Further Reading section for helpful articles on estate planning.

Stealth Wealth Rule #10: Read the room. Different environments require different modes of being. If the mood in the room is serious, but you're constantly cracking jokes at another's expense, you might not be invited to future brainstorming sessions. If the social setting is joyous, try not to be the downer who is always pointing out worst-case scenarios.

You must learn to read the room and act accordingly. Practice developing a poker face in order to better control your expressions. If you develop a good one, you'll be better equipped to change your expression as the situation warrants.

Tiptoe Away from the Spotlight

Feeling loved and acknowledged is wonderful. I get it. But it should come naturally, as a by-product of the good work that you're doing. Seeking fame as a key objective is a 30/70 move. Not only might you never gain the level of fame that you seek, making you perpetually dissatisfied, but you might also find out fame can be restrictive.

One day I got lunch at a corner bistro in Oakland with Shaun Livingston, winner of three NBA championships with the Golden State Warriors. If there's one person who has a difficult time going unnoticed, it's a six-foot-seven Warriors basketball player in Oakland. About every twenty minutes during our two hours sitting outside, a random stranger would come up to us and say hello and share stories about their own basketball-playing days. A couple of fans even offered bodyguard services and weed delivery at a discount!

It was the first time I had ever experienced what true fame felt like. On the one hand, it must be nice to be constantly recognized by basketball fans for bringing so much joy to the Bay Area. On the other hand, fame can take away one's freedom to simply eat in peace. But Shaun greeted every visitor with kindness and respect. He was a true professional and is one of the most inspirational people I know. Shaun battled back from injury to win it all multiple times. I bet he'd make a great general manager one day.

Instead of fame, what most people really want is admiration from the people who matter most to them. This could mean approval from a critical parent or close friends' recognition of a job well done. Do not seek the approval of strangers. They do not matter in the end.

Buy a Luxury Car or Stick with a Budget Car?

I just got through saying that a modest car is the number one easiest way to practice Stealth Wealth. Let's take a closer look at some optimal choices when it comes to buying a vehicle.

Back in 2009, I observed in amazement as a total of 690,000 new vehicles averaging $24,000 each were sold under the Cash for Clunkers program. Instead of helping, the government's $4,000 rebate for trading in your perfectly fine car ended up hurting people's finances. With a median household income barely around $50,000 at the time and heading lower, $24,000 was clearly too much to spend on a new car. Instead of buying a $24,000 car in 2009, you could have invested in the S&P 500 and tripled your money.

Buying a car you cannot afford is one of the most common 30/70 decisions the typical person makes. Besides the purchase price of a car, you've also got to pay insurance, maintenance, parking tickets, and traffic tickets. When you add everything up, the true cost of owning a car is much greater.

So let me introduce my One-Tenth Rule for Car Buying. I've mentioned it briefly in chapter 4. Let's take a closer look at it now. The rule states that you should **spend no more** than one-tenth of your gross annual income on the purchase price of a car. The car can be new or old, bought with cash or leased. It doesn't matter, so long as the car costs 10% of your annual gross income or less. You can also buy multiple cars using the One-Tenth Rule, so long as the total value of the cars equals 10% of your annual gross income or less.

In other words, if you make $65,000 a year, limit your car purchase to $6,500. If you desire a $70,000 luxury vehicle, then you've got to find a way to make $700,000. If you desire a $12,000 compact car and a $40,000 sedan, then your goal is to make $520,000. Ridiculous? Perhaps. But the One-Tenth Rule is there to help prevent overconsumption, and also to act as a motivator to make more money.

The median price of a new car today is over $40,000, yet the typical person makes nowhere close to $400,000. Therein lies the problem. Don't be like the typical consumer if you want to build greater wealth.

If you've already bought too much car, I suggest two options: (1) own it until its value becomes 10% of your income or (2) bite the bullet and sell it. If you've spent anything more than 30% of your gross annual income on a car, I'd sell it. It's acting as an anchor dragging along the seafloor as you try to swim to financial independence. Even if you have to take a financial hit, it's worth getting rid of your vehicle. Don't trade it in to the dealer because you'll get railroaded. Instead, try listing it privately on a free platform such as Craigslist.

To help you navigate the finances of owning a car, I've created a chart that explains car spending as a percentage of household income.

THE FINANCIAL SAMURAI ONE-TENTH RULE FOR CAR BUYING (SPEND NO MORE THAN 10% OF GROSS INCOME ON A CAR)

Percentage of Gross Income Spent on a Car	Analysis
10% or less	Financial hero destined for financial independence
11%–25%	Sound thinker who eschews consumerism
26%–50%	On the right track but can do better
51%–75%	Must want to work for a very long time
76%–100%	Cares too much about image and likely has huge debt
100%+	High risk of financial ruin, spending addiction, needs help

Source: FinancialSamurai.com

There is no shame in owning a car that's worth less than $10,000, unless it is unsafe. I bought a secondhand Land Rover Discovery II for $8,000, which was less than 3% of my income. Then I drove it for ten years until it was worth less than $2,000, while my income went up. The car was great and loads of fun. Sure, there were some dashboard lights that stubbornly stayed on. But nothing a little masking tape on the dashboard to block the light couldn't fix. With the money I saved by not buying a more expensive car, I diligently invested in the stock market. A decade later, that money had grown by over 160%.

Put your ego aside so you can have true wealth: all the freedom in the world. Be a time billionaire!

Once you buy a car following my One-Tenth Rule, aim to own it for around ten years if you bought it new. That will let you maximize the car's value while also minimizing any safety risks that tend to appear due to age. If you're buying used, look for a car that is three to five years old and also aim to drive it for ten years.

Both approaches aim for you to keep the vehicle until it is ten to fifteen years old. That may sound like a long time, but the average age of vehicles on American roads in 2021 was 12.1 years. You'll be right in the sweet spot for value and safety *and* on par with many vehicles out there.

In personal finance land, we always talk about using things for as long as possible.

But when it comes to cars, owning a car well past the fifteen-year mark should not be a badge of honor. For safety reasons, if you have the money, you should look for a new car after ten to fifteen years. I get the desire to save money by owning a car until the wheels fall off. However, if the wheels actually do fall off while you're driving, you're screwed.

Weigh your risks and use the One-Tenth Rule as a guiding principle. If you absolutely can't afford a safe and reliable car by spending 10% of your income, spend a bit more and keep the One-Tenth Rule in mind. Ideally you wouldn't spend more than 20%, and really, only go that high if you absolutely have to for safety reasons. And if you truly can't stick to even a 20% limit, it's time to figure out how to make more money with your career and side hustles.

DRIVING A BEATER HAS ITS BENEFIT

Although my father worked for the U.S. embassy as a foreign service officer, he always bought beaters. This mismatch between the comfortable housing the government provided us and our vehicles throughout the years was always quite jarring.

From 1986 to 1990, when I was in middle school in Kuala Lumpur, Malaysia, he drove a 1976 Nissan Datsun that had no paint and three missing hubcaps. I remember taking it out for an illegal joyride with my friends one day. We were thirteen years old. It was monsoon season, and the one remaining hubcap fell off as we drove through a massive rainstorm. It just rolled off and rapidly floated away down a three-foot-deep drain. By the time I got out of the car to try to retrieve it, it was gone.

I thought my dad was going to kill me. My friends and I snuck the car back home at 2:00 a.m. and I prayed he wouldn't notice. The next day he took the car to work and didn't say a thing. The missing hubcap never came up until I mentioned it over a decade later.

It was then that I realized there were great benefits to owning inexpensive things that you could easily afford. A dent in your car while parking at the grocery store? No sweat. A glob of ketchup splattering your old shoe? It gives it character.

What mattered most was that Dad wasn't frugal for frugality's sake. He passed over sodas and new cars because he was investing that money instead. Consider doing the same if you want to expedite your path to financial freedom.

Get Your Hands Dirty or Outsource It?

I mentioned at the start of this book that most of us were raised with financial advice focused on saving. The trouble with this thinking is that it keeps us stuck in a scarcity mindset. We do a much better job of building wealth when we embrace an abundance mindset.

I stress saving until it hurts, but that doesn't mean save at all costs. This is especially true when it comes to our everyday home life. For example, most people have been trained to believe that cooking and eating at home is the wisest financial move. But is it really? The best way to tell is by factoring in *all costs* of preparing meals at home—including, especially, the cost of your time.

Calculate what your time is worth per hour and then do the math. If you make $50 an hour and spend one hour cooking and one hour buying $30 worth of ingredients, your meal better be worth more than at least $130. Unless you enjoy cooking, it may not make sense to come home from a long day's work and spend an hour cooking. You could be using this time to unwind, play with your kids, or work on your side hustle.

When you factor in all of the costs, ordering meals several times a week may not be as indulgent as it seems, especially with the proliferation of food delivery apps. These food delivery companies are heavily subsidized by investors, which results in cost savings for you. Take advantage to buy yourself more time.

Use this same logic to determine whether it's worth doing any home task yourself, or if you should outsource it: house cleaning, laundry, lawn and yard work, pool maintenance, snow removal. Many of us default to thinking that outsourcing these everyday jobs is wasteful when we can do them ourselves. But remember—doing it yourself doesn't mean it's free. There is always the cost of your time and stress. Further, if you end up hurting yourself in the process, this is another cost to consider.

One day I carelessly peeled a mango too quickly and ended up slicing my left index finger. Not only was the cut painful, but it took me out of playing tennis and softball for two weeks. Another time I decided to dig a trench to plant a row of bushes in front of my house. During the process, my lower back gave out. As a result, I couldn't pick up my baby boy for a couple of days. I would have paid plenty of money to be able to do my favorite activities that my injuries prevented.

The opportunity cost of everything you're not doing could be the greatest cost of all. What if you took those few extra hours each week to finally work on your wealth-building strategy, think of ways to excel at work, or finally launch that website you've been struggling to find the time to do? The upside to taking action could be tremendous over time.

The 70/30 move when deciding whether to get your hands dirty or outsource a task is twofold: (1) Determine if it brings you joy. If you love to cook, then by all means, cook. (2) Do the math. If you don't enjoy the task and the true costs are high, then outsource it when you can.

Work to Live or Live to Work?

Despite their frigid temperatures for a third of the year, one of the reasons why European countries such as Finland, Iceland, and Denmark perpetually rank as some of the happiest countries in the world is because their citizens work to live. Although taxes may be high and income upside may not be as great, these countries' citizens tend to be happier because they have more control over their free time.

In comparison, the United States regularly ranks outside of the top ten to fifteen, partly because Americans have overemphasized capitalism at the expense of free time. When there is an insatiable desire to make more money and beat your competitors, it becomes harder to be satisfied. The goal, of course, is to find the optimal balance between free time and money.

It's been more than ten years since I left my day job, and I never plan to go back to the way things were. There are a plethora of new ways to invest and make money today.

Please do not spend forty good years of your life working at a job that you do not enjoy. Don't suffer from the sunk-cost fallacy like a partner in a loveless marriage who is too afraid to ever leave. You owe it to yourself to find work that provides you joy and purpose.

A colleague of mine, a vice president we'll call Mele, gave up her $200,000-base-salary job at age thirty-three to try her hand at baking. She went to baking school for almost a year and got a job working at a fancy restaurant making pastries for eight hours a day.

After six months, she quit because, she told me, "If I'm going to be getting yelled at all day, I might as well be getting yelled at all day in banking instead of in a crowded and hot kitchen making fifteen dollars an hour!"

She returned to banking two years later and continues to be in the industry today. Even though her stint as a world-renowned baker didn't work out, she will always be happy that she tried. Making choices is seldom an all-or-nothing proposition. If things don't work out after several years, you can usually go back to the way things were.

Just be careful about making your passion your main source of income. You might find out that doing it because you need to is no longer as much fun.

Once You're on the Right Financial Path, Your Goal Is to Live as Long as Possible

Strictly from a financial standpoint, the stronger your cash flow and the longer you can live, the more valuable your overall life will be. After all, an asset that can generate $100,000 a year for fifty years is more valuable than an asset that can generate $100,000 for only twenty years. Therefore, once you're on the right financial path or actually achieve financial freedom, it behooves you to try to extend your life for as long as possible.

Back in the good old days, a person might work until age sixty-five and enjoy retirement for ten years before kicking the bucket. With the advancement of modern medicine and the flexibility to earn in more ways, we might be able to achieve financial independence much sooner and live much longer.

It's hard to control for disease and rare illnesses. However, we can take care of our physical and mental health to the best of our abilities. In fact, the more wealth we have, the more time and money we should consider devoting to healthy foods, exercise, coaches, and therapists. If a healthier life means relocating to an area with cleaner air and more pleasant weather, you might want to consider that, too.

Back when I worked in finance, due to constant stress, I gained weight and developed chronic lower back pain, sciatica, and TMJ, which made speaking difficult. My jaw clenching got so bad that I once paid $700 out of pocket to a dentist to purposely drill down my back molars to try to ease the pressure on my teeth.

Nothing worked until I finally left the finance world behind. Over the next twelve months, I noticed my chronic pain gradually begin to go away. The white hairs that had begun to sprout a year earlier also went back into hibernation. I had experienced pain for so long that I thought waking up every day with some type of ailment was normal. But it is not normal. Pain is the primary way your body tells you to change your life.

Listen to your body.

All the money in the world means nothing if you don't have your health. Do whatever you can to protect and nourish it. Once you've won the lottery, aim to enjoy your winnings for as long as possible.

THE FINANCIAL SAMURAI WAY

- Optimize your online and offline profile for Stealth Wealth. The less attention you receive for your wealth, the happier you will be.

- Stop driving an expensive automobile to work or to any social gathering where you might be negatively judged.

- Calculate what your time is worth per hour. Now determine the true value of cooking or doing anything else that can be outsourced. Compare the cost of outsourcing with the value of what you could make or do, and make the appropriate choice. Always think in terms of opportunity costs. What could you be doing if you didn't have to do something else?

- Be mindful of the suffering of others. The more mindful you can be, the more you will appreciate what you have and the less you will take things for granted.

- The reality is, nobody yearns to retire from work they enjoy doing. Therefore, the 70/30 solution is to find an occupation that provides constant meaning and purpose. The money may be hard to quit, but you owe it to yourself to at least try. You can always go back to your old job if your new job doesn't work out.

Take Your Shot

One of my favorite people at work was a man named Conrad. He was in his midfifties and worked in the mail room and at the front desk. Every time I walked by him he would greet me with a cheerful smile. We'd always exchange stories about funny events that happened at work.

One day, in 2011, I asked him what he would do differently if he were my age. I was thirty-three at the time.

He said, "Sam, I wish I had taken more risks." He lamented how he was having a difficult time making ends meet on a $40,000 salary in San Francisco. Then he went on, "Over time, you will regret more of the things you don't try than the things you do."

Those were exactly the words I needed to hear as I was planning my escape from corporate America for good. After coming up with my severance-negotiation idea, I was excited to run my plan by Conrad. He always had some insightful feedback.

Unfortunately, Conrad never returned to the office. He was summarily let go during one of the many rounds of layoffs we had that year. I couldn't believe it. Cutting one managing director could have saved twenty-five Conrads. I was mad but also emboldened to make a change.

From then on, I decided I was always going to take leaps of faith. No matter what would happen next, at least I would never regret having tried. The thing is, nobody is going to push you to change. You must jump on your own.

As you navigate the many potential paths in your unpredictable life, work on making positive-expected-value decisions. Your decision-making skills will get better through practice and experience. If you can consistently make decisions with a 70% positive probability or greater, you will do very well over time. Waiting until you have 100% certainty is often impossible and unnecessary.

At the same time, let us be humble enough to realize that even with the best preparation, things can and will go wrong. The challenge is whether we learn from our mistakes and grow or give up and curse our bad luck.

To be a Financial Samurai is to be someone who follows these core principles.

The Core Principles of a Financial Samurai

1. **Never fail due to a lack of effort, because effort requires no skill.** You can fail because of superior competition, bad luck, or poor execution, but you cannot fail because you didn't try your best. When you look back on your life, your biggest regrets will be the things you didn't do and the things you did half-heartedly.

2. **Always maintain an abundance mindset instead of a scarcity mindset.** There are trillions of dollars in the world for the taking. There is no reason why you can't build your own fortune. Focus on wealth creation through investing, hard work, and entrepreneurship rather than just being frugal. There is only so much you can save and an endless amount you can make. Create your own opportunity!

3. **Depend on no one but yourself to succeed.** Nobody will save you, so you must save yourself. The world can be a very difficult place. We will inevitably face hardships along our path to financial independence. Most people are too busy fighting their own fires to help fight yours. By accepting that nobody will bail us out, we will end up

doing our best work because we have no other choice. And if a kind person or thoughtful institution does end up providing us assistance, all the better.

4. **Know that you deserve only what you have earned.** There is no better feeling than working hard for your success. Pity those who have had everything handed to them. Further, let go of your need to compare yourself with others. You will never fully know how hard someone tried or didn't try to achieve their results. Luck is a bigger factor than we realize.

5. **Give without asking for anything in return.** Give your time. Give your money. Give your kindness to those in need. You never know what someone is going through, so keep your judgment locked away. In return, people will want to help you succeed.

6. **Know there is often a solution to a difficult problem.** Instead of feeling stuck, always look at a problem as a fun challenge. You'll be surprised at the number of solutions that can lead you to the same goal. So long as you have "a chip and a chair," you still have a chance.

7. **Think in probabilities, not absolutes.** As soon as you start thinking in probabilities, a whole new world of opportunity opens up. No longer will you be too fearful to try new things because you will start seeing the potential in everything. By thinking in probabilities, you openly accept different viewpoints, which may further enhance your decision-making skills and overall outlook on life.

Once you adopt these core principles, your outlook will change for the better. Now let's recap some specific goals all of us should have on our path to financial freedom.

Specific Goals of the Financial Samurai

1. **Save until it hurts every month.** If the amount of money you're saving each month doesn't hurt, you are not saving enough. Once your savings amount stops hurting, it's time to save a little more. Ideally, you'll eventually save and invest 50% or more of your after-tax income.

2. **Always max out all tax-advantaged retirement accounts.** There is no excuse not to take full advantage of tax-advantageous vehicles. Tax is likely your greatest ongoing liability. Your goal is to defer and minimize taxes for as long as possible.

3. **Shoot to build a net worth equal to 20X your average gross income.** Once you have built a net worth of at least 10X your average annual gross income, you will begin to

feel true financial freedom. Using your average gross income keeps you honest as your income grows over time.

4. **Aim to generate a passive-income stream that covers 100% of your basic living expenses.** Once your basic needs are covered, you become more emboldened to do what you want, even if you haven't achieved a net worth equal to 20X your annual gross income. Assign a purpose to every single investment to keep you motivated.

5. **Never quit; get laid off.** When it's time to finally leave your job, negotiate a severance instead of quitting. If you quit, you are not eligible for unemployment benefits, WARN (Worker Adjustment and Retraining Notification) Act pay, or subsidized health care. If you were willing to quit your job anyway, there is no downside to trying to make the transition process as smooth for your employer as possible.

6. **Live a life of purpose as soon as financially possible.** After you've spent your initial years building up a strong financial base, make sure you do work that provides meaning to you and to others. If you feel an emptiness inside every time you go to work, you must change occupations.

7. **Work while others are playing.** Instead of watching sports all weekend, use that time to do something productive. Instead of sleeping in until 8:00 a.m., wake up an hour early to build your business. Work while others are playing long enough, and you might just be able to play for the rest of your life if you so choose.

8. **Empower those who are struggling or feel forgotten.** In every city and town across the world, there are people who need a helping hand. Although nobody is coming to save you, you should still allocate some time to help others, especially if you are one of the lucky ones.

9. **Fight ego by practicing Stealth Wealth.** It's only natural to want to shout from the rooftops how much you make, how much you are worth, and how successful you are. Instead, stay humble. By staying humble, you acknowledge the suffering all around you. You also recognize that not everybody was born with the same gifts or has the same opportunities as you.

    Boasting about your wealth will only make others feel bad and attract unwanted negativity. If you must disclose some of your successes, then do so in a manner that can help others improve their chances of success as well. In other words, provide some points of action.

10. **Never confuse luck with skill.** Always differentiate between luck and skill. In a long bull market, it's easy to think you are the greatest investor, employee, or entrepreneur on earth. In a bear market, it's easy to think of yourself as a fool and discredit all your

hard work. The luckier you are, the harder you should work and give back. Eventually, your luck will turn, so you will need to be prepared.

11. **Practice predicting the future.** Avoid letting your mind ossify through years of mundane thought and groupthink. Instead, spend at least an hour every month thinking about future trends in demographics, technology, labor, health, work, and life. Discuss your predictions with your family and friends. Seek out different points of view.

    Be where the potential opportunities are greatest. Further, if you can properly forecast your misery, you should end up happier because you'll seek positive changes before such misery comes.

12. **Create a perpetual giving machine.** Establish something that will keep on giving long after you are gone. Giving is the purest form of joy you will ever experience, so much more than financial success. When it's time for you to go, you will rest easier knowing that you did something to help others heal and grow.

Never Stop Learning

I'm confident that if you use the strategies I've outlined, ten years from now, you will have grown your wealth far more than you could have ever imagined. More important, you will *feel* richer because your life will be more meaningful. This book is your unfair advantage for navigating an extremely competitive world.

Too often we find ourselves not speaking up for what's right or not pursuing our dreams because we are too afraid of the financial repercussions. What a shame to go through life governed by fear. By actively working to achieve financial independence, you will be able to gradually attain the freedom you seek.

The journey will not be easy. Sacrifices will need to be made. But giving up is not an option. When times are tough, think about this famous Chinese proverb: "If the direction is correct, sooner or later you will get there."

Financial Samurai is not a level you finally attain. It is a way of life.

Thank you for reading *Buy This, Not That*. It has been one of my greatest honors to serve you.

Acknowledgments

First and foremost, thanks to Noah Schwartzberg, my editor, for taking a chance on me. I appreciate just having the opportunity to try to write a great book. You are truly one of the nicest people to work with. Thanks also to Kimberly Meilun, assistant editor, for smoothing the rough edges and to Hilary Roberts and Megan Gerrity for such thorough and thoughtful copyedits.

Thank you, Maria Gagliano, for helping me write and flesh out ideas. You've been a fantastic sounding board to help shine a bright light on my blind spots. I'm in awe of your work ethic as a mother of three kids during this entire process.

Thank you, Sydney, for always being there for me since college. If it weren't for your waking up at 5:00 a.m. to make sure I got to my first interview on time, I'm not sure where I'd be. Thank you for reviewing the entire book thrice! Our kids are incredibly lucky to have you as their mother. Your patience and kindness are second to none.

Thank you, *Financial Samurai* readers, for sharing your perspectives every time I publish a new post. Special thanks to Silvia V., Lily N., Joe U., Richard L., Wynn P., Ben M., Leah G., Jack A., Ben H., Jilliene H., Larry G., Anand R., Paul O., Jeremy S., Carl K., and Shaun L. Shout-out to my tennis and softball crew for providing a great outlet during a most difficult time.

Finally, I would like to acknowledge, with gratitude, the support and love of my family—my parents, Allen and Kathy; my sister, Colleen, who did all of the book's art; and my children. JJ and KK—since you two were born, all I've ever wanted to do was make you proud. It would be a great honor if you could bring this book to show-and-tell one day.

Further Reading

If you found this book valuable, please share it with your family, friends, and colleagues. Everybody deserves to achieve financial independence sooner than later.

For a deeper dive into some key topics covered in the book, as well as related topics, see the following posts at *Financial Samurai*.

In addition, please sign up for the free *Financial Samurai* Newsletter for exclusive content. Features include stock market insights, real estate strategies, career and business advice, early retirement guidance, entrepreneurship tips, and special promotions. Sign up at: **https://financialsamurai.com/newsletter**.

Part One: Adopt the Right Money Mindset to Get Rich

Chapter 1: Find Your Happiness Equation

Seeking Happiness: "Solving the Happiness Conundrum in Five Moves or Less," https://www.financialsamurai.com/solving-happiness-things-that-will-make-you-happier-and-wealthier.

Eliminate Back Pain: "The Book That Changed My Life and Made Me Rich Again," https://www.financialsamurai.com/the-book-that-changed-my-life-made-me-rich-again.

It Takes Courage: "Your Financial Independence Number Is Not Real if Nothing Changes," https://www.financialsamurai.com/financial-independence-number-is-not-real-if-nothing-changes.

What Is FIRE?: "The Fundamentals of FIRE (Financial Independence Retire Early)," https://www.financialsamurai.com/the-fundamentals-of-fire-financial-independence-retire-early.

Unhappy Smart Countries: "Why the Smartest Countries Are Not the Happiest," https://www.financialsamurai.com/why-the-smartest-countries-are-not-the-happiest.

That Rich Feeling: "When Will You Finally Feel Rich? It's Not Always About the Money," https://www.financialsamurai.com/when-do-you-finally-feel-rich.

A Strong Mind: "Do You Have the Strong Money Mindset to Get Rich?" https://www.financialsamurai.com/do-you-have-the-right-money-mindset-to-get-rich.

Chapter 2: Do the Math and the Plan Will Come

Net Worth by Age: "What Should My Net Worth Be at Age 30, 40, 50, 60?" https://www.financialsamurai.com/what-should-my-net-worth-be-at-age-30-40-50-60.

Rule 72(t): "Use Rule 72(t) to Withdraw Money Penalty Free From an IRA," https://www.financialsamurai.com/rule-72t-to-withdraw-money-penalty-free-from-ira-for-early-retirement.

Social Security: "When to Take Social Security? Make So Much It Doesn't Really Matter," https://www.financialsamurai.com/when-to-take-social-security.

Early Retirement Cons: "The Negatives of Early Retirement Life Nobody Likes Talking About," https://www.financialsamurai.com/the-negatives-of-early-retirement-life-nobody-likes-to-talks-about.

Risk Tolerance: "Financial SEER: A Way to Quantify Risk Tolerance and Determine Appropriate Equity Exposure," https://www.financialsamurai.com/seer-quantify-risk-tolerance-determine-appropriate-equity-exposure.

Chapter 3: Get the Cash, Put It to Work

401(k) Balances: "How Much Should I Have Saved in My 401(k) by Age?" https://www.financialsamurai.com/how-much-should-one-have-in-their-401k-at-different-ages.

Online Income: "Reflections on Making Money Online Since 2009," https://www.financialsamurai.com/reflections-on-making-money-online-since-2009.

Create a Blog: "How to Start a Blog: Insights into Building Your Own Website," https://www.financialsamurai.com/how-to-start-a-profitable-blog.

Passive Income: "How to Build Passive Income for Financial Independence," https://www.financialsamurai.com/how-to-build-passive-income-for-financial-independence.

Venture Debt: "What Is Venture Debt? An Investment with Higher Yields and a Lower Risk Profile," https://www.financialsamurai.com/what-is-venture-debt-higher-yields-with-a-lower-risk-profile.

Portfolio Weightings: "Historical Returns of Different Stock and Bond Portfolio Weightings," https://www.financialsamurai.com/historical-returns-of-different -stock-bond-portfolio-weightings.

1031 Exchange: "1031 Exchange Rules to Defer Your Real Estate Capital Gains Tax," https://www.financialsamurai.com/rules-1031-exchange-defer-real-estate-capital -gains-tax.

Chapter 4: Master Your Debt

U.S. Retirement: "Retirement Savings by Age Show Why Americans Are Screwed," https://www.financialsamurai.com/how-much-have-americans-saved-for-retirement.

Margin: "Buying Stocks on Margin Is a Bad Idea: You Could Easily Lose Everything," https://www.financialsamurai.com/buying-stocks-on-margin/.

Tax-Free Home Sale: "Clarifying the $250,000/$500,000 Tax-Free Home Sale Profit Rule," https://www.financialsamurai.com/tax-free-profits-for-home-sale-250000 -500000.

Early Mortgage Pay-Down Pros: "Why I'm Paying Down My Mortgage Early and Why You Should Too," https://www.financialsamurai.com/why-pay-down-mortgage-early -benefits-costs.

Early Mortgage Pay-Down Cons: "The Biggest Downside to Paying Off Your Mortgage Early," https://www.financialsamurai.com/the-biggest-downside-to-paying-off-your -mortgage.

Part Two: Put Your Money to Work

Chapter 5: Follow a Proper Allocation Model

Stocks Versus Property: "Real Estate or Stocks: Which Is a Better Investment?" https://www.financialsamurai.com/which-is-a-better-investment-real-estate-or-stocks.

Bonds: "The Case For Buying Bonds: Living for Free and Other Benefits," https://www.financialsamurai.com/the-case-for-buying-bonds-living-for-free-and-other -benefits.

Net Worth Structure by Wealth: "Net Worth Composition by Levels of Wealth: Build a Business Already," https://www.financialsamurai.com/net-worth-composition-by -levels-of-wealth.

Net Worth Case Study: "The Average Net Worth for the Above Average Person," https://www.financialsamurai.com/the-average-net-worth-for-the-above-average-person.

Couples' Net Worth: "The Average Net Worth for the Above Average Married Couple," https://www.financialsamurai.com/the-average-net-worth-for-the-above-average -married-couple.

Chapter 6: Optimize Your Investments

Investing Hierarchy: "The Right Contribution Order Between Your Investment Accounts," https://www.financialsamurai.com/right-contribution-order-between -your-investment-accounts.

Day Trading: "Day Trading Is a Waste of Time and Money, Don't Do It!" https://www .financialsamurai.com/day-trading-is-a-waste-of-time-and-money.

Passive-Income Forecasting: "Accurate Passive Income Forecasting Is Vital for Long -Term Happiness," https://www.financialsamurai.com/accurate-passive-income -forecasting.

Capital Gains Tax: "Short-Term and Long-Term Capital Gains Tax Rates by Income," https://www.financialsamurai.com/short-term-long-term-capital-gains-tax-rates-by -income-for-single-and-married-couples.

Structured Notes: "Not All Structured Notes Are Bad, but There Are Downsides to Know," https://www.financialsamurai.com/not-all-structured-notes-are-bad-but -there-are-downsides.

Chapter 7: Understand Real Estate Fundamentals

ARM Versus Fixed: "Why an Adjustable-Rate Mortgage Is Better Than a 30-Year Fixed -Rate Mortgage," https://www.financialsamurai.com/why-an-adjustable-rate -mortgage-is-better-than-a-fixed-rate-mortgage.

Median Home Buyer: "The Median Homebuyer Age Is Getting Older: We Better Live Longer!" https://www.financialsamurai.com/the-median-homebuyer-age-is-now -so-old.

Cons of Renting: "The Return on Rent Is Always Negative 100%: How to Live for Free," https://www.financialsamurai.com/return-on-rent-is-always-negative-100-percent -how-to-live-forfree.

Refinance Fees: "All the Mortgage Refinance Fees in a No-Cost Refinance," https://www.financialsamurai.com/all-the-mortgage-refinance-fees-in-a-no-cost -refinance.

Chapter 8: Choose Where to Live for Maximum Wealth Potential

Save Money by Moving: "The Proper Geoarbitrage Strategy: First Your City, Then Your Country, Then the World," https://www.financialsamurai.com/the-proper-geoarbitrage-strategy.

Dream Home: "The Best Time to Own the Nicest House You Can Afford," https://www.financialsamurai.com/the-best-time-to-own-the-nicest-house-you-can-afford.

Retirement Friendly States: "Which States Are Best for Retirement?" https://www.financialsamurai.com/which-states-are-best-for-retirement.

Housing Budget: "Housing Expense Guideline for Financial Independence," https://www.financialsamurai.com/housing-expense-guideline-for-financial-independence.

Home Remodeling: "How Much Should You Spend Remodeling a House for Max Profit?" https://www.financialsamurai.com/how-much-to-spend-remodeling-a-house-for-maximum-profit.

Housing Prices: "Go Up the Housing Price Curve to Find Better Value," https://www.financialsamurai.com/go-up-the-housing-price-curve-to-find-better-value.

Net Worth and Your Home: "Primary Residence Value as a Percentage of Net Worth Guide," https://www.financialsamurai.com/primary-residence-value-as-a-percentage-of-net-worth-guide.

Chapter 9: Go Long on Real Estate

An Incentive to Save: "Dear Minorities, Use Racism As Motivation for Achieving Financial Independence," https://www.financialsamurai.com/dear-minorities-use-racism-as-motivation-for-achieving-financial-independence.

Online Real Estate: "Real Estate Crowdfunding Learning Center," https://www.financialsamurai.com/real-estate-crowdfunding-learning-center.

No Financing Contingency: "No Financing Contingency Offer: A Way to Pay All Cash for a Property Without Having the Cash," https://www.financialsamurai.com/no-contingency-financing-offer-a-way-to-offer-all-cash-for-a-property.

Home Buyers Beware: "10 Warning Signs Before Buying a House: Be a Thorough Inspector," https://www.financialsamurai.com/warning-signs-to-look-out-for-before-buying-a-house.

Closing Costs: "Closing Costs When Paying All Cash for a Home," https://www.financialsamurai.com/closing-costs-when-paying-all-cash-for-a-home.

Letters to Sellers: "How to Write a Real Estate Love Letter and Save Big Bucks," https://www.financialsamurai.com/how-to-write-a-real-estate-love-letter-and-save-big-bucks.

Refinance Fees: "All the Mortgage Fees in a No-Cost Refinance," https://www.financialsamurai.com/all-the-mortgage-refinance-fees-in-a-no-cost-refinance.

Part Three: Work While Maximizing Your Wealth

Chapter 10: Think Strategically About Your Career

Cons of Start-ups: "Candid Advice for Those Joining the Startup World: Sleep with One Eye Open," https://www.financialsamurai.com/candid-advice-for-those-joining-the-startup-world.

Micromanagers: "How to Deal with a Micromanager Without Killing Yourself First," https://www.financialsamurai.com/how-to-deal-with-a-micromanager.

Expensive Cities: "Living in an Expensive City Can Make You Richer, Happier, and More Diplomatic," https://www.financialsamurai.com/living-in-an-expensive-city-can-make-you-richer-and-happier.

Get Rid of Negative Thoughts: "Abolish Welfare Mentality: Janitor Makes $235,812 Plus $36,652 in Benefits," https://www.financialsamurai.com/abolish-welfare-mentality-six-figure-bart-janitor.

Six-Figure Salaries: "How to Make Six Figures a Year at Almost Any Age," https://www.financialsamurai.com/how-to-make-six-figures-income-at-almost-any-age.

0.1% Incomes: "Who Makes a Million Dollars a Year? Exploring the Top 0.1% Income Earners," https://www.financialsamurai.com/who-makes-a-million-dollars-a-year-exploring-the-top-0-1-income-earners.

Chapter 11: Make Your Money and Then Make Your Exit

Severance Case Study: "How to Negotiate a Severance as a High-Performing Employee," www.financialsamurai.com/how-to-negotiate-a-severance-as-an-excellent-employee.

Negotiate a Severance: "How to Engineer Your Layoff eBOOK," https://www.financialsamurai.com/how-to-make-money-quitting-your-job-2.

State Unemployment Benefits: "States with the Highest and Lowest Unemployment Benefits," https://www.financialsamurai.com/states-with-the-highest-and-lowest-unemployment-benefits.

Chapter 12: Get Your Side Hustle On

Perseverance: "The Secret to Your Success: 10 Years of Unwavering Commitment," https://www.financialsamurai.com/the-secret-to-your-success-10-years-of -unwavering-commitment.

Retiring Before Your Spouse: "How to Convince Your Spouse to Work Longer so You Can Retire Earlier," https://www.financialsamurai.com/how-to-convince-your -spouse-to-work-longer-so-you-can-retire-earlier.

Early Retirement for Couples: "Achieving the Two Spouse Early Retirement Household," https://www.financialsamurai.com/achieving-the-two-spouse-early-retirement -household.

Never Sell Your Cash Cow: "Why I'll Always Regret Selling My Online Business for Millions of Dollars," https://www.financialsamurai.com/why-i-regret-selling-my -online-business-for-millions-every-single-day.

Taking the Leap: "How Much Do I Have to Make as an Entrepreneur to Replace My Day Job Income?" https://www.financialsamurai.com/how-much-do-i-have-to-make-as -an-entrepreneur-or-contractor-to-replace-my-day-job-income.

Part Four: Focus on the Most Important Things in Life

Chapter 13: Invest in Education

529 Plan Transfers: "Using a 529 Plan for Generational Wealth Transfer Purposes," https://www.financialsamurai.com/using-a-529-plan-for-generational-wealth -transfer-purposes.

School Rankings: "Why More Public Schools Will Eventually Rank Higher Than Private Schools," https://www.financialsamurai.com/why-public-schools-will-rank-higher -than-private-schools.

529 Plan Contributions: "Determining How Much to Contribute to a 529 Plan: Too Much No Good!" https://www.financialsamurai.com/determining-how-much-to -contribute-to-a-529-plan.

Chapter 14: Nurture Your Love

Marriage and Money: "Marrying Your Equal Is Better Than Marrying Rich," https:// www.financialsamurai.com/marrying-your-equal-is-better-than-marrying-rich.

Divorce: "Divorce After Kids: Try Bird Nesting for Stability," https://www .financialsamurai.com/divorce-after-kids-is-birdnesting-the-key-for-stability.

Au Pair Pros and Cons: "Hiring an Au Pair May Be the Best Childcare Decision a Family Makes," https://www.financialsamurai.com/hiring-an-au-pair.

Hiring a Night Doula: "What Is a Night Doula and Should You Hire One?" https://www.financialsamurai.com/what-is-a-night-doula.

Newborn Childcare Costs: "The Cost of Fourth Trimester Childcare: Potentially $40,000 and Up," https://www.financialsamurai.com/the-cost-of-fourth-trimester-childcare.

Starting a Family: "What's the Best Age to Have a Baby? 20s? 30s? 40s+?" https://www.financialsamurai.com/whats-the-best-age-to-have-a-baby-20s-30s-40s.

Marriage and Taxes: "The Marriage Penalty Tax Has Been Abolished, Hooray!" https://www.financialsamurai.com/marriage-penalty-tax-abolished.

"Do I Want Kids?" video by _Vox_: https://www.youtube.com/watch?v=4kfcsOhgzRA or Google "Vox Do I Want Kids?"

Benefits of Having Kids Late: "Dear Older Parents, Having Kids Late Might Be the Best Choice After All," https://www.financialsamurai.com/older-parents-having-kids-late.

Chapter 15: Live Like a Financial Samurai

Wealth and Luck: "Your Wealth Is Mostly Due to Luck: Be Thankful!" https://www.financialsamurai.com/your-wealth-is-mostly-due-to-luck-be-thankful.

Estate Planning: "Three Things I Learned from My Estate Planning Lawyer Everyone Should Do," https://www.financialsamurai.com/three-things-learned-from-my-estate-planning-lawyer-everybody-should-do.

Living Trusts: "The Benefits of a Revocable Living Trust," https://www.financialsamurai.com/revocable-living-trust-benefits.

Importance of a Death File: "The Death File and Why You Need One," https://www.financialsamurai.com/death-file.

Estate Tax: "Historical Estate Tax Exemption Amounts and Tax Rates 2022," https://www.financialsamurai.com/historical-estate-tax-exemption-amounts-and-tax-rates.

Leasing a Car: "Multiple Options for Terminating a Car Lease Early," https://www.financialsamurai.com/multiple-options-for-terminating-a-car-lease-early.

Wealth Versus Fame: "Be Rich, Not Famous: The Joy of Being a Nobody," https://www.financialsamurai.com/be-rich-not-famous.

Notes

Chapter 1: Find Your Happiness Equation

9   **A recent World Happiness Report:** John F. Helliwell, Richard Layard, Jeffrey Sachs, and Jan-Emmanuel De Neve, eds., *World Happiness Report 2021*, New York: Sustainable Development Solutions Network, https://happiness-report.s3.amazonaws.com/2021/WHR+21.pdf.

Chapter 2: Do the Math and the Plan Will Come

21   **The "4% Rule" was first:** William P. Bengen, "Determining Withdrawal Rates Using Historical Data," *Journal of Financial Planning*, October 1994, 171–80.

21   **It was subsequently made:** Philip L. Cooley, Carl M. Hubbard, and Daniel T. Walz, "Retirement Savings: Choosing a Withdrawal Rate That Is Sustainable," *AAII Journal* 20, no. 2 (February 1998): 16–21.

23   **In 2021, Vanguard came out:** Paulo Costa, David Pakula, and Andrew S. Clarke, "Fuel for the F.I.R.E.: Updating the 4% Rule for Early Retirees," Vanguard, June 2021, p. 4, https://personal.vanguard.com/pdf/ISGFIRE.pdf.

26   **Let's dig into what risk:** Ned Davis Research, "10 Things You Should Know About Bear Markets," HartfordFunds, December 15, 2021, https://www.hartfordfunds.com/practice-management/client-conversations/bear-markets.html.

Chapter 3: Get the Cash, Put It to Work

44   **Since Jackson's death:** Eamonn Forde, "Death & Taxes: The Michael Jackson Estate, the IRS and Posthumous Celebrity Valuations," *Forbes*, May 4, 2021, https://www.forbes.com/sites/eamonnforde/2021/05/04/death--taxes-the-michael-jackson-estate-the-irs-and-posthumous-celebrity-valuations/?sh=4dc90c08a8da.

45   **The purpose of the JOBS Act:** U.S. Securities and Exchange Commission, "Spotlight on Jumpstart Our Business Startups (JOBS) Act," no date, https://www.sec.gov/spotlight/jobs-act.shtml.

Chapter 4: Master Your Debt

57   **It is sad that the average:** Janelle Cammenga, "Facts and Figures 2021: How Does Your State Compare?" Tax Foundation, March 10, 2021, https://taxfoundation.org/2021-state-tax-data.

58   **According to an analysis:** First Trust Advisors, "History of U.S. Bear and Bull Markets," no date, https://www.ftportfolios.com/Common/ContentFileLoader.aspx?ContentGUID=4ecfa978-d0bb-4924-92c8-628ff9bfe12d.

59 **annualized returns by asset class between 2001 and 2020:** J.P. Morgan Asset Management, "Guide to the Markets," September 30, 2021, p. 64, https://am.jpmorgan.com/content/dam /jpm-am-aem/global/en/insights/market-insights/guide-to-the-markets/mi-guide-to-the -markets-us.pdf.

60 **A year later, it was worth:** Davide Scigliuzzo and Gillian Tan, "Airbnb Lenders Reap $1 Billion Windfall on Pandemic Lifeline," *Bloomberg*, December 11, 2020, https://www .bloomberg.com/news/articles/2020-12-11/airbnb-lenders-reap-1-billion-windfall-on -pandemic-lifeline.

61 **Under Regulation T:** "Part 220 - Credit by Brokers and Dealers (Regulation T)," Code of Federal Regulations, accessed April 12, 2022, https://www.ecfr.gov/current/title-12/ chapter-II/subchapter-A/part-220.

62 **retirement account balance in 2019:** Federal Reserve Board, "Changes in U.S. Family Finances from 2016 to 2019: Evidence from the Survey of Consumer Finances," *Federal Reserve Bulletin* 106, no. 5 (September 2020), https://www.federalreserve.gov/publications/files/scf20.pdf.

Chapter 5: Follow a Proper Allocation Model

68 **only about 53% to 56%:** Jeffrey M. Jones and Lydia Saad, "What Percentage of Americans Owns Stock?" Gallup, August 13, 2021, https://news.gallup.com/poll/266807/percentage -americans-owns-stock.aspx.

70 **By 2010, the median net worth:** Alfred Gottschalck, Marina Vornovytskyy, and Adam Smith, "Household Wealth in the U.S.: 2000 to 2011," U.S. Census Bureau, p. 4, https://www .census.gov/content/dam/Census/library/working-papers/2014/demo/wealth-highlights -2011-revised-7-3-14.pdf.

71 **The S&P 500 index, for example:** Vanguard, "Vanguard Portfolio Allocation Models," no date, https://investor.vanguard.com/investing/how-to-invest/model-portfolio-allocation.

71 **Returns were just as manic:** Fei Mei Chan and Craig J. Lazzara, "Returns, Values, and Outcomes: A Counterfactual History," September 2021, S&P Global, Inc., https://www .spglobal.com/spdji/en/documents/research/research-returns-values-and-outcomes-a -counterfactual-history.pdf.

82 **That said, the median:** Farida Ahmad, Elizabeth Arias, and Betzaida Tejada-Vera, "Provisional Life Expectancy Estimates for January through June, 2020," National Vital Statistics System Vital Statistics Rapid Release, Report No. 010, February 2021, https://www .cdc.gov/nchs/data/vsrr/VSRR10-508.pdf.

Chapter 6: Optimize Your Investments

96 **Roth IRA or Traditional IRA?:** IRS, "Retirement Plans," accessed March 17, 2022, https:// www.irs.gov/retirement-plans.

Chapter 7: Understand Real Estate Fundamentals

115 **However, the net worth data:** Neil Bhutta et al., "Changes in U.S. Family Finances from 2016 to 2019: Evidence from the Survey of Consumer Finances," *Federal Reserve Bulletin* 106, no. 5 (September 2020), https://www.federalreserve.gov/publications/files/scf20.pdf.

121 **According to the National Association:** Jessica Lautz, "Age of Buyers Is Skyrocketing . . . but Not for Who You Might Think," *Economists' Outlook* (blog), National Association of Realtors, January 13, 2020, https://www.nar.realtor/blogs/economists-outlook/age-of -buyers-is-skyrocketing-but-not-for-who-you-might-think.

122 **Over the course of 2021, for example:** Chris Salviati et al., "Apartment List National Rent Report," Apartment List, November 1, 2021, https://www.apartmentlist.com/research /national-rent-data.

125 **Back in 2009, the average:** ATTOM Staff, "U.S. Home Seller Profits Dip Slightly in First Quarter of 2021 but Remain Higher Than Year Ago," ATTOM Data Solutions, April 29, 2021, https://www.attomdata.com/news/market-trends/home-sales-prices/attom-data-solutions-q1-2021-u-s-home-sales-report.

128 **data from Redfin:** Lily Katz, "Share of Homes Bought with All Cash Hits 30% for First Time Since 2014," Redfin, July 15, 2021, https://www.redfin.com/news/all-cash-home-purchases-2021.

Chapter 8: Choose Where to Live for Maximum Wealth Potential

144 **data says the average homeownership tenure:** ATTOm Staff, "U.S. Home Seller Profits Dip Slightly in First Quarter of 2021 but Remain Higher Than Year Ago," ATTOM Data Solutions, April 29, 2021, https://www.attomdata.com/news/market-trends/home-sales-prices/attom-data-solutions-q1-2021-u-s-home-sales-report.

Chapter 9: Go Long on Real Estate

155 **median home price in America:** U.S. Census Bureau and U.S. Department of Housing and Urban Development, "Median Sales Price of Houses Sold for the United States," Federal Reserve Bank of St. Louis, accessed March 2, 2022, https://fred.stlouisfed.org/series/MSPUS

155 **According to the Survey of Consumer Finances:** Federal Reserve Board, "Changes in U.S. Family Finances from 2016 to 2019: Evidence from the Survey of Consumer Finances," Federal Reserve Bulletin 106, no. 5 (September 2020), https://www.federalreserve.gov/publications/files/scf20.pdf.

155 **according to digital wealth adviser:** Megan DeMatteo, "The Average American's Portfolio in 2021," *Daily Capital*, January 4, 2022, https://www.blog.personalcapital.com/blog/investing-markets/average-american-financial-portfolio.

158 **Roughly 15% of the world's population:** World Health Organization, "World Report on Disability 2011," December 14, 2011, https://www.who.int/teams/noncommunicable-diseases/sensory-functions-disability-and-rehabilitation/world-report-on-disability.

158 **Check out the employee racial:** Facebook, "Annual Diversity Report," July 2021, https://about.fb.com/wp-content/uploads/2021/07/Facebook-Annual-Diversity-Report-July-2021.pdf.

163 **For reference, the heartland comprises:** Joel Kotkin et al., "The Emergence of the Global Heartland," Heartland Forward, May 2021, https://heartlandforward.org/wp-content/uploads/2021/05/GlobalHeartlandFinal_Web-2-Updated-bio.pdf.

164 **The heartland's share of:** Kotkin et al., "Emergence of the Global Heartland."

164 **For a fascinating look:** Jennifer Bradley, "The Changing Face of the Heartland," Brookings Institution, March 17, 2015, http://csweb.brookings.edu/content/research/essays/2015/changingfaceoftheheartland.html#.

Chapter 10: Think Strategically About Your Career

177 **There are more than 400,000:** Ralph R. Smith, "Agencies with the Most Federal Employee Salaries above $100,000 and $200,000," FedSmith.com, October 14, 2021, www.fedsmith.com/2021/10/14/federal-employee-salaries-above-100k.

177 *MarketWatch* **reported that:** Silvia Ascarelli, "The Average Defense Department Contractor Is Paid Nearly $200,000," *MarketWatch*, December 6, 2016, https://www.marketwatch.com/story/the-average-defense-department-contractor-is-paid-nearly-200000-2016-12-06.

178 **The average salary for an elementary:** "How Much Does an Elementary School Principal Make?" Glassdoor, no date, https://www.glassdoor.com/Salaries/elementary-school -principal-salary-SRCH_KO0,27.htm.

186 **When Wooden started coaching:** Bill Dwyre, "Steve Alford's Salary Is 14.8 Times Higher Than John Wooden's Pay," *Los Angeles Times*, July 12, 2013, https://www.latimes.com /sports/la-xpm-2013-jul-12-la-sp-sn-ucla-steve-alford-money-20130712-story.html.

187 **Miami offered him five:** Associated Press, "Saban: 'I'm Not Going to Be the Alabama Coach,'" ESPN.com, December 21, 2006, https://www.espn.com/nfl/news/story?id=2705288.

187 **After two years of a mediocre:** Michael Casagrande, "The History of Nick Saban's Rising Salary, How It's Been Viewed," AL.com, January 13, 2019, https://www.al.com /alabamafootball/2017/05/the_10-year_history_of_nick_sa.html.

187 **Then in 2021, after winning:** Michael Casagrande, "Putting Nick Saban's New $84.8 Million Contract into Context," AL.com, August 3, 2021, https://www.al.com /alabamafootball/2021/08/putting-nick-sabans-new-848-million-contract-into-context.html.

Chapter 11: Make Your Money and Then Make Your Exit

196 **For parents without a university:** Esteban Ortiz-Ospina, "Are Parents Spending Less Time with Their Kids?" Our World in Data, December 14, 2020, https://ourworldindata.org /parents-time-with-kids; Giulia M. Dotti Sani and Judith Treas, "Educational Gradients in Parents' Child-Care Time Across Countries, 1965–2012," *Journal of Marriage and Family* 78 no. 4 (August 2016): 1083–96, https://doi.org/10.1111/jomf.12305.

202 **Legally, most companies:** "Can I Get COBRA if I Quit?," COBRAInsurance.com, no date, https://www.cobrainsurance.com/kb-questions/cobra-insurance-402.

Chapter 13: Invest in Education

229 **According to the Education Data Initiative:** Melanie Hanson, "College Enrollment & Student Demographic Statistics," Education Data Initiative, November 22, 2021, https:// educationdata.org/college-enrollment-statistics.

229 **Under *Forbes*'s new methodology:** Christian Kreznar, "America's Top Colleges 2021: For the First Time a Public School Is Number One," *Forbes*, September 8, 2021, https://www.forbes .com/sites/christiankreznar/2021/09/08/americas-top-colleges-2021-for-the-first-time -apublic-school-is-numberone/?sh=284aa22f41ad.

231 **a chart outlining the costs:** "Tuition and Adjusted Tuition," Chinese American International School, accessed November 28, 2021, https://www.cais.org/admissions/tuition -and-adjusted-tuition; "Tuition and Additional Costs," San Francisco University High School, accessed November 28, 2021, https://www.sfuhs.org/admissions/tuition-and -additional-costs; "Admission & Aid," Princeton University, accessed November 28, 2021, https://www.princeton.edu/admission-aid.

231 **According to researchers from the Georgetown:** "Ranking ROI of 4,500 US Colleges and Universities," Center on Education and the Workforce, Georgetown University, accessed December 8, 2021, https://cew.georgetown.edu/cew-reports/CollegeROI.

238 **in the mid-$70,000 range:** "2022 Best Business Schools," *U.S. News & World Report*, accessed November 28, 2021, https://www.usnews.com/best-graduate-schools/top-business -schools/mba-rankings?_mode=table.

Chapter 14: Nurture Your Love

244 **The data hurts:** Shelby B. Scott et al., "Reasons for Divorce and Recollections of Premarital Intervention: Implications for Improving Relationship Education," *Couple & Family Psychology* 2, no. 2 (2013): 131–45, https://doi.org/10.1037/a0032025.

244 **Based on one calculation:** "Marriage Calculator," Tax Policy Center, accessed November 28, 2021, https://tpc-marriage-calculator.urban.org.

245 **The U.S. Social Security Administration allows:** "Social Security Benefits," U.S. Social Security Administration, accessed November 28, 2021, www.ssa.gov/oact/quickcalc/spouse.html.

247 **average cost of a wedding in America:** Esther Lee, "This Was the Average Cost of a Wedding in 2020," *The Knot*, February 11, 2021, https://www.theknot.com/content/average-wedding-cost.

248 **With the median household:** "Income and Poverty in the United States: 2020," U.S. Census Bureau, September 14, 2021, https://www.census.gov/library/publications/2021/demo/p60-273.html.

251 **According to the 2021 WeddingWire:** Kim Forrest, "This Is How Much an Engagement Ring REALLY Costs," WeddingWire, March 3, 2021, https://www.weddingwire.com/wedding-ideas/engagement-ring-cost.

255 **Between 10% and 25%:** "Miscarriage," March of Dimes, no date, https://www.marchofdimes.org/complications/miscarriage.aspx#.

256 **By age twenty-eight:** "Do I Want Kids?" *Glad You Asked*, season 2, episode 6, July 28, 2021, https://www.vox.com/22577373/do-i-want-kids-parenthood-baby-childfree.

256 **According to the U.S. Department of Agriculture:** Mark Lino, "The Cost of Raising a Child," U.S. Department of Agriculture, February 18, 2020, https://www.usda.gov/media/blog/2017/01/13/cost-raising-child.

257 **According to Princeton economist:** Daniel Kahneman and Angus Deaton, "High Income Improves Evaluation of Life but Not Emotional Well-being," *Proceedings of the National Academy of Sciences* 107, no. 38 (September 2010): 16489–93, https://doi.org/10.1073/pnas.1011492107.

258 **family of four with an income of $117,000:** "Poverty in San Francisco," City and County of San Francisco, no date, https://sfgov.org/scorecards/safety-net/poverty-san-francisco.

258 **Nathan Yau of FlowingData:** Nathan Yau, "Divorce Rates and Income," FlowingData, no date, https://flowingdata.com/2021/05/04/divorce-rates-and-income/.

265 **However, overall, about 50%:** "Divorce Rate by State 2021," World Population Review, no date, https://worldpopulationreview.com/state-rankings/divorce-rate-by-state.

Chapter 15: Live Like a Financial Samurai

272 **Be aware that the median:** Emily A. Shrider et al., "Income and Poverty in the United States: 2020," U.S. Census Bureau, September 14, 2021, https://www.census.gov/library/publications/2021/demo/p60-273.html.

275 **With a median household income:** Amanda Noss, "Household Income for States: 2008 and 2009," U.S. Census Bureau, *American Community Survey Briefs*, September 2010, https://www2.census.gov/library/publications/2010/acs/acsbr09-02.pdf.

276 **The median price of a new car:** "Average New-Vehicle Prices Hit All-Time High, According to Kelley Blue Book," Kelley Blue Book, July 19, 2021, https://mediaroom.kbb.com/2021-07-19-Average-New-Vehicle-Prices-Hit-All-Time-High,-According-to-Kelley-Blue-Book.

277 **That may sound like:** Colin Beresford and Caleb Miller, "Average Age of Vehicles on the Road Rises above 12 Years," *Car and Driver*, June 21, 2021, https://www.caranddriver.com/news/a33457915/average-age-vehicles-on-road-12-years.

279 **Despite their frigid temperatures:** John F. Helliwell et al., "World Happiness Report 2021," Sustainable Development Solutions Network, 2021, https://worldhappiness.report/ed/2021.

Index

Note: Italicized page numbers indicate material in tables or illustrations.

and home-buying rules, 114,
116–20, *117–18*
and job-hopping, 186–88
passion vs. money in career choice,
180–81
ranked passive-income options,
39–47
and refinancing mortgages,
129–31
and savings plans, 33–36, *36*,
38–39, 68, 188
and side hustles, 209, *217*, 218–19
start-ups vs. established
companies, 181–84
and Stealth Wealth, 272
and tax-efficient investing
strategies, 92
tethering, 30–31
and value of education, 231–32
and value of real estate
investments, 164
See also after-tax income; salaries;
taxable income
independence, 9, 252–53
index funds, 155
Index Plus strategy, 101–2
inequalities, xix
inflation
and annualized asset returns, *58*
and bond yields, 23
and costs of having children, 258
and home ownership costs, 143
and home-buying rules, 121, 122
impact on rents, 112
and investing risk tolerance, 87
and paying down mortgages, 131
and real estate investments, 46
inheritances, xix, 33, 69, 161–62, 166
injuries, 86
Instacart, 38
insurance
and cost of living by location
choice, *11, 135*
and financial independence in
couples, 253
and home purchases, 113–14, 119,
123, 126
and refinancing mortgages, *130*
interest rates
and asset allocation models, 83
and debt management, 50
and home-buying rules, 114, 116,
122–23, 126
and margin investing, 63, *63*
and mortgages, 62, 124–26, 131
paying down debt vs. investing,
52–55
and ranked passive-income
options, 43, 47
and teaching children about
finances, 262–63
and value of pensions, 78
internal rate of return (IRR), 106n
internal salesmanship, 192
international private schools, 229
internet companies, 177
interviewing for jobs, xxi, 180, 227

investing
active vs. passive funds, 80,
100–102
angel investing, 105–8
and author's financial success, xxi
growth vs. dividend stocks, 102–5
investment targets by age, *69*
IRA options, 96–100
key questions, 89–90
losses, 28
and net worth targets, 17
and refinancing mortgages, 131
taxable vs. tax-advantaged
accounts, 90–96
teaching children about finances,
263–64
See also stock market investing
investment banking, 177
IRAs
and age of retirement, 18
and asset goals by age, *69*
401(k)s compared to, 96–97
and investing misconceptions, 34
investing options, 96–100
Roth IRAs, 91, 96–100, 159–60
SEP-IRAs, 91, 97, 100
SIMPLE IRAs, 91
and stocks vs. bonds balance, 80
IT consulting/accounting firms, 177

Japan, 43
Jefferson County, Texas, 169
job-hopping, 186–88
JOBS Act (Jumpstart Our Business
Startups Act), 45
Jordan, Michael, 3
Journal of Financial Planning, 21
junior colleagues, 195

Kahneman, Daniel, 257
Kawaja, Carl, 5
Kelly, Brian, 187n
Kleiner Perkins, 108
Kuala Lumpur, Malaysia, 278

labor costs, 148
law enforcement careers, 178
layoffs
firings contrasted with, 200–202
and global financial crises, 142
and goals of a Financial Samurai,
286
and home-buying rules, 115
and risk-taking, 284
strategizing for, 199–203
and value of job-hopping, 187
Lean FIRE lifestyle, 7, 12
legacy retirement philosophy, 21
Lending Club, 40
lending practices, 131
letters of instruction, 274
leveraged buyouts, 60
life expectancy, 220
life insurance, 253, 259–60
lifestyle
businesses based on, 219
and debt management, 49

and goals of financial success,
279–80
hobbies and interests, 39,
180–81, 237
living with purpose, 9, 286
personal freedom, 165–68
and 70/30 philosophy, xv–xix
and side hustles, 220–21
and value of financial success, xv
See also family life
limited liability corporations
(LLCs), 273
liquidation preference, 107
liquidity of assets, 39–47, 107.
See also cash assets
living expenses
and net worth allocation by age, 77
and net worth/passive-income
balance, 19
and quantifying happiness, 10–12
and risk tolerance, 27
living space requirements, 147–49
living trusts, 274
Livingston, Shaun, 275
loan defaults, 115
location, 169, 171, 258
Los Angeles, California, 122
love, xvi, 246–47
loyalty to companies, 186–88
luck, 286–87
luxury spending, 121–24, 272
Lyft, 208

maintenance costs, 123, 149
management of companies, 185
Mandatory Provident Fund, 68
margin investing, 60–64, *63*
marginalized groups, 156–60, 210
market conditions
downturns, 156
and global financial crises, 13, 60,
70, 142, 154, 167–68, 200,
247, 271
and home-buying rules, 115
and value of real estate
investments, 171
See also bear markets; bull markets
marketing, xviii, 251
marriage
and capital gains taxes, *94, 95*
cohabitation contrasted with,
244–46
and cost of living by location
choice, 139
and divorce, 244, 245–46, 253,
258, 265–66
and goals of financial success, 280
for love vs. money, 246–47
matching funds, 35, 96
maximizing wealth potential, xv.
See also income; salaries
MBA programs, xiv, xix, 238–40
McLean High School, 235
median incomes, 272
medical expenses, 50, 86
meritocracy, 191
midlife crises, 74

and divorce rates, 245
and maximizing wealth
    potential, 133
and pension values, 179
and proper asset allocation, 67
and 70/30 philosophy, xvi–xviii, 13
and value of education, 232
Proctor & Gamble, 182
product creation, *41,* 43–44, 47, 215
productivity, 187. *See also* work ethic
profession choice, 175–76
profit sharing, 96
promotions, 87, 191, 192–95, 257
property management, 149, 151, 165
property taxes, 271
property values, 159, 168–71, 271
Prosper, 40
public schools, 138, 229–35
public-sector careers, 178
purchasing power, 131
purpose, 9, 286. *See also* lifestyle

quitting jobs, 129, 199–203

racism, xx, 156
real estate careers, 178
real estate investment trusts (REITs)
    and asset-to-liability ratios, *58*
    and career choices, 177
    eREITs, 72, 73, 93, 165
    forms of, 161
    and net worth allocation by age,
        72, 73
    and ranked passive-income
        options, *41, 45*
    tax-efficient investing
        strategies, 93
real estate investments
    adjustable vs. fixed-rate
        mortgages, 124–28
    and asset goals by age, 69
    and asset-to-liability ratio, 57
    establishing correct values, 168–71
    and historically marginalized
        groups, 156–60
    home-buying rules, 112–20
    local vs. from afar, 165
    and net worth allocation by age,
        71–77, *73, 75, 77,* 83
    and net worth/passive-income
        balance, 19
    1% Rule for investments, 172
    physical vs. online, 161–63
    and ranked passive-income
        options, *41,* 42, 44–45
    real estate crowdfunding (REC),
        41, 45–46, 93, 161, 163
    real estate ETFs, *41,* 45, 161, 165
    real estate tech companies, 177
    refinancing mortgages,
        128–32, *130*
    renting vs. buying, 120–24
    role in financial freedom plans,
        111–12
    stock investing compared with,
        70–71, 104–5, 155–56
    syndication deals, 163–64

three key types, 112
vacation properties, 165–68
value of heartland real estate,
    163–65
value of long real estate investing,
    153–54
See also real estate investment
    trusts
reality checks, xv
recruiting practices, 227–28
Reddit, 136
Redfin, 170, 271–72
refinancing loans, 128
Registered Retirement Savings Plan
    (RRSP), 34, 68
Regulation T, 61
relationship skills in workplace, 192,
    273–74
relocating, 139–41
remodels, 147–48
rental properties/income
    and cost of living by location
        choice, 135, 141, 142
    and financial support for children,
        261–62
    and fundamental value of real
        estate, 63
    and heartland real estate
        investments, 164–65
    and home-buying rules, 117
    and impact of inflation, 112
    and living expenses, 10
    and net worth allocation by age, 73
    and proper asset allocation by
        age, 81
    and property location choice,
        144–45
    and ranked passive-income
        options, 44, 46
    and rent-control laws, 151
    and renting vs. owning, 120–24
    and side-hustle income, 209
    and value of real estate
        investments, 154, 157, 159,
        168–72
replacement employees, training,
    201–3
required minimum distributions
    (RMDs), 97
retirement savings
    and age of retirement, 18
    and appropriate wedding costs,
        248–50, *249*
    and asset-to-liability ratio, 57, 59
    and cost of living by location
        choice, 135, 139
    delaying retirement, 25
    early retirement, 6–8
    and matching funds, 35, 96
    misconceptions about, 34
    and net worth allocation by age,
        71–75
    philosophies for, 20–21
    and refinancing mortgages, 129
    Registered Retirement Savings
        Plans, 34, 68
    and school tuition, 234, 235–38

self-invested personal pensions,
    34, 68
and value of real estate
    investments, 164
See also 401(k) accounts; IRAs;
    Roth IRAs
returns on investment (ROI)
    and education choices, 229
    and physical vs. online real estate
        investing, 161–62
    and ranked passive-income
        options, 39–47
    and value of education,
        231–32, 240
revenue streams, 206, 208, 209, 214,
    218–19. *See also* passive
    income; side hustles
revocable living trusts, 274
rewards points, 64
The Rideshare Guy (website), 208
ridesharing, 146, 208
Riley, Lincoln, 187n
risk
    and angel investing, 105–8
    and asset allocation by age, 84–85
    and bond yields, 23
    and cultivating side hustles, 211,
        218–19
    and education choices, 227
    and goals of financial success, 283
    and investment return
        expectations, 23–25, *24,* 58
    and net worth/passive-income
        balance, 19
    and ranked passive-income
        options, 39–47
    risk premiums, 23, 169
    risk tolerance for equities,
        25–29, *28*
    risk-appropriate debt, 61–64
    value of taking risks, 283–84
risk-free rate of return
    and bond yields, 23
    and investing risk tolerance,
        86–87
    and net worth allocation by age,
        72, *73, 75, 77*
    and optimal investment
        choices, 39
    and paying down mortgages, 131
    and real estate investing, 123
    and retirement withdrawal rates,
        21–22
    and teaching children about
        finances, 262
    and value of real estate
        investments, 169
    See also bonds and bond yields
roommates, 261
Roth IRAs, 91, 96–100, 159–60
Rover app, 208
royalties, 43–44

Saban, Nick, 187
sabbaticals, 74–75
sacrifice, 211. *See also* work ethic
safety factors, 277

Sam Dogen founded *Financial Samurai* in 2009. One of the pioneers of today's financial independence movement, he was previously at Goldman Sachs and Credit Suisse, from which he retired at age thirty-four to focus on his writing. Dogen is a graduate of William & Mary and received an MBA from University of California, Berkeley. He now lives in San Francisco with his wife and two children. In his free time, you can find him playing tennis or trying to hit line drives on the softball field.